IB £19.?

John Blake Dillon, Young Irelander

John Blake Dillon,
Young Irelander

BRENDAN O'CATHAOIR

IRISH ACADEMIC PRESS

The typesetting of this book
was produced by Gilbert Gough Typesetting
for Irish Academic Press,
Kill Lane, Blackrock, Co. Dublin

BRITISH LIBRARY CATALOGUING IN PUBLICATION DATA
O'Cathaoir, Brendan
John Blake Dillon: Young Irelander.
1. Ireland. Politics. Dillon, John Blake, 1814-1866
I. Title

ISBN 0-7165-2467-8

A C K N O W L E D G E M E N T
Publication of this book has been generously assisted
by a grant in aid from the
Senate of the National University of Ireland

Printed in Ireland by
Betaprint International Ltd.

To Eva

In a higher world it is otherwise, but here below to live is to change, and to be perfect is to have changed often.
JOHN HENRY NEWMAN

Contents

List of Illustrations

All except numbers 1 and 10 are courtesy of the Dillon family and Irish Times photographers. Numbers 1 and 10 are reproduced with the permission of the National Library of Ireland.

Preface

I am grateful to all who helped during the eight years this book has been in preparation. My first debt is to Professor John Myles Dillon, who introduced me to the papers of his family in Trinity College, Dublin. Regrettably, James Mathew Dillon—who represented the third generation of his family in Irish public life—did not live to read this biography of his grandfather. His widow, Mrs Maura Dillon, was a source of inspiration; his son, Mr John Blake Dillon, also provided information.

The Irish Times Ltd granted sabbatical leave at a crucial stage of research. Mr Liam Hynes placed his work generously at my disposal.

The following assisted or encouraged: Pádraig Ó Snodaigh, Ulick O'Connor, Revd Professor Donal Kerr, Professor Kevin B. Nowlan and Professor Tomás P. Ó Néill; the monks of Mount Melleray Abbey, Cappoquin, County Waterford; my sister, Brid Cahir; and the late F.S.L. Lyons, Eileen O'Brien and Leon Ó Broin. I am grateful to my parents and to all who inspired me with a love of history.

I wish to thank the Board of Trinity College for permission to quote from the Dillon papers. (A note on quotations: in conformity with modern usage, capital letters used originally for emphasis have been lower-cased; the spelling of surnames and placenames has been standardised; the few spelling errors encountered were corrected silently.)

My thanks to the staffs of the TCD Manuscripts Room, particularly Stuart Ó Seanóir; of the National Library, especially Gerard J. Lyne; of the Royal Irish Academy and Bray public library.

Professor Donal McCartney and Dr C.J. Woods read my manuscript and made valuable comments. Michael Adams, of Irish Academic Press, treated it with sensitivity and skill.

It would not have been possible to write this book without the support of my wife, Eva, who not only cared for our children while I communed with Blake Dillon, but made important discoveries in the course of her own research.

I am glad to have completed a task first mooted by Dillon's widow to Charles Gavan Duffy. Adelaide Dillon then suggested to her son, William, that he write a biography of his father. John Mitchel advised him (from New York on 11 May 1873) 'to leave the memoir of John B. Dillon to some one else. . . . There were indeed few nobler lives—finer nature there never was. . . . When forced into publicity he abhorred it. The fruit of such a life is in its friendships and its gracious influences, which die not.' Hopefully this monograph transcends, in the words of Professor Joe Lee, 'the fragmentation of perspective characteristic of the contemporary mind'.

Introduction

*John Dillon whom everybody knew and who was a repealer
and a gentleman . . . and my own darling.*
ADELAIDE HART, 2 AUGUST 1847

John Blake Dillon is remembered chiefly as a co-founder of the *Nation* newspaper. He was, furthermore, a leading Young Irelander, a rebel and a fugitive in 1848, a political refugee in New York, a liberal Catholic, and subsequently a member of parliament. He died suddenly in 1866, aged fifty-two, after little more than twelve months at Westminster (the arena where his son, John, was to be a leading figure for nearly forty years). During his brief parliamentary career, however, he made a decisive contribution to the Irish-Liberal understanding which led to the disestablishment of the Anglican Church in Ireland and to the land act of 1870.[1]

His wife, Adelaide Hart, was a remarkable person, too. She was born in Dublin on 20 May 1828. Her family had links with the United Irishmen and her father, William Francis Hart, was a solicitor whose firm, Hart and O'Hara, was one of the first Catholic law partnerships to begin practice after the relaxation of the penal laws. In their youth Adelaide and her sister wrote, as 'Two Irish girls', to the *Nation* urging Irishwomen to forgo selfish interests and become fosterers of disinterested patriotism.[2] She told Dillon (28 July 1847) that reading Theobald Wolfe Tone's autobiography 'has always an enlivening effect on me'. Adelaide Hart and John Blake Dillon were married in October 1847, and their union conformed to the Romantic ideal that lovers should be intellectually congenial.[3]

After her husband's death Adelaide tried to interest his friend, Charles Gavan Duffy, in writing a memoir. Duffy, then a successful politician in Victoria, Australia, replied seeking copies of Dillon correspondence and outlining his literary plans (expanded later when he returned to live in Europe in 1880): 'The idea in my mind is one volume as readable as I can make it, containing portraitures as true and vivid as I am capable of producing, of the men who kindled a soul in Ireland in 1843—and a rapid

panorama of the affairs of Ireland for twenty years after.'[4]
Duffy left a pen-portrait of Dillon:[5]

> His generous nature made him more a philanthropist than a
> politician. He was born and reared in Connaught amongst the most
> abject and oppressed population in Europe, and all his studies and
> projects had direct relation to the condition of the people. Codes,
> tenures and social theories were his familiar reading, as history and
> biography were an inspiration to the more powerful imagination
> of Davis. He followed in the track of Bentham and de Tocqueville,
> and recognised a regulated democracy as the inevitable and right-
> ful ruler of the world; and he saw with burning impatience the
> wrongs inflicted on the industrious poor by an aristocracy prac-
> tically irresponsible. Davis desired a national existence for Ireland
> that an old historic state might be raised from the dust, and a sceptre
> placed in her hand, that thus she might become the mother of a
> brave and self-reliant race. Dillon desired a national existence
> primarily to get rid of social degradation and suffering, which it
> wrung his heart to witness without being able to relieve. He was
> neither morose nor cynical, but he had one instinct in common with
> Swift, the villainies of mankind made his blood boil.

Duffy continued: 'Under a stately and somewhat reserved demeanour
lay latent the simplicity and joyousness of a boy'. Dillon was ardent but
not without a sense of humour; he shrank from self-display; he 'was a man
of remarkable talents carefully cultivated, of lofty purpose sustained by
steady courage, and of as pure and generous a nature as ever was given to
man. . . .'

Adelaide had started to edit his correspondence for publication before
she herself died, probably of tuberculosis, in May 1872, having acknowledged the limitations of her project: 'He wrote and spoke very little,
the influence he exercised was mainly personal; the power, I think, of a
very noble and very perfect character. He loved to work through others.
He would originate, suggest, arrange, and then rejoice when success was
achieved by others, who carried off all the credit. "What matter who gets
the credit so the good is done?" he would say laughing. . . . He hated
letter-writing and never wrote but the shortest business letters *excepting
to his wife.*'[6]

Even allowing for Adelaide's hyperbole, Dillon was no ordinary
politician. Although many other papers have come to light in the course
of research, this monograph is based primarily on Dillon's letters pre-

served by his wife; some of hers are also extant. Their weekly epistolary conversations, during lengthy periods of separation stoically endured, were made possible by the advent of steamships.

The emigrant letter is a difficult, if rewarding, text to handle. Dillon's perception differed radically from the hordes who, fleeing hunger and pestilence, 'landed in the United States like tired migratory birds'.[7] Prisoners of poverty, the vast majority of Irish immigrants experienced intolerable conditions: in 1849, for instance, 18,456 (mostly Irish) people, or four per cent of the population of New York, lived in cellars.[8] By 1850 the number had risen to 30,000.

At the turning point in his career, with a price of £300 on his head, Dillon escaped to join an Irish-American élite which regarded the US as 'the great asylum of the wronged beyond the Atlantic'. He belonged to an estimated two per cent of professional people among the Irish in New York.[9] While he avoided Irish-American entanglements, this did not prevent him from writing perceptively (and entertainingly) about them.

Dillon's letters contain material of intrinsic significance. Moreover, he possessed the hall-marks of a good letter-writer—natural reflectiveness and a tendency to self-examination. But he had no idea of the power-lessness of poverty. His exile coincided with a phase of disillusionment, after the failure of the 1848 insurrection, with Ireland and the Catholic Church.

As a liberal he was outside the main stream of Irish Catholic opinion. For example, he supported the Italian Risorgimento against the temporal power of the papacy. He had difficulty reconciling his views with the ultramontane church, which in 1864 condemned liberalism as one of the errors of the age. If Cardinal Paul Cullen had read some of Dillon's observations to his wife in the 1850s, he might not have co-operated politically with him after his return to Ireland and written at his death: 'Poor Mr Dillon . . . was well prepared, but he is a great loss. There is no one to take his place.'[10]

With Alexis de Tocqueville and other middle-class intellectuals of his day, Dillon believed that Europe was in transition from an aristocratic to a democratic era. The Young Irelanders were concerned about the condition of the people in a volatile, Carlylean sense, but they had not experienced hunger. They failed to understand the extent to which the cataclysm of the Great Famine had weakened the Irish people. The unrealistic expectations raised by the French Revolution of 1848 were not shared by a nation in agony.

The Young Irelanders, in hoping for a rerun of the events which had secured Grattan's constitution, underestimated the determination of the British government to retain control of Ireland. Lacking every military quality except bravery, they blamed the people and, more unreasonably, the priests for ensuring that the rising of 1848 ended in fiasco rather than in bloodshed.

Dillon's departure in the wake of the rising encapsulated the flight from a stricken land. The renewed failure of the potato crop broke the will of many small farmers who had survived 'black '47'. During the famine years (1845-51)) the population of Ireland declined by about 2.25 million; between 1849-52 the annual emigration never fell below 200,000, and in 1851 it reached 250,000.[11] In New York, where there was no shortage of Irish clients, Dillon prospered as a lawyer. In 1856 he was induced by his wife to return to Ireland. Otherwise, the Dillon dynasty would probably have grown up in America.

Despite his flirtation with revolution, Dillon was essentially a political realist and a constitutional nationalist. When persuaded to re-enter politics, he took a prominent part in founding the National Association of Ireland. Significantly, this had been the original title of O'Connell's Loyal National Repeal Association in 1840.

John Blake Dillon was reflective, cautious and unassuming. A man of wide culture, he entered public life from a sense of duty. He lacked robust health and was prone to despondency. His transition from romantic nationalist to Catholic nationalist coincided with the changes which shaped modern Ireland. Although remaining untainted by sectarianism, he became a tribune of the nation called into being by O'Connell. He began and ended his career as an advocate of the tenant farmer. Dillon believed in social justice, not social equality. A millennial vision recorded shortly before his death, however, suggests he was moving towards Christian socialism.[12]

Boyhood

My family have not as you will perceive much refinement about them, but they have many solid virtues. They have always been strictly honest and very charitable. I cannot call to mind any act of any of them in their dealings with the world which I would be ashamed to have mentioned. As for public spirit they were I believe the only people in that region who ever exhibited any. These solid and substantial virtues are more than sufficient with me to cover some oddities from which some of them are not free, and on the whole I not only love them but I am proud of them.

JOHN TO ADELAIDE DILLON, 26 JUNE 1849

John Blake Dillon was born on 5 May 1814 in Ballaghaderreen. The Dillons regarded the town as being in County Mayo because it was only four miles from their ancestral home beside the Lung river. In the fragment of a biography written after her husband's death, Adelaide said 'he always retained a love and remembrance for the river.'[1]

John Dillon, *fils*, used to say that he was the son of a rebel and the grandson of an evicted tenant.[2] This colourful generalisation obscures the reality of considerable family resources even in the eighteenth century. Luke Dillon, John Blake Dillon's father, held approximately 150 Irish acres at Blenaghbane, in the townland of Lissiane[3]—a substantial farm, given that in County Mayo in 1841 nearly three-quarters of all holdings were under six acres.

The information available about John Blake Dillon's background and early life is sketchy. His family belonged to that neglected class of Irish Catholics who were neither landlords nor peasants. Luke Dillon was born *c*.1756 and became a tenant on the Waldron estate—a sub-estate of Viscount Dillon, of Loughglynn. According to Adelaide's memoir, he was evicted because his farm was coveted by a man (named Clarke) 'who made interest with the landlord.' The likelihood is that Luke refused to renew his lease on terms which he considered exorbitant—thus showing characteristic shrewdness, for the agricultural boom of the Napoleonic war years ended shortly after he gave up his holding and moved to Ballaghaderreen about 1812. A number of leases involving John and James Dillon, of Lung, and James Hughes of Ballaghaderreen, had been registered during 1779–1812.[4] Hughes built the house which the Dillon family would occupy until 1986. Luke was probably related to John Dillon, of Lung, the eldest son of James, who may have been the Captain James Dillon described as a gentleman and the eldest son of John Dillon, of Cappagh, County Mayo, in a lease dated 1744.[5]

According to family tradition, Luke Dillon drilled the United Irishmen at night and the Yeomanry by day, but it is more likely that he was associated with the Defenders as there is no evidence of United Irish activity in Mayo before the French landing in 1798.

John Blake Dillon's father remains an enigma. He may have been a member of Loughglynn Cavalry in 1796; he is said to have taken part in the fleeting victory known as the 'Castlebar races'; and we know he was at one point agent to Patrick Dillon, 11th earl of Roscommon.[6] He was evidently a prosperous farmer, who after *c.*1812 became a successful merchant. He 'kept a large shop' in Ballaghaderreen, where he was appointed sub-postmaster before his death in 1825.

Luke Dillon was renowned as a hurler and a horseman. Another part of the family legend is that when Arabelle (Anne) Blake, of Dunmacrina, County Mayo, saw him vault into a saddle she decided to marry him. They were married around 1797 and his wife outlived him by forty years. They had seven children: Andrew, who became a doctor; Thomas, the mainstay of the family business; Valentine, who became crown solicitor for Sligo and lived until 1904, thus meriting three not altogether accurate references in Joyce's *Ulysses*; John, the subject of this biography; Monica, who married a man called Duff; Jane, who became Mrs McDonagh; and Bridget, who joined the Sisters of Mercy in Derry.

John Blake Dillon attended a hedge school and later was tutored privately by a 'classical' master. According to his widow's narrative—a devotional retrospect—he grew up in a house 'where the rosary was said every night, and no poor person ever allowed to pass the door without assistance'. His birthday coincided with the feast (under the old Roman calendar) of the conversion of St Augustine—'to whom he had always a special devotion'. More likely this came with spiritual maturity, after

'Ady' had played the role of St Monica. She also claimed that Carolan's music remained dear to John, 'with whom love for Irish music was a passion.'

In 1830—the year after Catholic Emancipation—Dillon was sent to Maynooth College, 'not that he felt any vocation to the priesthood, but that his mother wished him "to try" seeing that he loved books and was of a serious disposition.'[7] The matriculation requirements included a knowledge of Latin and Greek. In Maynooth he studied the medieval curriculum of rhetoric, humanities and philosophy. He was intended for the diocese of Achonry in a still predominantly Irish-speaking Mayo.

Dillon showed an early capacity for friendship. During his two years in Maynooth he made lifelong friends (some of whom would help him to escape after the 1848 rising). Finding he had no priestly vocation, he left but retained an 'affectionate remembrance' of the college.

He entered Trinity College, Dublin, on 17 October 1834, an unusual transition in those sectarian days. He registered as a son of Luke Dillon, *agricola defunctus*. Initially he was a sizar—a student paying reduced fees in return for performing certain duties. Dillon read ethics and mathematics at university, and also studied for the bar. He was admitted as a student at King's Inns in 1836 and to Gray's Inn, London, two years later. While in London he attended a protest meeting against a pogrom in Syria; those present included Daniel O'Connell and the Irish historian and humanitarian, Richard Robert Madden.[8]

Dillon's years of study were crowned with achievement in 1841, when he was a prize-winner in political economy, was conferred with a BA (second senior moderatorship) degree in logic and ethics,[9] and was called to the Irish bar.

In the Historical Society at TCD he met, 'and added to his friendships for life', John Edward Pigot and John O'Hagan—the sons of Catholic lawyers. But the most important friendship of his political career was with Thomas Davis (1814–45), whom he succeeded as president of the Historical Society. While fellow students they dabbled in political journalism, and together they joined O'Connell's Repeal Association in April 1841.[10]

Dillon followed Davis's pedagogic line in his presidential address to the Historical Society, delivered extra-murally on 8 November 1841. His address, scarcely less than that of Davis (who spoke about education the previous year), set the tone for the fledgling Young Ireland group.

O'Hagan, for example, declared: 'The night before I read Dillon's address I was a whig; next morning and ever after I was a nationalist.[11]

Dillon's subject was 'Patriotism', in which he emphasised Davis's doctrine of duty to one's country. His oration reflected the integrity and naivety of youth. He believed that 'the fate of our country is in the balance; when a little mutual forbearance on our parts, and the removal of a few prejudices, may put an end perhaps for ever to her misery and humiliation'; the time was not far distant 'when our hearts shall unite, and our dissensions and our degradation shall depart together'.[12] He called for a revival of the spirit of 1782, yet he regarded as overrated the intellectual powers of Henry Grattan and the other leaders who had won legislative independence in that year: 'At a time when they had the enemy completely at their mercy, and might have dictated whatever terms they pleased, they should have insisted on something more than permission to meet and amuse one another with elaborate orations, and to make laws which they had no power to enforce. The should have known that ... a parliament is nothing more than a debating club if it be not sustained by the sympathy and, if needs be, by the arms of the people.' This was as near as he went to criticising the Protestant parliament which survived in Dublin until 1800.

On the same occasion Dillon asserted that sincerity was the key to eloquence: they should love their country as Demosthenes had loved Athens.

> You must all have observed that a notion has gone abroad, and has been for some years gaining ground very rapidly—less rapidly, I am happy to say, amongst the humbler classes of our fellow-countrymen, than amongst the class to which you belong—that the spirit of nationality is an unreasonable and a mischievous prejudice; that national glory is but a mockery and a phantom; that instead of preserving national recollections and national customs, and diffusing amongst our population a respect for, and a knowledge of their country's history, it were better to draw a veil over the past, and to obliterate it from their memory. ...
>
> The man who loves his country, and knows how much more its future greatness and happiness are dependent on the spirit and the dispositions of its people, than on the quality of the food which they eat or the clothes they wear, will view with more alarm the progress of such opinions amongst them, than a pestilence or a famine, or the presence of a hostile army on their shores. For the effects of these things are speedily effaced; the ravages of pesti-

lence and famine are soon repaired, and fields laid waste will soon grow green again; but when cold and grovelling selfishness takes possession of the minds of a people, and draws them away from virtue and from honour, there is then a wound inflicted which festers at the heart, and which centuries may not heal.

The excesses of nationalism did not disprove the merits of nationality, any more than bigotry was a reason for abandoning religion. The character of Ireland 'has not been produced in a day, or in a year, or in a hundred years. Long centuries of trial and affliction have made it what it is. ... And is it not vexatious to hear little assimilating politicians talk about bending and fashioning this ancient tree, as if it were a twig?' Dillon distinguished between love of country and love of empire: 'I never could understand the patriotism of those men who exhaust the little stock of enthusiasm that nature has given them in admiring and praising a people, every page of whose history is stained with some villainous perfidy or savage atrocity practised on their country. ... It is, no doubt, the duty of a Christian to forgive the man who does him an injury; but, if he sees the same man about to inflict a similar injury on a third party, it is not his duty to assist him, or to wish that he may succeed in his wicked attempt.'

Although he had absorbed a considerable amount of Benthamite utilitarianism, in this valedictory student address Dillon identified with the Romantic movement: 'The patriot revels in a thousand pure delights which the cold cosmopolite can never taste.' The worshippers of 'commerce and manufactures' would strip us 'of those lofty affections that raise the soul above present and material pleasures, and connect our hearts with one another, and with heaven.' He was 'not one of those sentimentalists who cannot be made to feel the importance of providing for the physical wants of mankind; but it is no sentimentalism to assert that the gratification of his physical desires forms but a very insignificant portion of the happiness to which man is capable of attaining.'

Dillon was a spiritual man who believed the material world is insufficient to satisfy the human heart. This vision of life 'moves us to take an interest in those political and social improvements, the effects of which cannot be felt until long after the grave shall have closed over us.' He rejected the 'what-has-posterity-done-for-me' syndrome. He criticised the utilitarians as short-sighted and ungenerous; if love of country was abandoned people would cease to be concerned about future generations: 'Patriotism is the great link which connects the future with the present, which binds, as it were, the interests of posterity to our hearts.'

He concluded:

> If the observations I have made on the subject have the effect of
> raising a doubt concerning the wisdom of those politicians who
> make light of nationality, who think that they serve their country
> by depreciating her power and resources in the estimation of her
> own people and of the world, and by representing her as unfit to
> enjoy, and unable to defend, her freedom; if anything I have said
> should cause you to think that national patriotism and common
> sense are by no means inconsistent with one another, as they are
> very commonly supposed to be; then my object is accomplished.

Davis claimed that the doctrine associated with the Young Irelanders—
a nationality 'indifferent to sect and independent of party'—was '*made* in
the historical societies of Dublin and belongs to Trinity College
Protestants and a few Roman Catholics of TCD.'[13] This group included:
Davis, Dillon, Pigot, O'Hagan, Thomas MacNevin, Denny Lane, Denis
Florence MacCarthy, Colman O'Loghlen, Richard O'Gorman, John
Mitchel, John Martin, Thomas Devin Reilly and Thomas Charles Wallis.

Most of them belonged to comfortable, middle-class families, and, on
the Catholic side, represented the first generation to reach manhood
knowing the penal laws only by tradition. This Catholic middle class
asserted its new social status by having sons educated at Trinity College,
where young Catholics and Protestants, such as Dillon and Davis, met as
equals and formed enduring friendships. Dillon was the earliest
confederate of Davis.

Another decisive Trinity influence was Thomas Wallis, a graduate and
prominent member of the Historical Society, who claimed he 'changed
John Dillon from a whig and utilitarian to a nationalist and a popular
leader.'[14]

The whig *Morning Register* provided these young intellectuals with a
training ground in journalism.[15] In February 1841 Davis had an article
published denouncing the British government for withdrawing a parliamentary grant to the Royal Dublin Society, which had disgraced itself by
a display of Protestant bigotry. He admonished the public not to look on
quietly and see an 'old, useful *Irish* institution sacrificed to the rashness
or caprice of an English minister.'[16] Writing on the same issue Dillon said
that no honesty on the part of an imperial administration could compensate
for Irish independence.[17]

The government relented and the two friends, elated by their success, persuaded the owner of the *Register*, Michael Staunton, to let them run his paper as an experiment. The dull whig-Catholic journal suddenly adopted an exciting nationalist tone, to the bewilderment of its regular readers.

The trial period lasted only four months but it led to Dillon and Davis taking the momentous step of entering the Repeal Association on 17 April 1841. O'Connell, who lacked substantial middle-class support, had them at once appointed to the executive of the association.

It was around this time that Dillon met Gavan Duffy, a self-educated Ulster Catholic, who was then studying for the bar while editing the *Vindicator*, a biweekly paper in Belfast. On a visit to Dublin he called at the *Register* office, which had given him, too, an apprenticeship to journalism. Dillon was seated in the sub-editor's chair: 'The sweet gravity of his countenance and the simple stately grace of his tall figure struck me at once. His dress was careless and his carriage had not then acquired the ease and firmness which afterwards became so natural that they seemed born with him; but he was a man whom a casual observer could scarcely overlook.'[18]

Next day Dillon introduced Duffy to Davis in the committee room of the Repeal Association. Duffy found Dillon sympathetic and confident. Dillon admired Duffy's writing and told Davis: 'a weekly paper conducted by that fellow would be an invaluable acquisition.'[19] Davis recorded: 'A desire to start a paper more decided than Mr O'Connell's organs, and less Romanist than the *Freeman's Journal*, had long existed in the minds of Mr Dillon and myself'; Dillon wished to create a higher kind of journalism, and they had many earnest talks about the *Nation* project.[20]

Returning to Dublin in the spring of 1842, Duffy met Davis and Dillon in the Four Courts, and they

> proposed that we should walk away together to some place fitter for frank conversation. The young barristers put off their gowns, and we strolled into the neighbouring Phoenix Park. ... After a long conversation on the prospects of the country we sat down under a noble elm within view of the park gate leading to the city, and there I proposed to my new friends a project which had been often in my mind from the first time I met them—the establishment of a weekly newspaper.[21]

Duffy 'was to find the funds and undertake the editorship, and we were to recruit contributors among our friends. ... Dillon named two young men in college, who afterwards did valuable work—John O'Hagan and John Pigot.'[22]

Thus begun what T.W. Moody called 'the most notable journalistic venture in Irish history.' The three founders were all under thirty. Dillon 'was then in his twenty-ninth year, full of youth, hope, enthusiasm, and in person singularly prepossessing. He was tall, slight and thin but broad-shouldered; dark as a Spaniard in complexion, with regular noble features, and great dark melancholy eyes.'[23]

The editorship was assigned to Duffy as the most experienced journalist, 'but Davis was our true leader. Not only had nature endowed him more liberally, but he loved labour better, and his mind had traversed regions of thought and wrestled with problems still unfamiliar to his confederates.'[24]

Davis outlined a coherent philosophy of Irish nationalism, which had an immense influence then and on subsequent generations:

> Nationality is their first great object—nationality which will not only raise our people from their poverty by securing them the blessing of a domestic legislature, but inflame and purify them with a lofty and heroic love of country—a nationality of the spirit as well as of the letter—a nationality which may embrace Protestant, Catholic and Dissenter—Milesian and Cromwellian—the Irishman of a hundred generations, and the stranger who is within our gates: not a nationality which would prelude civil war, but which would establish internal union and external independence; a nationality which would be recognised by the world, and sanctified by wisdom, virtue and prudence.[25]

The *Nation's* print-run of 12,000 copies sold out on the first day of publication, 15 October 1842, and, though costing sixpence, it had within a short time a higher circulation than any other newspaper in Ireland. Duffy calculated it was read by a quarter of a million, because of its wide distribution through reading rooms and from hand to hand.

The paper attracted a talented array of contributors who, in reaction to bourgeois sobriety, romanticised the past and looked forward to an heroic future. The nationalism which they preached reflected many of the ideals shared by young intellectuals in the Europe of their day. They rejected the economic laws of the market place as the determinants of social relationships.[26]

Responding to the spirit of the age which gave a mystical sense to the idea of nationality, they advanced the values of Ireland's ancient civilisation and ransacked Irish history for episodes which could be romanticised; contemporary politics were expounded in martial songs. The *Nation* succeeded in providing for the great mass of the people a myth, a romantic history and an aspiration.[27]

The men who set about 'regenerating the spirit of Ireland' met on Saturday evenings—'at a frugal supper, seasoned by wit and friendship and generous hopes'—to plan the next week's issue. Occasionally, a Sunday excursion to visit antiquities replaced the weekly suppers. (Dillon lived in 20 Great Charles Street next door to George Petrie, the antiquary.) Of all the group, Mitchel rated Dillon the tallest 'in body and mind. In our many gay and genial meetings he was always quiet and unassuming; never keeping himself on the stretch for an opportunity to say a good thing.'[28]

Despite O'Connell's skills in mobilising clerical support, the repeal agitation did not begin to gain momentum until late 1842. Distress was widespread owing to a bad harvest and the *Nation* harnessed it to the political campaign. At the outset O'Connell welcomed the vigorous propagandists of the *Nation*, while they accepted him as the patriarchal leader of the national cause. Ultimately, he would tire of the earnest, self-righteous young men in stove hats. Initially, however, they concentrated on spreading the gospel of nationality and left the practical politics of repeal to O'Connell.

The nationalism of the *Nation* derived from Grattan and O'Connell, but it was more intellectual, comprehensive and intense. Furthermore, its latent 'tone' was Wolfe Tone. It took up the United Irishmen's concept of a new nation to be founded by merging the identities of Catholic, Protestant and Dissenter. But the task of uniting the Irish people had grown even more difficult since Tone's day. In supporting O'Connell's repeal agitation the Young Irelanders were backing a movement regarded by Protestants in general as threatening them with a Catholic ascendancy.[29] Irish Protestants had reacted against the Catholic revival by swinging round to a policy of maintaining the Union as a guarantee of their interests.

The undercurrent of 'no popery' in English life had, moreover, bubbled to the surface in the mid-1830s. Pulpit, press and parliament contributed to the renewal of anti-Catholicism, which was exacerbated by the 'creeping Romanism' of the Oxford movement.[30] On the other hand, the French writers, Alexis de Tocqueville and Gustave de Beaumont, expressed surprise at the radical spirit which they found among the Irish Catholic clergy. In vain the mild archbishop of Dublin, Daniel Murray, reminded his fellow prelates of their pledge in 1834 to keep priests out of politics. Catholic emancipation had not proved the boon forecast and the times were not conducive to clerical disengagement.

Sir James Graham, home secretary at the height of the repeal agitation in 1843, characterised the movement as 'a Catholic struggle directed by the Roman Catholic hierarchy and priesthood'; twenty of the twenty-seven bishops, headed by the archbishop of Tuam, John MacHale, supported the campaign with varying degrees of enthusiasm. Before he left office in 1846 Robert Peel, the Conservative prime minister, warned that 'the spirit of popery, and its alliance with democratic feelings and institutions, will constitute a very formidable combination against the peace of Ireland, and the maintenance of cordial union with this country.'[31]

The more formidable the repeal movement seemed to become, the less inclination there was among Protestants to respond to the *Nation's* call for reconciliation. The Young Irelanders vitalised the repeal cause, but were not much more successful than O'Connell in uniting Irishmen. Their only notable Protestant converts were: William Smith O'Brien, John Mitchel, John Martin and, for a time, Samuel Ferguson.[32]

The group which founded the *Nation* was termed, at first ironically, 'Young Ireland'—after 'Young Italy', with which it had obvious affinities. Its enthusiasm was not reciprocated by Camillo Benso Cavour and Giuseppe Mazzini, who dismissed Irish nationalism and courted British goodwill.[33]

Although the *Nation* was in part Davis's translation of German romantic nationalism, with O'Connell most Young Irelanders saw in repeal of the Union and a return to the constitution in 1782, purged of its abuses, the goal of their endeavours.[34] Repeal for them meant something much more than the restoration of Grattan's parliament, or the home rule programme of the later nineteenth century. The parliament they envisaged was to be a representative assembly, drawing its strength from a popular franchise and equality between Protestants and Catholics. They demanded of England effective sovereignty for Ireland: the only connection between the two countries to be the equivalent of today's Commonwealth status.[35]

Besides echoing the sentiments of romantic nationalism then sweeping through Europe, the *Nation* school sprang directly from Irish conditions: it was conscious of economic and political realities as well as national ideals. This was especially true of Dillon, who was less literary and more practical then either Davis or Duffy.[36] Davis said (1 October 1844) the *Nation* succeeded because it 'was written by men smarting under the sight of the people's misery and mad at their country's degradation.'

Nation Contributor

It is impossible to express all that there is to love in that man.
DAVIS ON DILLON

John Blake Dillon contributed an estimated 51 articles to the *Nation*.[1] Most of these were written before May 1843, when he withdrew to concentrate on his legal career. Unlike Davis and Duffy, Dillon practised at the bar.

According to John O'Hagan, he 'had not the abounding and restless energy of Davis, but he united a lofty enthusiasm with great lucidity of intellect and an unvarying candour. He seemed incapable of the least sophistry or insincerity. ...'[2] Many of Dillon's pieces were brief political commentaries, reflecting the priggish certainties of youth. Several essays contain, however, evidence of his strong logical mind, passion for social justice and grave charm. He emerges as an enlightened, compassionate, if unoriginal, thinker.

Dillon began his article in the first issue of the *Nation*, 'Aristocratic institutions', by quoting Mirabeau: 'Society is composed of three classes—those who work, those who beg and those who rob.' A landed aristocracy was the cause of the 'unnatural, monstrous combination of poverty and profusion' in his native Connacht. He contrasted the lives of the idle rich with 'the condition of the people who produce by their labour the materials of all this splendour—the state of abject slavery to which they are reduced—the unlimited power which landlords and their agents have over them—their uncultivated minds—their physical sufferings—their haggard looks—their naked children—their wet potatoes—their hovels—their rags—and their beds of straw.'

Dillon concluded (28 January 1843): 'Land reform should hold the first place in the thoughts of every man who wishes to better the condition of the people.' In an article in the second issue of the *Nation* he emphasised that his hostility was directed against the landlord system: 'The Irish aristocracy is what our laws have made it—it is what every aristocracy has been which has existed long enough to reach its maturity of rottenness. It is the very same compound of frivolity, luxury and rapacity, which in 1789 drove France to madness at first, and then to freedom.' (Thomas Carlyle's history of the French Revolution (1837), with its underlying philosophy that aristocratic regimes ultimately meet the fate they deserve, was essential reading for the Young Irelanders. Carlyle was a social prophet of the 1840s before the loss of humanity in his later writings.)

Dillon delineated a Connacht landlord as

> a man upon whose iron heart the sufferings of his fellow-man made no impression; whose ear is deaf to the cry of anguish; who sacrifices the peace, the happiness, the lives of thousands, to the gratification of the meanest of his desires; who can, without a pang, drive the widow and the orphan houseless upon the world—greedy and griping—mean at once, and haughty—a slave and a tyrant— the grovelling sycophant of power, and the grinder of the poor man's face. A Connaught landlord sees but one object in creation, and that is himself. He alone is made for enjoyment—all things else are made for him. He counts the potatoes on which the poor man lives. His horses are better lodged, and his hounds better fed, than the most comfortable tenant on his estate.
>
> Even his own interest is sacrificed to the gratification of his short-sighted avarice. If any man should be so desperate as to expend his money or his labour in improving his land, he raises the rent or turns him out. He is without even the most vulgar sort of benevolence; squanders the patrimony of his own children in ostentation and luxury, and leaves them beggars. As for patriotism, he either fears or laughs at it. A Connaught landlord has no country.[3]

Dillon asserted (29 October 1842) that Irish tenants were 'poor beyond comparison with any people, civilised or savage, in the universe ... only one degree above the starving point'. In the prevailing distress rents should be reduced: 'We respect the rights of property as highly as men can, but we respect the rights of human nature more.' The farmers could not agitate for themselves: 'They are at the mercy of their masters; and the punishment of resistance, in the agrarian code, is extermination, which is the popular synonym among the landed interest for death by cold and hunger.' Irish landlords were hated and despised because they had 'neglected the common duties of humanity'.

When advocates of fixity of tenure 'insist upon the right of the people to an interest in the soil of their own country, we are generally met with a cry about the rights of property', Dillon argued; real property rights were incompatible with landlord claims because 'the rights of property encourage production, while landlord rights impede it'. A landed aristocracy was an 'insurmountable obstacle' to progress. He declared (3 December 1842): 'The only legitimate object of property is to secure to the man who works the fruits of his labour.' But in Ireland 'protection of property' meant enabling one man to live in idleness on the industry of others; aristocracy was 'the result of conquest' and 'the descendants of those robbers have contrived to keep their feet upon the necks of the people'.

Dillon also rejected socialism: 'There never will be a community in which perfect equality will reign until universal benevolence shall become the sole activating principle of men's conduct.' He favoured a meritocracy: 'Distinctions of rank are no more inconsistent with democracy than aristocracy—the only difference is that, under the former, these distinctions are bestowed according to merit, under the latter they are allotted by chance.'

Reflecting on recent agrarian murders in County Tipperary, he blamed the barbarous rack-renting system 'for the sufferings of the people and for their crimes'. He continued:

> Let us put ourselves in their place—let us suppose that we were after spending our whole lives in unceasing toil and suffering—that want and sickness were the constant inmates of our miserable homes—that we worked day after day, from morning till night, to save a wife and children and aged parents from perishing—and that, after all this, some heartless scoundrel, who had been rioting in profusion and luxury on the fruits of our labour, had thrown us out with a helpless family upon the world—let us suppose all this, and although we cannot justify these deeds of blood, we will at least cease to be surprised by them.[4]

He added, quoting Tacitus: 'We value peace much, but we value freedom more—we have no sympathy with those who would "made a desert and call it peace".'[5]

Dillon went on to ask: 'What are the poor people to do ... for the extermination is the cruellest of murderers? Are they to lie down quietly and die? It is the course, no doubt, which the spirit of Christianity and the example of its divine author would recommend; but ... it is not everyone who can be a martyr.' (When the people lay down and died during the Famine, and failed to respond to the Young Ireland resistance, Dillon would despise the apathy of the masses.)[6]

In 1842—anticipating the Land League—he urged tenant farmers 'to join together and call with one voice for a complete remodelling of the laws affecting landed property. Instead of committing unmeaning murders, which every good man must condemn, however he may pity the unhappy wretches who are driven to these dreadful deeds—instead of breaking out into partial insurrections, which only expose them to the vengeance of their oppressors, let them unite and work with a common purpose, and their combined strength cannot be resisted.'[7]

For Dillon, 'the grand grievance which a foreign government has inflicted upon this country was the support it uniformly gave to a rapacious squirarchy. ... We wish for a domestic and a democratic government chiefly because we expect that such a government would cut down the powers and privileges of this class, and bring about its total abolition as soon as it could be effected with safety'.[8]

He denounced as 'impious doctrine' and 'sham morality' the view that it was 'the proper business of the people to learn to submit to their miseries with patience'. He told 'the working people of Ireland, Protestant, Catholic and Presbyterian', that the evils which they endure do not come from God 'but rather from the wickedness of your oppressors, and still more from the want of union and brotherly feeling amongst yourselves'.[9] At the same time Dillon regarded 'the priests as the natural advisers of the [Catholic] people'; together they had overcome sectarian ascendancy; united they would overthrow 'aristocratic tyranny'.

He believed that without morality political action was of little worth: 'We may agitate and spout about liberty, but we cannot be free ... we may destroy, but we can never build up.' He deplored the Irish toleration of 'rascality'. In its task of moral education, Young Ireland joined forces with the temperance crusade of Father Theobald Mathew, who, according to Dillon, had 'effected a great reformation, without the aid of law or superstition, by the mere majesty of virtue'. Davis considered Father Mathew's success bore witness to the dawn of a new era: 'Irish intoxication was the luxury of despair—the saturnalia of slaves. Irish temperance is the first fruit of deep-sown hope, the offering of incipient freedom.'[10] The diarist, Amhlaoibh Ó Súilleabháin, who was closer to the popular mind, wrote that the people had got it into their heads that Father Mathew's crusade was 'preparing the country for that national uprising which they supposed would be imminent should O'Connell's parliamentary tactics fail'.[11]

In reflections on a monument to Father Mathew, Dillon suggested a museum 'or a college in which our native language, literature and arts might be revived and extended'.[12] He maintained that 'we have no literature of our own—none, at least, to which we have access,' and began a scheme of translating extracts from contemporary French literature into English for readers of the *Nation*.

In a population of eight and a half million, more than 3,700,000 were illiterate (little account being taken then of the rich oral tradition). Irish, Davis pointed out, was still the language of about half the people west of a line from Derry to Waterford, yet it was excluded from the 'national' schools. He also observed that among the middle classes to speak Irish was regarded as a mark of vulgarity.[13]

Dillon differed with the O'Connells on the new Poor Law system. Daniel O'Connell had voted against the measure in 1838, asserting that relief of the destitute should be a matter for private charity rather than state provision.[14] Dillon, for his part, thought the system better than the absence of any help in a country suffering from chronic destitution—where the largest proprietors were absentee landlords—and insisted that the poor law should not be abolished but amended. He declared that the great majority of the Irish people were treated not as citizens 'but as enemies to be intimidated and subdued'. However, 'the hairs of the poor man's head are counted as carefully as those of the rich and as strict a reckoning will be demanded for his blood by Him who values not these distinctions, but looks down upon all His children with the same eye of concern and of love.'[15]

A poor law was not what Ireland wanted, Dillon wrote.

> It is a blundering system of legislation, which converts the whole population of the country into paupers, by taking away the produce of their labour and giving it to idlers, and then sets up a costly machinery for the purpose of relieving their distress. Let the people be relieved from their intolerable burdens—let the taxes which are spent in plundering Afghanistan and China, to enrich a sordid and heartless aristocracy, be reduced—let the army and constabulary, which are paid by the people for the purpose of keeping themselves in unwilling subjection to this same aristocracy, be disbanded and sent to earn their bread in some more honest way—in fine, let the swarms of idlers, who under various denominations infest the country and devour the fruits of the people's industry, be made work.[16]

Nevertheless, he disagreed 'unwillingly' with O'Connell's son, John, about the poor rate: it was 'the only tax which has for its object the good of the poor'. He explained why he supported the scheme in principle: 'Under the present system of tenure, and with the present race of landlords, the real question is between rents and the poor rate—whether all the plunder ought to be given to the landlord, or a little of it secured for the poor—whether it is better that £12 million should be spent on the vanities and luxuries of our worthless aristocracy, or that £1 million should be subtracted from that sum, and devoted to the clothing and feeding of our naked and starving people.'[17]

In Ireland, where 'the land which God made for all is monopolised by a few' and the people lacked employment, the poor law was a necessary evil, Dillon concluded. 'It is a clumsy device for conveying back to the people a small portion of that wealth which of right belongs to them, and of which they have been plundered by tax-eaters and landlords.'[18]

In November 1842 O'Connell ended his term as lord mayor of Dublin, having been the first Catholic to fill that office in 150 years. On the basis of corporation dinner speeches by O'Connell and Isaac Butt, a rising Protestant lawyer, Dillon asked: 'Is it too much to hope that a few more years will see the end of those absurd prejudices—that the religion of love will soon cease to be a source of dissension and hatred, and that the many parties into which Irishmen have been hitherto divided will soon be merged into two parties—the national and the anti-national—the friends of the country and the friends of the stranger?'[19] (Butt defended the Union in a three-day debate with O'Connell the following spring and would hesitate until 1870 before embracing nationalism.)

Meanwhile, Dillon urged O'Connell to 'fling himself upon the bosom of the people'. On repeal 'the English parliament will never yield, unless to necessity and fear. It is on Irish ground ... that the battle for nationality must be fought; and to be fought with success, and without blood, it must be fought by him.'[20]

On 7 January 1843 Dillon welcomed O'Connell's announcement that he was embarking on a series of 'monster' meetings: 'A year devoted to such an undertaking would be, indeed, a repeal year. One such year would do more for the national cause than ten spent in the British parliament.' A fortnight later he wrote: 'Ireland for the Irish is our creed; and that creed is based upon the conviction that the resources of our country are sufficient for the support of our people, and that the intellect of our people is sufficient for the full development of those resources.'

The 1840s was a disturbed period in Britain. Although Dillon referred to Chartism as 'a poor thing', he thought O'Connell had blundered in alienating the British radicals, and advised Davis 'to speak with all respect and civility of those who stretch out the hand of friendship to us'.[21]

There was always the danger—from the establishment perspective— that British and Irish radicals would join forces. John Bright, after his by-election victory in 1843, warned government ministers of the need for reforms 'with insurrection threatening them more or less near in Ireland, in Wales and in the north of England'.[22]

Furthermore, difficulties with France and US suggested that a situation might arise which would make it necessary for the British government to conciliate Ireland. 'After all it was Yorktown which had set the stage for Grattan's victory in 1782.'[23]

Dillon indulged in the Irish propensity for wishful thinking: '... if '82 be not a fable then was there never a moment more propitious than the present. It would seem as if the new world and the old had conspired to create the opportunity by accumulating embarrassments upon England.' Commenting on the first Afghan war, he pointed out (24 December 1842) that £18 million had been 'taken from the hard-working and half-starved people of Great Britain and Ireland, and spent in exterminating the poor Afghans, because they would not submit to wear what we, my friends, have worn too tamely and too long—the livery of a foreign master'. But the people

> are beginning to feel that those laws which doom the millions to starvation and unremitting toil, in order that the uttermost regions of the earth should be searched to gratify the morbid appetites of a few, are based not upon natural justice or the will of God, but upon mere brute force. And feeling this, the countless sons of labour look upon their sinewy arms and ask in a voice always growing louder—what are these men that we should be their slaves.[24]

Dillon asked: 'What are the feelings with which true Irishmen ought to look upon those dangers and embarrassments which beset, not the *people* of England who share in our sufferings—nor the throne of Britain and Ireland, to which our allegiance is due—but that plundering aristocracy which torments and tyrannises over both? What ought they be but triumph and hope and bright anticipations of approaching freedom?' He continued: 'Why should we not seize upon the moment when doubt and confusion prevail in the councils of our enemy, to rescue our country from a connection into which she was driven by force and fraud, and which has ever been to her a source of suffering and calamity.'[25]

Nationalist euphoria was increased by the foreign support for repeal. Leading American politicians, including Robert Tyler, a son of the US president, spoke on Irish platforms, while President John Tyler came out strongly in favour of repeal. Alexandre Ledru-Rollin, a prominent French radical, went so far as to promise military aid if Britain suppressed the movement, and O'Connell had to persuade him not to come to Ireland at the height of the agitation. Cavour admitted: 'The present singular condition of Ireland has excited the attention of all in Europe who are interested in politics.'[26]

Pro-repeal meeting were held in industrial areas of England, while advocates of complete suffrage expressed sympathy with the Irish cause. Feargus O'Connor's *Northern Star* said no Chartist would 'lift his finger against Ireland'; the whig *Morning Chronicle* asserted that England would not pour out its armies and money to maintain 'the cruel injustice' of the established church in Ireland.[27]

During the summer and autumn of 1843 hundreds of thousands attended more than forty meetings, held usually in places of Irish historical significance. Dillon said that O'Connell, in his speeches on such sites, searched 'the depths of the nation's memory'. By autumn Ireland was at a fever pitch of excitement, and the attitude of the British government had changed from one of contempt to fear.

Dillon thought Britain would be unable to resist 'the unanimous determination of the Irish millions' for repeal: 'Hated by France, humbled by America, with a discontented people and a failing revenue, an English government could not afford to drive Ireland to a civil war.'[28] Ominously, Peel declared on 9 May that the government would, if necessary, prefer civil war to dismemberment of the empire.

Dillon reported on the monster meeting in Roscommon addressed by O'Connell, then at the height of his power:

> there was the meeting of multitudes in the noblest of causes—there was the reconciliation of old enemies, the grasping of hands that had been often raised against each other in mad and ruinous strife—there was the smile of pride and of tenderness more than filial, when O'Connell dwelt upon the excellencies and beauties of their fatherland; and when he asked was there one who would not die for it, there was the gloom of deep enthusiasm passing across the upturned faces of that mighty mass, and the bursting of 100,000 voices in one deafening cheer.

And then the reflection arose that this people, now so menacing, so terrific, so irresistible, were a few months ago a parcel of degraded serfs, without intellect, without spirit and without hope, submitting to wrongs and indignities without a murmur, incapable apparently either of understanding their rights or of combining to uphold them. It was a consoling and a cheering reflection to the friend of universal happiness and freedom, who could hardly fail to discern in that sudden transition the present interference of the power who promised long ago that the bruised reed should not be broken, and that the sufferings which are endured for the sake of righteousness will have an end.[29]

In August Dillon spoke at a banquet in Castlebar, Co Mayo, before O'Connell and Archbishop MacHale, in response to the toast: 'The people, the only true source of legitimate power.' He said the logic of the Saxon was: 'Poor, ignorant and debased under our domination you have become; and now, because you are poor, ignorant and debased, under that domination you shall remain.'[30] He confessed 'that he belonged to that class of wild enthusiasts who hate the Union by a sort of instinct, without ever waiting to inquire into its effects—who think that independence is a thing worth having for itself—or to speak perhaps more correctly, who believe that the loss of independence is a loss for which no advantages can compensate. His creed was that a country, like a man, had a character of its own, to which its government and its laws ought to be adapted, and that this character can be thoroughly comprehended by itself alone.'

He was also a repealer because of the degrading effects of the Union: 'I am but a humble individual, and yet I can afford to pity the man who could see without emotion such indignities heaped upon his country.' The enemy was not young Queen Victoria or the people of England, 'whose interests are perfectly identical with our own; but a section of an aristocracy, hated through the world for its restless avarice and unjust aggressions. ...'

To oppose 'this feeble, tottering power', Dillon added breathlessly,

we have the eternal force of justice, and the sympathy of all who love it; we have wisdom that never failed us, at our head; we have hands made strong by labour, and hearts that never paled at the face of danger (loud cheers). We have fallen upon auspicious times. The principle of rational democracy is advancing in every land. No longer deformed by revolutionary frenzy ... it comes proclaiming, with the lips of an angel, hope to the oppressed, protection to industry, the downfall of odious privilege, and the near end awakens strong healthful thoughts and holy passions which long lay slumbering there; it speaks of the unforgotten dead, no longer in whispers to the faithful few, but in accents of thunder to the people, commanding us to walk in their footsteps; it cautions us against the errors which led to their overthrow; it tells us to shun rash councils, to beware of promises that are made but to be broken; it preached kindness, conciliation and union; it recalls the mind of the Protestant to the contemplation of those days when Protestants stood foremost in the battle which we are fighting now; it reveals to his mind the glory of that night when, through the patriotism of a Protestant, parliament, inflamed by the eloquence of a Protestant, "rose as it were from its bed, and came nearer to the sun".

To the Irish Catholic it says look into the history of your country; count if you can the tears which she has shed since the time when, invited by domestic discord, the invader first set foot upon the soil, and learn that disunion is the bitter source from which all those tears have flowed. Hate disunion then as you love your country. Put an end to disunion if you would see her free. It is in your power; it is easier than you suppose. The truth is already dawning upon the mind of your Protestant brother, that his wealth cannot be safe in the midst of poverty; that he cannot be happy where all is misery; that if the edifice even of his prosperity would be permanent its foundation must be laid at home. Like yourself, he placed too much reliance on the promises of strangers and he, like you, has been abandoned and betrayed (hear, hear). Seize him by the hand with the strong cordial grasp of Irish friendship, and approaching triumph of truth, freedom and justice through the world (cheers).

Turning to O'Connell, Dillon ended on a note of characteristic generosity: 'Seeing what is passing around and amongst us, it is not too much to hope that heaven will repay that man who is with us tonight for his long years of fidelity and toil, by enabling him to behold with his own eyes the prosperity and the freedom of a country which he loves, and which owes everything to him. ... Even now, from the graves which the tyrants have opened like wounds upon her bleeding breast, there comes a voice instructing, encouraging, purifying the people for the trial through which they have to pass.'

Dillon wrote a number of memorable articles for the *Nation*, but his prose—like his oratorical style—was marked by overstatement.

Repeal Bubble

*Look into our hearts—they were made for love and kindness
and confiding friendship—what fatal power has changed their
nature, and converted them into dark dwelling-places of
hatred, bigotry and distrust? ... The degrading consciousness
of provincialism paralyses our energies and chills our hopes.*
DILLON, 19 NOVEMBER 1842

The repeal bubble burst when the British government called
O'Connell's bluff. Disturbed by the symbolism of the Clontarf site,
Dublin Castle proscribed a mass meeting scheduled to take place there on
8 October 1843. O'Connell, faced with the alternatives of surrender or
bloodshed, capitulated. His most powerful weapon—presenting himself
as holding vast revolutionary forces under leash—was spiked.

Twice the Liberator organised great numbers of people and stirred their
passions. In 1829 he had compelled the Duke of Wellington and Peel to
concede Catholic emancipation. The second essay in brinkmanship failed
because the British ruling class was determined to maintain control of
Ireland. The repeal agitation withered after the web of delicately contrived
impressions was roughly torn away.[1]

As a strong military force was deployed outside the Pro-cathedral in
Dublin, Archbishop Murray commented to his vicar-general:

> I long foresaw, and it required no spirit of prophecy to do so, that
> if the agitation was persisted in the whole power of England would
> as far as necessary be employed to crush it. ... The dream of moral
> influence as able to accomplish everything was clung to in
> opposition to the plainest dictates of common-sense ... and but for
> the prudence evinced by our poor people ... the shores of Clontarf
> would be again steeped in torrents of blood.[2]

The Clontarf surrender, Duffy wrote with hindsight, deprived the repeal
movement of half its dignity and all its terror. At the time he said

O'Connell's decision prevented a massacre: 'There was no butchery—there was no human sacrifice upon the altar of the Orange Moloch that was gloating over the anticipated offering of the day.' (Wellington, a pillar of the tory establishment, had proposed that Northern Protestants be armed and trained as a yeomanry force.[3])

Encouraged by its easy victory, the government had O'Connell, his son, John, Duffy and five others arrested and charged with conspiracy. Although O'Connell appealed successfully against conviction to the law lords, he emerged from prison his vitality diminished.

During the Clontarf show-down Davis was touring the west. He spent two days with Dillon and on 10 October enrolled him in his '82 Club, which Davis envisaged as a sort of senate.[4] (In *Mise agus an Connradh*, Douglas Hyde records that Davis stayed with the Dillons for some time in Mayo attempting to learn Irish.) Dillon later defended his deceased friend against John O'Connell's charge that Davis had left Dublin in 1843 to avoid arrest; he pointed out that Davis began his tour a month before the Clontarf débâcle 'when no person dreamed of arrests'.[5] He said Davis had expected an insurrection would follow the arrests. Furthermore, 'I fully participated in his anticipations, or his *hopes*, if you will. ... If those hopes had been realised—if the people of Ireland had risen as one man at that moment, and in the blood of their tyrants had washed out the shame of 600 years, Mr O'Connell or any other man would not now dare to say they had done wrong'.

When the *Nation* was launched Dillon and Davis had agreed to write a political article each week, but in May 1843 Thomas MacNevin replaced Dillon as a regular contributor.[6] It is not altogether clear why Dillon abandoned journalism. With his uncertain health, he alternated between bursts of energy and dejection. Moreover, he was interested primarily in a legal career. He told Duffy early in 1843 'to succeed at the bar I must be almost altogether a lawyer. However, I will not lose sight of politics entirely; but you must not depend too much on me'.[7] In one of the few references to Dillon's performance in court, Davis recorded that he 'was called on suddenly to speak for prisoners at Castlebar and succeeded admirably I'm told. He says not, but you know him.'[8] Dillon ceased to write for the *Nation* 'except for an occasional spurt'; he remained, none the less, 'a constant critic of his friends, and his lenient and sympathetic strictures sank deep'.[9]

Dillon spent most of the disappointing years of 1843–6 in legal practice.

In March 1844 he described himself as 'an impartial spectator', who advised on *Nation* policy. By September Pigot hoped Davis would make him 'take a subject for publication in the winter'. Five days later he exclaimed: 'Would anything shame that incarnate indolence, John Dillon?'[10] A judgment later to be echoed by Arthur Griffith, who argued that Dillon's literary assistance to the *Nation* 'was not great, his temperament being on the indolent side'.[11] The founder of Sinn Féin, a journalist of prodigious energy, did not take Dillon's health into account.

In the atmosphere of anti-climax after the collapse of the repeal agitation differences in age, experience and outlook emerged between O'Connell and the Young Irelanders. The preoccupations of 'repeal year' had allowed few opportunities for discord to develop; strains in the movement increased when it became clear that repeal would not be achieved quickly and that O'Connell was out of sympathy with romantic nationalism.

Initially, however, the Young Irelanders were pleased with the choice of Smith O'Brien as deputy leader during O'Connell's imprisonment. O'Brien was a liberal aristocrat, who joined the Repeal Association in protest at the government's attitude. Descended from the ancient line of the O'Briens of Thomond, he was born in County Clare in 1803. He became MP for County Limerick, where he owned an estate.

Davis found O'Brien 'though cold in manner ... true, friendly and laborious'.[12] Tall and handsome, he was a throw-back to the Protestant patriots of 1782. This grave, quixotic figure resolved on 30 May 1844— the date O'Connell was sentenced to a year in jail—to abstain from intoxicating liquor until the Union was repealed. O'Brien's stark disinterestedness impressed Dillon.

O'Brien was extremely reluctant to question O'Connell's leadership, but increasingly his sympathies lay with the idealism and religious tolerance of the Young Irelanders. Essentially, they sought a pluralist Ireland, while O'Connell's movement had an overwhelmingly Catholic character.

Although opposed to physical violence, O'Connell had used verbal violence. The Young Irelanders' rhetoric, on the other hand, expressed their commitment to the politics of principle. After forty years in politics O'Connell was ready to adapt his course to circumstances; he viewed repeal pragmatically, whereas for Young Ireland it was a spiritual necessity. Already in September 1844, the month of O'Connell's release, Pigot was complaining about his 'damned whiggery'.[14]

O'Connell, deciding that repeal was not then attainable, began to cast around for new options. He considered a federalist compromise, until stopped by the *Nation*, and was also engaged in sounding out the whigs on the possible terms of a future alliance (his previous compact, with the Melbourne administration, had been beneficial to Ireland).

Young Ireland and O'Connell also differed on Peel's reform programme. Having defeated O'Connell on the constitutional issue, the tory prime minister set about detaching middle-class Catholics from what he still regarded as 'a sullen and formidable confederacy against the British connexion'.[15] A Charitable Bequests Act—which Davis thought a useful measure and O'Connell opposed—placed Catholic charities on an equal footing with other charities. Peel also increased the grant to Maynooth.[16]

The most significant feature of the government's Irish policy, however, was the lack of attention given to social and economic issues. While the Devon Commission represented the first official acknowledgement of the evils of the land system, its report in 1845 was overshadowed by the 'Godless' colleges controversy. The Colleges Bill proposed to establish non-denominational institutes in Belfast, Cork and Galway. By 1845 O'Connell had moved away from his earlier support for mixed education, and he fixed on the colleges Sir Robert Inglis's stigma of 'a gigantic scheme of Godless education'.[17] The Young Irelanders, committed to the principle of integrated education, welcome the bill with reservations. It was suggested they favoured the measure because of indifference to religion.[18] This was a wounding charge in the prevailing atmosphere. Dillon stood by Davis in his resolve to keep the repeal movement separate from denominational interests. He differed with O'Connell on the Colleges Bill, claiming it encouraged religious instruction; he and his brother, Valentine, were among 170 signatories of a petition supporting mixed education.[19] Davis was, however, slightly paranoid about a Catholic ascendancy taking the form of a 'Browne and MacHale government'. (Robert Dillon Browne was a bankrupt Mayo MP addicted to sherry, who sometimes had to borrow a suit before appearing in parliament.)[20]

Davis and O'Connell debated the education question at a meeting of the Repeal Association on 26 May. Davis irritated O'Connell and reduced himself to a state of nervous exhaustion. O'Connell launched a stinging attack on the Young Irelanders; Davis wept and Dillon burst a blood vessel.[21] A reconciliation followed but it did not end the dispute.

Overstrained and disheartened by his failure to heal the breach between the rival factions, Dillon went to recuperate in the country. He advised Davis to 'avoid any further encounter with the O'Connells for some time'. Regarding John O'Connell: 'It is impossible latterly to bear with the insolence of this little frog. There is no man or country safe from his venom. If there be not some protest against him, he will set the whole world against us.' Dillon could find only one priest in Mayo still friendly to the *Nation*.[22]

The Young Irelanders overreacted to John O'Connell's denunciation of 'the infidel colleges'. The Liberator's favourite son was a minor figure, who, as Dillon observed, inherited 'all the cunning without the genius of his father'.[23] At a meeting in November, 19 Catholic bishops decided to oppose the Colleges Act while eight were prepared to accept the scheme provisionally.

On 22 July 1845 Dillon wrote inviting Davis to spend a week with him at the seaside: 'I have a piper there that will put life into you for the next seven years. The lodge in which I stop looks straight across the bay at the spot where Humbert landed, and we shall make a pilgrimage to the place. I will also take you to see Downpatrick which they speak of as a curiosity. You will see a description of it in Otway's tour.'[24]

In his *Sketches of Erris and Tyrawly* (1841), Caesar Otway described Downpatrick Head as a spectacular promontory on the north Mayo coast. According to tradition, St Patrick visited it on his way to Croagh Patrick. Patterns were held there before the Famine. At Kilcummin strand near by, a French expeditionary force under Jean Joseph Amable Humbert landed in 1798. Kilcummin was a tangible link for Dillon with the French revolution, the ideals of which he had absorbed, and the '98 rising. During the repression which followed the French surrender, 25 local men fleeing from the Redcoats had drowned in a sea cave below Downpatrick.

In his letter to Davis, Dillon added: 'In this country as far as I can see repeal is all but extinct. One cause of this is a very general dissatisfaction about the accounts [of the association], but the principal cause is the universal rottenness of all classes: gentry, priests and people. One must have a most sanguine temperament to be able to hope in the centre of the county of Mayo.'

Davis did not heed the piper 'that will put life into you for the next seven years'. On 9 September he was struck down by scarlet fever and died seven days later. Dillon wrote to Duffy (19 September):

Your letter was like a thrust from a dagger. I had not even heard
that he was unwell. This calamity makes the world look rather
bleak. God knows I am tempted to wish myself well out of it. I am
doing you a grievous wrong to leave you alone at this melancholy
time. I was preparing to be off by the post-car, but my friends have
one and all protested against it, and I verily believe that they would
keep me by force if nothing else would. God help us, my dear
fellow; I don't know how we can look at one another when we
meet.[25]

The death of Davis coincided with the beginning of the greatest
cataclysm in the history of modern Ireland. It deprived the Young
Irelanders of the one leader who might have directed their energies
effectively during the terrible famine years which followed, when
O'Connell lost his grip on the situation.

Dillon's health deteriorated rapidly after his friend's death. 'I have got
a return of that ugly cough which brought on some startling symptoms
[spitting blood] before I left town', he reported to Duffy. The doctors
ordered him to spend the winter in Madeira as the only chance for his
life.[26] Before leaving Ballaghaderreen he wrote a piece for the *Nation*.
'But the stamp of his malady was on it and for the first time, and when his
aid was most needed, he found himself a rejected contributor, and thanked
me for rejecting him', Duffy recalled; 'for many months his wise counsel
and effectual aid were lost to the party which he had helped to create.'[27]
In Madeira Dillon hoped to complete a biography of Tone begun by
Davis. He listed the sources to Duffy:

Besides the 'Life of Theobald Wolfe Tone', edited from his papers
by his son, published at Washington in 1826 in two large octavos,
and since reprinted in a mutilated form in London, I have had the
use of several unpublished letters now in the possession of Dr
[John] Gray (proprietor of the *Freeman's Journal*), and of a great
number of minute personal memorandums collected at great
labour by Dr Madden, for the third series of "The United Irishmen"
and placed by him in the kindest and frankest manner at my
disposal.[28]

He also enlisted the aid of John Mitchel, a rising man in the *Nation*
office. Mitchel wrote providing information; his letter continued: 'And
now, my dear Dillon, I must tell you that nothing almost has occurred since

I came to live in Dublin which I regretted so much as your departure, both for public reasons and personal ones. I wished to know you more thoroughly, because I have an idea that there is none of our friends with whom I would have more sympathy. And I sincerely trust that your health is improving and that next summer you will return to Ireland as well as I wish you.'[29]

On returning from Madeira Dillon was invited to Mitchel's home and afterwards in the United States they became more intimate friends. The friendship which developed between the two families transcended political differences.

Although it was announced in the *Nation*, Dillon made little use of the source material and his life of Tone, planned for Young Ireland's library series, never appeared.[30] But his health and spirits were restored in Madeira—an island resort off the coast of Africa fashionable among wealthy people threatened by tuberculosis.[31]

Dillon rode home through Morocco and southern Spain with a Scottish companion. In Seville he contemplated a carved figure of the crucifixion by Montañez: 'The half-closed eyes, the strained sinews, and the relaxed and powerless limbs make death fearfully present; and on the face there still lingers a blended expression of agony, patience, purity and love. ... But then with my admiration of great works of art, there is always mixed up a sense of their vast inferiority to those of nature.'[32]

In Gibraltar he wrote to his sister, Jane: 'I am quite a different sort of being from what I was when I left home—able to endure any conceivable hardship.' He expected to be home at the end of June 1846: 'Have the old lady in Castlerea and as many of the B'derrin folk as you can make room for and we shall all spend a jolly week there.'[33]

While in Madeira, Dillon had been friendly with Richard Lalor Sheil, an old ally of O'Connell. Nevertheless, on returning to Ireland he wrote an article in the *Nation* protesting at Sheil's election for Dungarvan.[34] Sheil had been offered an appointment under the new whig government and O'Connell—intent on an alliance with Lord John Russell's administration—prevented a repeal candidate from opposing him.

The Young Irelanders were indignant. They wanted national independence, not whig reform. On the other hand, they were an obstacle to O'Connell reaching an accommodation with Russell, who considered the *Nation* was preaching separation. The clash between O'Connell's pragmatism and Young Ireland came to a head in July 1846. O'Connell

decided to silence his young critics, either by compelling them to acknowledge his leadership or by forcing them out of the Repeal Association.
His choice of weapon was the peace resolutions. He insisted that a pledge
repudiating the use of physical force in any circumstances be adopted by
every member of the association.[35]

Although no one seriously contemplated using force at the time, this
proposition was unacceptable to the Young Irelanders. It opened the way
for Thomas Francis Meagher's speech in praise of the sword when the
peace resolutions were debated. On 28 July John O'Connell interrupted
Meagher's oratorical flight; O'Brien came to his defence and after further
dissent led the Young Irelanders present out of Conciliation Hall, the
headquarters of the association.

Earlier, Mitchel had protested that the question was an abstract one:
'Nobody is the least afraid of physical force but there are some of us
mortally afraid of whiggery.' He declared: ' I am one of the Saxon
Irishman of the North, and you want that race of Irishmen in your ranks
more than any other. ... Drive the Ulster Protestants away from your
movement by needless tests and you perpetuate the degradation both of
yourselves and them.'[36]

Fledgling Politician

*... dressed as he always was in solemn black ... calm, gentle,
brave; his broad brow expanding with the enthusiasm that
swelled within it, and his dark eye half concealing, half
emitting the fire of which it was a fountain, as he leaned
forward to take note of that wonderful assembly.*

DUFFY ON DILLON AT THE
ROTUNDA MEETING OF DECEMBER 1846

John Blake Dillon took an active part in politics after his return to Dublin
from Madeira. As before he tried to unite repealers but found the
divisions even more intense. The queen's colleges controversy had opened
a deep fissure in the repeal movement; by 1846 it was becoming clearer
that two different concepts of nationality were confronting each other:
O'Connell's moderate constitutionalism and the sterner creed of Young
Ireland, which did not rule out the possibility that freedom might have to
be won by force of arms. The initiative passed from O'Connell when, with
Ireland reeling under the impact of the Famine, it became apparent that
little beyond inadequate expedients could be expected from the whigs.[1]

Although middle-class supporters replaced priests as repeal organisers
in Dublin, the O'Connell name remained a bulwark between Young
Ireland and the country people. Insofar as the clergy were actively involved
in politics during the Famine years, their sympathies lay with the Repeal
Association before and after O'Connell's death in Genoa on 15 May 1847.
Nevertheless, it was from the ranks of the confused young men that the
repeal movement made its final contribution to the shaping of modern Irish
nationalism.[2]

The success of a restricted government food distribution system in 1845
blunted an appreciation of the magnitude of the problem which emerged
in the autumn of 1846 with the total failure of the potato crop. To provide

relief ideologues of the new whig regime designed public works so as not to enter into competition with private enterprise.

Charles Edward Trevelyan—'custodian of the British treasury during the Famine and a prime example of those in history who have created or sustained suffering on a large scale from more or less disinterested motives'[3]—was concerned that the starving should not be demoralised by becoming dependent on government hand-outs. Even when he acknowledged the reality of famine, Trevelyan resisted state intervention: 'If the Irish once find out there are any circumstances in which they can get free government grants ... we shall have a system of mendicancy such as the world never saw.'[4]

During the winter of 1846-7, the harshest in living memory, hunger tightened its grip on the Irish poor. The wretched people who had existed on the margins of society died in their tens of thousands. (In the 1830s the poor law commissioners had estimated there were 2,385,000 destitute people in Ireland.[5])

The public works system collapsed: in County Mayo, for instance, only 13,000 of an estimated 400,000 people in want were employed.[6] The government, still relying on 'market forces', refused to open its food depots which in any case were inadequately stocked, other European countries having bought up available supplies of Indian corn.

Much unnecessary suffering was caused by leaving the poor at the mercy of a small number of speculators. Despite the virtual monopoly enjoyed by those merchants, the local relief committees were instructed not to under-sell the traders but to follow the general movement of prices.[7] Early in 1847 bewilderment was succeeded by panic, and the headlong flight to the New World got underway. After a deplorable delay in switching from public works to soup kitchens, the government—forced to abandon its policy of limited intervention—fed 3,000,000 in the summer. But the free distribution of food, it was stressed, could be regarded only as an emergency measure until the revised poor law came into operation.

Under the Poor Relief (Ireland) Bill the full burden of supporting the destitute would fall on the Irish poor law unions—an ominous prospect for the poor as many of the unions were known to be bankrupt. The poor law had never in fact been successful in Ireland, where poverty was too deep-rooted to be remedied by pauper relief. A mere revision of the 1838 act, in the cruel circumstances of 1847, totally under-estimated the degree of economic and social collapse. Incomprehensibly, it was assumed that a poor law based on the English model and supported exclusively from local funds could function by the autumn of 1847.[8]

The new poor law was in part a reaction to the hordes of Irish paupers flooding into Britain. Parliament, in a spirit of retribution, transferred the cost of relieving the destitute from the exchequer to Irish property owners. In October, after the last distribution from the soup kitchens, Lord Clarendon, the viceroy, told Lord John Russell the Irish would starve if left to their own resources. The prime minister replied: 'The state of Ireland for the next few months must be one of great suffering. Unhappily the agitation for repeal has contrived to destroy nearly all sympathy in this country.'[9]

The relentless severity in rate collecting increased the depopulation. The government had accepted a tory amendment to the poor law bill which required that an applicant for relief should surrender his holding, if it exceeded a quarter of an acre in extent. This provision, the notorious 'Gregory clause', facilitated the clearances of 1847-8. Furthermore, as landlords were liable for rates on farms valued at £4 and under, many chose to evict rather than pay their tenants' rates. Estimates of the number of evictions vary from 90,000 people in 1849,[10] to 90,000 families between 1847-80.[11] The number of families evicted increased from 6,000 in 1847 to nearly 20,000 in 1850; in the period 1851-3 alone, 136,106 men, women and children were evicted.[12]

While the traditional view of Irish landlords as a rapacious class has been modified by recent research, the overwhelmingly majority of them had neither sympathy with nor understanding of their tenants.[13] In the early stages of the Famine it was the British government, rather than Irish nationalists, which sought to fix responsibility on the landowners; but Trevelyan blamed '... the moral evil of the selfish, perverse, and turbulent character of the people'; and Clarendon claimed 'their idleness and helplessness can hardly be believed'.[14]

Moreover, there was a strong community of interests between British ministers and the Anglo-Irish aristocracy. Almost one peer in four owned Irish land.[15] On the other hand, a high proportion of people on Irish estates were squatters or sub-tenants; Lord John Russell voiced the prevailing view of property rights when he said: 'You might as well propose that a landlord compensate the rabbits for the burrows they have made.'[16] Within the cabinet Lord Palmerston resisted the measures which even Russell realised were necessary in 1847-8.

Palmerston, who had inherited 6,000 acres, received half his income from Irish rents; he considered 'any interference with the right of eject- ment' infringed the rights of property; furthermore, the changes required in Irish agriculture necessitated 'a long and continued and systematic ejectment of smallholders and of squatting cottiers'.[17] (As foreign secretary, Palmerston was an influential agent of reaction in 1848.) In vain the Catholic bishops deplored that 'the sacred and indefeasible rights of life are forgotten amidst the incessant reclamations of the subordinate rights of property'.[18]

Cecil Woodham-Smith, observing that markets flourished throughout the Famine, concluded that high prices and lack of money placed food out of reach of the starving.[19] Gearóid Ó Tuathaigh has pointed out that it was the payment of rents which separated the people from food in the first instance.[20] In the absence of a suspension of rents—dismissed as an unthinkable infraction of property rights—containing the Famine demanded a highly synchronised intervention: beyond the intellectual and physical resources of the Victorian state as far as Ireland was concerned.

English incomprehension of Ireland reached its tragic climax in the Great Famine. Victorian respectability was like a curtain cutting off the propertied classes from the misery of the poor. The provision of public relief on terms less favourable than obtainable by the lowest paid worker was the optimum envisaged by those who understood poverty as the result of some defect of character. Irish workhouses, Carlyle observed, resembled human swineries.

A natural disaster—the repeated failure of the Irish potato crop— became a national catastrophe as British reliance on *laissez-faire* capitalism was compounded by racist attitudes. Official correspondence adopted the euphemism 'distress' to describe the Famine, reflecting government policy which was that the Irish should look after themselves. Rather than an integral part of the United Kingdom Ireland might have been Bengal, where the London *Times*, reporting a cyclone which killed an estimated quarter of a million people, reassured its readers: '... no large sums of money will be spent and care will be taken to leave everything as far as possible to private trade.'[21]

O'Connell created a diversion on the largely irrelevant issue of physical force at a crucial stage of the Famine, while by appearing to support violence the Young Irelanders presented 'a fatal image of Ireland when the time of her greatest need was just at hand'. Rumours about arming the peasantry steeled many hearts to the suffering of the Irish. In reality, as James Hack Tuke, a Quaker philanthropist, wrote in January 1847 on returning from the west, it was the fairly well-to-do who bought arms for the protection of property; the starving, even if weapons were put into their hands, had not the strength left to use them.[22]

John Pigot, Dillon's friend, wrote from London: 'God knows no man with human feeling can easily think of anything but the Famine just now: the accounts of it make me sick and excited and often sleepless, and nervous beyond description. The very first thing to be done is anything (not in its nature criminal) that can alleviate that.'[23]

Pigot held that outdoor relief—not having to enter a workhouse—was 'the only not inhuman species of poor law'. He was a son of Chief Baron David Richard Pigot, who at the end of 1847 formed part of a special commission appointed to expedite the trial of hundreds charged with agrarian offences under the new Outrages Act.

The Young Irelanders, too, were products of their time and class. They tended to think in terms of principles rather than people. They had no effective remedy, except the panacea of repeal, for what is now seen as the worst human disaster of 19th-century Europe.

Dillon continued to seek a 'union of repealers', realising that clerical antagonism was fatal to the Young Ireland cause. Shortly after the secession from the Repeal Association he wrote to Duffy saying he had sent a hurried article answering an attack in the O'Connellite journal, the *Pilot*: 'The most outrageous lies will be believed if they are constantly repeated without contradiction, and I really believe that if this infidelity howl had been promptly and boldly met in the commencement and the hypocrisy of its vile authors exposed, the *Nation* and the cause would be greatly the better of it. … Besides, this question as to whether controversy and bigotry are to form part and parcel of the repeal agitation must be met and answered.'[24]

He outlined a 'plan for reconciliation' in the *Freeman's Journal* on 27 October 1846:

> The position in which the country is now placed presents to the repeal leaders a noble opportunity of pushing forward the repeal cause by giving practical demonstration of the utility of home legislation. The whole people of Ireland are at length united in one sentiment—dissatisfaction with things as they are, and a desire for change. The landlords, in terror for their estates, are compelled in self-defence to consider the condition and necessities of the country, and are prepared to enter on any safe and honourable course that leads out of the difficulties which surround them.
>
> If the committee of the Repeal Association could now stand before the country as the instructors of the English government—if

it possessed wisdom to originate useful measures and influence to compel their adoption, the advantages of self-government would be made plain to all, and decency itself would compel our English rulers to abandon duties which they discharged under the guidance of others. ... The only way to demonstrate the utility of repeal is by showing that we can do our own business better than others can do it for us.

Dillon feared that the increasingly sectarian tone of the association's committee, of which he had ceased to be a member, was causing apprehension about a Catholic ascendancy: 'that the same bell which would toll for the advent of national independence would sound the death-note of free opinion. The growing enlightenment of the country appears to me a sufficient safeguard against this danger. I would take repeal, and do most sincerely wish for it, with all its perils. And so disinterested is my attachment to that cause, the first that awakened any political interest in my mind, that I would gladly see it prosper, even though I have been excluded from its councils.'

He pointed out that O'Brien had urged measures 'whose only fault was that of being too large for the limited generosity of English statesmen'; nothing had emanated from the association except exhortations to patience. He appealed for an end 'to these wretched dissensions, which now engross so much of the time of the committee and which have robbed it of so much of its intellectual strength'. Everybody was 'willing to declare that he is resolved to seek the repeal of the Union by peaceable means alone'. But nobody of Dillon's acquaintance, except the pacifist James Haughton,[25] 'could truly say that a recourse to arms is not justified under any circumstances'. Dillon proposed submitting the question to a panel of lawyers, a suggestion taken up by O'Connell.

A month after the secession a politically conscious section of the Dublin working class, called Friends of Freedom, drafted a remonstrance attacking the whig alliance, the administration of the association and the new test which was driving honest men out of the repeal movement.[26] On 2 December, having as the *Nation* claimed endured four months' vituperation from Conciliation Hall, the leading seceders accepted an invitation from a 'committee of the citizens' to speak in their own defence.

The *Nation* report of the meeting organised by the Dublin remonstrants was published as a pamphlet entitled *Proceedings of the Young Ireland party*. ...[27] It stated: 'Upwards of 2,000 of the most intelligent of the artisan and trading classes filled that portion of the spacious Round Room of the Rotunda set apart for them; and the reserved seats and platform, capable of containing 600 persons, were crowded to inconvenience by as respectacle a body of gentlemen and ladies as we have ever seen at any public demonstration.' In retrospect Duffy summed up the Young Ireland following: 'A few priests, a dozen or two professional men, but mostly artisans of a comfortable class, mercantile assistants, and the students of the schools of law and medicine.'[28]

The attendance included new, talented members of the *Nation* group: Meagher, Patrick James (P.J.) Smyth, Thomas Devin Reilly, Richard D'Alton Williams, Michael Doheny and Thomas D'Arcy McGee; John Martin, from County Down, a figure of secondary importance in the pantheon of Protestant patriots; Eugene O'Curry, who became the first professor of 'Irish archaeology' at the Catholic University, Dublin; and James Cantwell, 'an intelligent and devoted Confederate' who had signed the remonstrance and would accompany Dillon after the rising.

Richard O'Gorman, junior, Dillon's future law partner in New York, made one of the few references to the Famine in his speech repudiating physical force. Born in County Clare, he was the son of a prosperous merchant who had been associated with the emancipation campaign. O'Gorman said:

> Sad and dreary is the picture that this winter sets before our eyes: famine is under the land. The peasant faints from hunger; the landlord sinks under the load of increased taxation; cultivable lands lie idle, while elsewhere population crowds in ruinous pro-fusion: a starving people have seen borne from their shores the best fruits of the earth which they toiled to raise. ... And famine will come on us again, as it did before, and again find a government unprepared to avert it, unless we at once exert ourselves to change that government; to put new men in their places ... men imbued with Irish feeling and sprung from the Irish soil ... united by a sense of national honour and acting in the pride of national independence.

It was reported that 'Dillon's maiden speech could not be better done'.[29] He asserted there was only one crime 'of which we have never been accused, that is begging places from the whigs. Long and laboured orations have been made to prove us guilty of the grievous crime of treason against the queen; but the more shameful and detestable crime of treason against the liberties of our country we stand confessedly guiltless.'

O'Connell stood charged with having broken up the association for an alliance with the whigs. 'How does he answer that accusation?' Dillon asked. 'Why, he comes down with the old story about physical force.'

It was a sad end to so noble a career. The Young Irelanders wanted the association to remain independent of the British government. Dillon avoided 'the futile and fruitless controversy respecting the relative merits of physical force and moral force', and professed his faith in 'an awakening nation': 'I do most sincerely believe in the possibility of achieving the legislative independence of Irish without violence or bloodshed, by uniting all classes and creeds in a demand for it. I have never shared in that vulgar partisan intolerance which loves to represent as insurmountable and eternal the puny barriers that separate the children of the same soil. I cling to the belief in the convertibility if all Irishmen to the cause of Ireland.'

Admonishing O'Connell's crumbling autocracy, he declared:

> When I see an association tolerant and comprehensive in its principles; dignified, rational and pure in its conduct—undegraded by buffoonery, unsullied by petty practices of corruption—free from all taint of sectarian bigotry, free from all suspicion of revolutionary designs—when I see an association, based upon such principles, conducted in such a spirit, appealing in vain to the whigs, tories and Orangemen of Ireland, then I too will think that they have hearts and heads unlike the hearts and heads of other men, and I will begin to despair for a country that is cursed with such a people.

On 15 April 1848, Thomas Francis Meagher would present a tricolour of orange, white and green to the Irish people as a new national flag, in the hope 'that beneath its folds the hands of the Irish Protestant and the Irish Catholic may be clasped in generous and heroic brotherhood'.[30] In the meantime, the Young Irelanders decided to meet in January 1847 'for the purpose of adopting means to revive the struggle for Ireland's nationality, on a basis equally above the reach of anarchy and the corrupting influence of power'.

O'Connell responded swiftly to the display of support for the Young Irelanders. On 7 December he denounced the government's parsimonious measures and proposed a conference to discuss repeal unity. He named a panel comprising the eminent barristers, Sir Colman O'Loghlen and Thomas O'Hagan, Smith O'Brien and himself, 'and I must add Mr Dillon.

... He is a Young Irelander; but I would not hesitate one moment in leaving the question to him'.[31]

The old Liberator liked Counsellor Dillon and considered he posssessed talents 'entitling him to a success in his profession which, I believe, ought not to be far distant'.[32] Moreover, neither had been present when the Young Irelanders staged their walk-out.

Dillon earnestly sought a reconciliation with O'Connell on 'good and honest terms'. He wrote a succession of letters to O'Brien urging him to come to Dublin to lead the inexperienced young men and curb 'our impetuous town supporters', some of whom had Chartist leanings.

O'Brien, who was engaged in trying 'to secure employment and food for famishing thousands' in Cahirmoyle, his west Limerick estate, refused to attend a conference on the peace resolutions alone. He wanted the discussions broadened to include the general policy of the association, and believed no reconciliation was possible until O'Connell threw 'overboard the whigs'.[33]

The seceders, meeting in the *Nation* office, agreed to O'Brien's conditions and added two of their own: 'The exclusion of sectarian questions and the formation of an effective committee.' Dillon commented 'I was always of opinion that O'Connell rendered the former committee unfit for business of any sort, in order that he might be himself completely free from any controlling power. If a committee could be got together consisting of 50 persons of character, he could never occupy the position which he has held up to this.'[34] O'Connell was evidently still a formidable negotiator and not the senile figure depicted in Duffy's later writings.

Dillon urged conciliation: 'Perhaps a general statement that the future policy of the association, and not physical force, is the real subject to be discussed might do no harm; but I cannot persuade myself that the country will not be disgusted by a detailed enumeration of abuses at the present moment. Whatever we may think, very many amongst the best of our supporters regard this offer of O'Connell as a magnanimous act, done in defiance of the parasites who surround him; and they would expect to see us assisting to cover his retreat instead of industriously exposing his weakness.' The people were impatient for concord; 'expecting that it will enable the association to force upon the government some effective measures of relief'.

He continued next day:

> We shall lose favour (justly) with the country if we do not use all reasonable diligence in expediting a reconciliation. The necessity

of a strong popular association is deeply felt just now and I think
we ought not deprive the country of the protection of such an
association for one day longer than we can help it. There is another
danger in delay. O'Connell, I feel persuaded, has taken his step
with a serious purpose of effecting a reconciliation. It is notorious
that his son, John, and all the wretches who have access to him are
doing their utmost to induce him to retreat. ... A vigorous agitation
for a redress of the financial grievances of Ireland would be sure
to attract all the landlords now that they are thoroughly frightened
by the immediate prospect of overwhelming taxation.[35]

Dillon appreciated O'Brien as an untypical aristocrat, but along with
the majority of Young Irelanders he accepted that an essential harmony
of interests existed between landlord and tenants. He had prepared a report
on Famine legislation for the 'Irish Party'—the seceders' description of
themselves at this time. His paper was a feeble response to half-hearted
government attempts to induce landlords to provide employment on land
reclamation.[36]

Young Ireland flexed its muscles. The *Nation* asserted that the Repeal
Association had become powerless for good, offensive to Protestant
members, under obligation to 'an English faction'; and its committee,
'which even in its best days had not that control which it ought to have
over the operations of the body, has now no control at all'.[37]

Dillon tried to persuade O'Brien to meet O'Connell, whose motives he
now suspected:

If he can delude the country into a belief that we wish to perpetuate
dissension he will drain away vast numbers of our friends. My
belief is that this proposal originated in this and no other motive.
I think the proper way of meeting it would have been to have closed
with his offer and to place him in the position of the party refusing.
I am not able to see that it would have done us any harm to go into
conference, to get the opinion of the lawyers on the question of
physical force (which would be unquestionably in our favour); and
then propose *our* terms to Mr O'Connell, and so put him as I have
said in the position of the refusing party. If we adopt this course
still, it is my belief that he would not dare to refuse us any
reasonable reform we might demand. If he did refuse then no man
would have a pretext for adhering to him. Our refusal to enter into
the conference will give him a weapon which he will not fail to
wield dextrously against us.[38]

O'Brien refused adamantly to renew discussion of the peace resolutions on their own. Furthermore, he wanted the tough-minded Mitchel on any delegation, or Dillon as sole negotiator.[39]

A delegation consisting of Duffy, Dillon, O'Gorman and Haughton met O'Connell on 15 December. O'Connell made it clear he would not abandon his peace resolutions, although he was prepared to restrict their scope to Anglo-Irish relations. The Young Irelanders wanted to widen the agenda, but O'Connell insisted that they must first accept the modified resolutions and return to the association. They refused and the meeting was terminated. Dillon explained to O'Brien:

> Many letters reached us from leading seceders and from private friends, imploring us to close at once with O'Connell's proposal; and intimating that if, in the present awful condition of the country, we should throw any obstacle in the way of a reunion of the popular body, we would expose ourselves to universal hatred and execration. ... Our desire for reconciliation has been all through *our strong position*. O'Connell saw this and made an attempt to dislodge us from it. It became necessary for us promptly to apply all our strength to its defence. You will probably relish this way of putting the matter, being *a man of the sword*. I think we have succeeded in demonstrating to the most stolid Old Irelander that O'Connell is *not* for reconciliation and that his conference was a humbug.[40]

'So be it', the *Nation* trumpeted.[41] A meeting of the committee of the Irish Party, at which Dillon presided, issued an address to the people of Ireland. This joint composition of Dillon and Mitchel was intended as 'a final answer' to O'Connell: 'Those of the seceders who upheld the principle of mixed education are responsible only for this opinion—that Catholics and Protestants can sit on the same form, read out of the same book and play over the same grounds, without contamination to the morals or peril to the religion of either'. But the Young Irelanders had been excluded from the Repeal Association 'chiefly because they warned the country against the whig alliance, denounced the surrender of Dungarvan and set their faces against place-hunting'.[42]

Their address concluded:

> The horrible famine which consumes our people, and threatens society with utter dissolution, loudly calls on all Irishmen to direct every thought and every effort to the preservation of social order

and of human life. As an ultimate remedy for Irish famine, we can propose nothing but self-government, that so the island may be ruled for its own benefit, not farmed for the profits of a foreign people. But to relieve the present season's calamity will soon, as we foresee, need the best exertions of all. We dare no longer bandy recrimination with our brother Irishmen on what is now past and over. Henceforth our faces must be turned *forward*. We devote ourselves now to ceaseless labour, and ask your zealous assistance until Ireland shall stand amongst the nations of the world a self-protecting and independent state. By what specific organisation or peculiar application of the moral force of our country we are to bring about that glorious end, it is not the purpose of this address to indicate. ... We must cherish the virtues of personal and public independence—truth, courage and devotion—without which no great national movement ever yet succeeded or deserved success.

But the debates in the Irish Confederation, founded on 13 January 1847 with Dillon and Duffy as secretaries, were divorced from the Famine experience. James Fintan Lalor summed up the Confederation as 'a decently-conducted Conciliation Hall' which was 'essentially just as feeble, inefficient and ridiculous'.[43] It had a bilingual motto: 'Bíodh a thír féin ag gach fear—Let very man have his own country.' As Smith O'Brien was agreeing reluctantly to lead the new movement, G.H. Moore and the sons of O'Connell were attending a levée in Dublin Castle.[44]

This Young Ireland attempt to relaunch the repeal agitation failed because the masses were crushed by hunger, while the more prosperous formed an inert mass of lower middle-class Catholic respectability. 'Old Ireland' remained powerful and hostile, even though the association was disintegrating as it became irrelevant in a famine-stricken land.

At the first meeting of the confederation there was general agreement with John Mitchel that legislative independence could be won by constitutional means 'if honestly, boldly and steadily carried out'. He still hoped to convert landlords to repeal.

The Young Irelanders looked to nationality as a unifying force which would transcend sectional interests. But in the bitter months ahead the vision of a comprehensive movement, embracing Catholics and Protestants, gentry and farmers, proved illusionary. While clinging to their objective of national independence, they never seemed able, or perhaps never had the opportunity in the short lifetime of their confederation, to clarify their methods and define secondary aims.[45]

Lalor emerged from obscurity to analyse the crisis in a series of letters to the *Nation* in 1847. He asserted that under existing circumstances an agitation based exclusively on the national question was doomed to failure; it must be coupled to the engine of agrarian revolution. His most notable convert was Mitchel, whose recurring theme of social dissolution formed a bridge between a conservative nature and revolutionary zeal.[46] He believed that 'when hundreds of thousands of people were lying down and perishing ... society itself stood dissolved'; and he now desired 'by any means to alter the system of government and distribution of property in this land'.

Although Lord Clarendon considered that 'distress, discontent and hatred of English rule are increasing everywhere', Mitchel's programme was rejected by nearly all the leading Young Irelanders. They thought a refusal to pay rates would deprive the poor of relief, while his proposal to withhold rents undermined their efforts to win resident landlords to the repeal cause.[47] After the British government withdrew its commissariat and ended the public works and soup kitchen schemes, the miserable relief provided by the poor rates alone stood between tens of thousands and starvation.

Dillon clung to the belief that 'they do not seek to subvert the law but rather to establish it in the affections of the people; that they do not aim at the confiscation of property, but are in pursuit of what they believe to be the only means of averting that confiscation; that, in fine, their efforts and their hostility are not directed against the aristocracy of Ireland, but against the system which has made them what they are'.[48]

At the three-day debate which opened on 31 January 1848 and ended in Mitchel's temporary withdrawal from the confederation, O'Brien said his policy of resisting the poor rate would 'increase the deaths by starvation by hundreds of thousands' and if his advice to arm 'was acted upon the end would inevitably be a massacre'. Dillon cited from Tone's memorial to the French the opinion that to raise a mere peasant insurrection in Ireland would be to deliver up the people to the British government.[49]

Dillon continued 'making an effort to unite all the friends of repeal in some safe and practical plan for its achievement'. He placed great emphasis on the return of genuine nationalists to parliament, at a time when O'Brien had lost faith in Westminster justice. If they had 'the 40 shilling fee franchise of England I think we could carry every constituency in Ireland in a few years'. Some Young Irelanders talked— Dillon had written in December 1846—

of spending five years in 'educating' the people. I do not under-
value the importance of this object, but I have a strong notion that
the five years might be better spent in getting a parliament. If
parties could be thoroughly reconciled and the association would
enter vigorously upon the career that is now open to it, I sincerely
believe that five years would not elapse until we should have a
parliament of some kind in Ireland.[50]

Repeal could be achieved constitutionally only by a united parliamentary party remaining independent of every minister 'and arresting the
progress of all public business until this question is settled to the satisfaction of the Irish people'[51] (Parnell would later come close to success
with this same policy).

He formed part of a delegation which met John O'Connell for more
fruitless talks. At Dillon's suggestion, the confederation intervened in the
Galway by-election of February 1847. Mitchel recalled that Dillon was
deeply affected by the sight of the starving multitudes which crowded into
the city to crave charity: 'and now and then I saw his dark eyes brimming
with tears; but they were tears of wrath as well as pity'.[52] The 'national'
candidate, Anthony O'Flaherty, failed by four votes to defeat the solicitor-
general, James Monaghan. Dillon described how the government victory
was secured: 'Enormous bribery, horrible perjury, unlimited exercise of
landlord intimation. ... The power of the state was applied without
disguise or decency in the service of the government candidate. Throughout the election the town was filled by armed servants of the crown, who
acted as election agents for the solicitor-general.'[53]

O'Flaherty was returned unopposed in a general election in August
1847 and represented Galway borough until unseated on petition a decade
later. In a letter to Duffy, Dillon expressed the hope that the new MP would
'effect a reunion (not between us and the Conciliation Hall jobbers) but
between the honest repealers through the country'. Observing that the
confederation received little clerical support, he added: 'The more I think
of the matter the more fruitless I think it is to persevere in our present
course.'[54]

He attended a dinner for O'Flaherty and spoke on his usual theme: '...
if an honest effort be made to establish upon sound and honest principles
an organisation which may combine both sections of our divided party—
no feeling of personal animosity—no vain ambition for a leadership to
which, with very few exceptions, none of us are by years or position
entitled to aspire—no mean, selfish or malignant consideration shall

prevent us from lending our cordial co-operation in effecting a union of the repealers of Ireland.'[55] Dillon wrote (9 August 1847) to his fiancée, Adelaide Hart: 'There is good reason to hope that something may be done. This dinner was altogether a very respectable and successful affair.'

But the general election of that month was an incongruous interlude to a nation fighting for survival, with the hungry people more inclined to stone the Young Irelanders than listen to their rhetoric. Moreover, they were denounced for having embittered the last years of the Liberator's life. John O'Connell delayed his father's obsequies until August to coincide with the election.[56] He refused a Young Ireland request to ask candidates to pledge against place-hunting, saying it would give Orangemen a mono- poly of public offices.[57] O'Brien and a protégé were the only confederates elected among the 39 repealers of doubtful allegiance returned to parlia- ment.

Paradoxically, this was a time of personal happiness for Dillon who had fallen in love with Adelaide Hart. They had met since his return from Madeira through William O'Hara, her uncle and guardian and a partner in the firm of solicitors, Hart and O'Hara. Adelaide and her sister, Pauline, 'entertained a hero-worship so ardent that it might have excited Carlyle's admiration for all the prominent men in the repeal agitation, particularly those in any way connected with the *Nation*'. Dillon became a frequent visitor to Druid Lodge, the house which O'Hara had built (it still stands) overlooking Killiney Bay, County Dublin.

O'Hara 'exercised in the private counsels of the [Young Ireland] party a notable influence', according to Duffy. In the relaxed moral climate of regency days he had maintained a mistress on an O'Hara estate in Clare.[58] His niece would become a paragon of Irish Victorian womanhood: devout and patriotic.

Adelaide was also a spirited woman. She noticed that, while 'it is now generally considered so fashionable and lady-like to be quite cool and unmoved in your manner, in fact most perfectly to conceal your feelings (if any you have) especially between men and women ... it's a *Young Ireland fashion* to appear fond of a person when you really are so, even tho' you be a woman and your friend a man'.

Adelaide recognised in John 'a great purity and delicacy of feeling and a high sensitive notion of what is right and noble'. Without his love she 'would be in such affliction about dear Ireland and very unhappy at the present prospects of the country. ... I sometimes wish I could feel for even a few minutes as I did in '43, or like when we were quite full of hope and pride and all countries were looking in astonishment at Ireland, thinking we really meant to be "A nation once again".'[59]

Ady—as she was affectionately called—wrote of their 'union of feeling'. She considered 'anything like ostentation or pride in charity is peculiarly disgusting'. The more she read of Tone's autobiography 'the more I am delighted with him, he is a man exactly after my own heart. I love him from his writings with something [of] the same affectionate love which I feel for Davis; reading his life has the effect of putting me into the best possible humour with myself and the whole world'.[60]

John wrote: 'My whole soul is full of you and I cannot without an effort think or speak of anything else.' He never knew 'what pure felicity may be enjoyed in this world until those calm sweet eyes began to look on me with affection and to reveal to me the secret of your love. For you must know that when I spoke to Mr O'Hara in March I had no more doubt that you loved me than I had of my own existence.' They must always be grateful to O'Hara 'who has been instrumental in making us so happy. And I feel towards your Mamma [Christiana Teresa Hart] too the same gratitude, as if it had been for my special advantage she bestowed so much care upon your education, and adorned your mind with those virtues and charms that have made you the idol of my heart.'

'As for my poor simple old mother', he wrote pompously (5 August 1847), 'she would as soon think of doubting the pope as of questioning my judgment in this or any other transaction. The only thing she wanted to know was "were you a good Catholic", being quite satisfied (in her own phrase) "to leave the rest in the hands of God". She will love you as dearly as she loves myself and I believe I could not say more.'

While in London on legal business for William O'Hara, Dillon read Johann Fichte, whose *Wissenschaftslehre*—that the purpose of life is to know and love God—appealed to his philosophical mind. He looked forward to reading Fichte in translation to Adelaide.

She reported (21 September 1847)—a month before their marriage—having told her 'favourite nun' that 'I hope I would never allow any feeling to interfere with that "gentle bearing" which is certainly most admirable in a woman but that I had always felt that to love Ireland and, irrespective of any party feeling, to take a deep interest in all that concerns her welfare and try to promote it by all gentle and womanly ways was not an amusement but a duty, and one which she would be the last to dissuade me from if she lived in Ireland and could see and feel as I do her misery.'

After his death, Adelaide started to edit Dillon's correspondence to her with the letter: 'Longford, August 1847. We arrived here at 9 o'clock after a pleasant journey, having travelled twenty miles by rail, twenty by canal and twenty by car. ...[61]

On the train Dillon had met a Maynooth professor of theology, Patrick Murray (1811-82), 'who delighted me vastly by the way in which he talked of that abomination, Conciliation Hall'. This was the Murray who in 1844, under the pseudonym 'An Irish priest', had accused the *Nation* of displaying 'an un-Catholic and infidel spirit'. He had written letters, Dillon recorded, 'under a conviction that the *Nation* was established and conducted with a deliberate view to undermine the faith of the Irish people. Having discovered through some private sources that he was mistaken in this, he at once went to Duffy and expressed his regret for having attacked him; and since then he has lost no opportunity to repair any damage he may have caused.'

Dillon now compared him to John Kenyon, one of the few active supporters of the confederation among the Catholic clergy. Murray 'has the advantage in print of discretion, and he is moreover quite free from eccentricities. He abominates the O'Connells chiefly, he says, because they are doing all that such reptiles can do to damage the Catholic faith and to render it odious to all virtuous and reflecting minds. In fact this Mr Murray is a man quite after my heart *and yours*.'

Dillon was writing after the Liberator's death and during the bitter general election campaign of 1847. He declined to be a candidate himself, Adelaide approving of his decision not to allow politics to interfere with his legal career, 'unless there were an opportunity of rendering some very important service'. He agreed with her that

> the *Nation* does not handle the elections with as much vigour and earnestness as one might expect from it, but at the same time I acquit Duffy and Mitchel of all blame in the matter. Under the circumstances it would be almost impossible for them to write with energy or spirit seeing the unhappy condition in which these elections have found the country. Is it not a reflection to make one sad that the military power of England, which three years since seemed hardly sufficient to cope with our united strength, now finds occupation in endeavouring to keep the peace between us? What do Englishmen say? That if we had repeal, the fury which is now exhausted upon England and the Saxon would be speedily turned against each other; and that we would never cease cutting each others throats until our old benefactor and pacificator

(meaning England) would step in again to put an end to our broils and our independence. Now I greatly fear that is the view of many well-meaning persons in Ireland and out of it; this answer to our demand will acquire great plausibility from the fierce animosity which now exists between Young and Old Ireland. Surely they will be universally regarded as a nation of children who deserve to be whipped into civilisation.

As for the idea of 'turning out' with a set of fellows who could break each other's heads about moral and physical force, I will only say of it—that he who could seriously entertain it would be a commander worthy of such an army. The upshot of all this is that unless I see moral force and physical force, and Young and Old Ireland all utterly abolished by the common sense of the country (if any there be in it) within the next six months; I will then feel myself bound in conscience to withdraw all aid and countenance from what I will then consider a mischievous delusion, viz: any agitation for repealing the Union. However, I do not despair, but on the contrary have considerable hope that within the period I have mentioned something effective will be done, and I lose no opportunity of contributing towards that result.[62]

Dillon had a long conversation with the local bishop and lobbied every priest he met.

Young Ireland's last parliamentary campaign was the Waterford by-election of February 1848 (occasioned by the resignation of Daniel O'Connell, junior, who had accepted a post in the consular service). Dillon hoped the return of Thomas Francis Meagher would decide the issue of repeal leadership between the confederates and John O'Connell.[63] But Meagher's father, who held one of the two borough seats, deplored 'Tom's' radicalism and refused to support his candidacy. Meagher, born in Waterford in 1823, entered politics while a law student in Dublin, having attended Jesuit colleges in Clongowes Wood, County Kildare, and Stonyhurst in Lancashire. He quickly achieved prominence as an orator and was a leader in the revolt of the younger men against the Liberator.

Acknowledging O'Brien's 'munificent' subscription to Meagher's election fund, Dillon reported that the people were 'all with Meagher'.[64] His popularity did not extend to the enfranchised, however, as he came at the bottom of the poll; a local landowner won the seat.

Dillon reported to his wife from the hustings, where he had been joined by William O'Hara and his brother-in-law, Charles Hart:

The day is lost. I am sorry to have to announce this because I know you will be all much grieved. However, if you were here to witness the enthusiasm of the people and the foul agencies by which we have been defeated, you would be apt to regard it as almost a triumph. ... Of course we are all rather low but I am not apt to be cast down. You know I have my philosophy to fall back upon. Mr O'H. swears that Mitchel shall henceforth be his prophet.[65]

This letter is one of the first of many attempts to reassure Adelaide. Dillon added a significant postcript: 'We are all in great glee about the French news.'

Great Expectations

[The Paris revolution] created a storm of excitement
[in Ireland] and carried all before it—even the wise
and calm resolves of moderate men.

ADELAIDE DILLON

John Blake Dillon reached the dramatic climax to his political career in 1848. What turned out to be the most momentous year of the nineteenth century began quietly, with Ireland still passing through the agonies of the Famine. The Irish Confederation adoped Gavan Duffy's proposal for an independent parliamentary party to put the country's case at Westminster. In disgust at this tame policy John Mitchel resigned from the council of the confederation and launched his *United Irishman*, advocating in Carlylean prose a revolution to achieve a republic which would destroy landlordism and secure 'the land for the people'.[1]

Most of the Young Irelanders were basically constitutionalists like O'Connell, but as we have seen their more ardent nationalism precluded an unconditional renunciation of physical force. The middle-class patriots of the Irish Confederation were nearly as distrustful of English Chartism as the Liberator had been. The Chartists aimed at redressing the inequities of a class-divided industrial society by securing a proportionate share of political power for working people. According to Duffy, they illustrated the 'hopeless errors' of a mere class agitation.[2] Mitchel, on the other hand, welcomed the Chartists as 'brothers and allies' against their common enemy 'the gold-broking, blood-bartering government of England; and the main task for us both is one—to pull down that Moloch and trample it under our feet'.

The sudden overthrow of the French monarchy sent reverberations throughout Europe. On 22 February the Paris masses demonstrated in the streets. On the 23rd and 24th, the bourgeois national guard having declared for reform, regular troops fired on the people. The mob invaded the chamber of deputies and Louis Philippe abdicated the throne. The Second

Republic was declared with the poet, Alphonse de Lamartine, as head of the provisional government.

The year of revolutions had already begun with an uprising in Palermo. Riots now occurred in Berlin and the liberal congress in Heidelberg decided to convene a parliament. Prince Metternich, a symbol of repression and reaction, was dismissed as Austrian chancellor on 13 March; two days later a revolution broke out in Budapest, while in Vienna the emperor promised a constitution.

The success of an almost bloodless revolution in France gave new hope to the divided and dispirited repeal movement. Factionalism subsided and even the more cautious confederates perceived a possibility for revolutionary action. The *Nation* became nearly as militant as the *United Irishman*.

Dillon suggested a consultation with Mitchel, whose popularity had soared in the Dublin clubs. But Duffy found after a conference with him 'that there was no common ground to us'; Mitchel wanted a spontaneous rising to bring about a social revolution; Dillon, Duffy and Smith O'Brien sought a peaceful settlement, while preparing for a British refusal to grant legislative independence.[3] Nevertheless, Mitchel returned to the confederation. Although Dillon admired Mitchel's ability, he deplored his extremism almost as much as he despised the timidity of John O'Connell.

Duffy urged the reluctant O'Brien to lead the revolution in Dublin, where

> the trades are organising a movement and Dillon, O'Hara and I are trying to draw the middle classes into it. ... Events march on at such a pace that every hour produces something. ... Mitchel means (I am told by Dillon) to declare for a republic in his paper tomorrow. There will be an outburst sooner or later, be sure of that. But unless you provide against it, it will be a mere democratic one, which the English government will extinguish in blood. Or if, by a miracle, it succeeds, it will mean death and exile to the middle as well as the upper classes. As Ireland lies under my eye now I see but one safety for her—a union of the Old and Young Irelanders, an arraying of the middle class in the front of the millions, and a peaceful revolution attained by watching and seizing our opportunity. By peaceful, I mean without unnecessary or anarchical bloodshed. It *may* be won without a shot being fired. But trust me, if there is no such junction, and if things are let to take the course they are tending towards, we will see the life of the country trampled out under the feet of English soldiers, suppressing a peasant insurrection.[4]

The proprietor of the *Nation* wanted the MP for County Limerick to emulate the moderate Lamartine.

The repealers greeted the French revolution rapturously. The *Nation* declared: 'Ireland's opportunity, thank God and France, has come at last.'[5] Mitchel addressed the small farmers: 'The earth is awakening from sleep: a flash of electric fire is passing through the dumb millions.'[6] The moderate nationalist *Freeman's Journal* asserted: 'In the present condition of Europe, no just and constitutional demand made by a unanimous Ireland could or dare be refused.'[7] Dillon said: 'The leading article in the *Freeman* has given me great satisfaction. We sail before the wind.'[8]

Meagher wrote to Dillon from Waterford, where he had been confined to bed since the election: '... our time, I firmly believe, has at last come, and we should grasp it with a greedy and a wicked hand. Let us bring matters to a crisis.' He affirmed publicly:

> As to the old routine of petitions, reports, getting men into parliament, and all that sort of work—I am heartily sick of it since my defeat. The contest in which I was recently engaged has clearly proved to me that the will of the people has no effect whilst we appeal to the weapons of the franchise. Besides, I think, it would be a crime in me to waste any further, in obscure election squabbles, that fine enthusiasm by which I was sustained and which, surging and swaying round me to the last moment—strong and passionate even when the cloud had lowered upon it—convinced me that it was an element destined to give life to a nobler struggle, upon a wider field.[9]

Although Meagher had received only 150 of the 750 votes cast, '10,000 artisans of Waterford with banners and music accompanied him to the hustings, through streets white with waving handkerchiefs and crowds hoarse with cheers.'[10]

The people of Paris, it was argued, had overthrown a repressive despotism by their moral indignation rather then by force of arms. With France as a model it appeared as if the armed yet peaceful peoples of Europe were to be led to victory not by soldiers and men of violence, but by poets, reformers and workers. The initial harmony in France impressed Irish nationalists profoundly, because it was such a union of interests they had long sought but failed to find. Old and Young Ireland joined in congratulating the French people.

In March the opinion was held widely in repeal circles that the British government, fearful of attacks by France, would capitulate to a united Irish demand, in a desire to avoid having to suppress social unrest in Britain and a national revolution in Ireland. This analysis, however, overestimated the missionary ardour of revolutionary France and the strength of Chartism.[11]

As revolutions broke out on the continent the anxiety of Lord Clarendon, the viceroy, grew: 'Every steamer that arrives bringing the news of some fresh and easy popular triumph adds to our difficulties by increasing and spreading disaffection'; they could not expect to escape unscathed from the hurricane which was 'desolating' Europe; he reported to the prime minister, Lord John Russell, that the 'lower orders' in Dublin were excited 'and say now that the French have got their liberties they will come and help us to get repale [*sic*]'.[12]

The ancient Duke of Wellington advised the commander-in-chief, General Sir Edward Blakeney, to have three or four howitzers prepared in case barricades should be erected in Dublin on the French model. Sir George Grey, the home secretary, wrote to Clarendon: 'I hope your artillery is in good order'; and Inspector-general Duncan McGregor issued secret instructions on 11 March placing his 10,000 strong constabulary force on military-style alert.[13]

In a memorandum to Grey on 27 March the lord lieutenant stated that the Young Irelanders had become much more influential since the death of O'Connell, and the Famine encouraged ideas of change. Such was the state of public opinion

in a country which for years had been the scene of continued political agitation in favour of an independent legislature and 'nationality' as it was termed—when the grave events of the recent French revolution occurred, and the power of a people was so impressively displayed by its rapid and easy triumph over old constituted authority. These events gave a sudden shock to public feeling in Ireland. At once the wildest dreams of every political agitator appeared to be realised; and that change which had long been promised to the masses of the people, was looked upon by all as on the eve of being accomplished.[14]

Irish nationalist hopes were not entirely without foundation. The new minister for the interior, Ledru-Rollin, was a known supporter of repeal. In its foreign policy manifesto the provisional government asserted it had a right to assist 'nationalités opprimées'. There were three oppressed nations in Europe, Dillon told a meeting of the confederation: Poland, Italy and Ireland. He drafted a council address to the Irish people in which 'courage, forgiveness and fraternity' were listed as the required virtues.[15]

> Be prudent; when boldness risks the safety of a cause, it becomes rashness. Be prudent, but not for yourselves. The man who now shrinks from personal risk must stand aside—he is fit neither to lead nor to follow. To what purpose do we express our admiration of the heroes who braved death for liberty, if we ourselves are frightened by the 'meshes of the law'? Freedom smiles not upon cowards; she turns her radiant face away from those who will not woo her in the midst of danger.
>
> For ourselves, brother Irishmen, we have but one request—that we may be suffered to share the labour and the danger of your struggle, as we hope to participate in the fruits of your triumph. We are ready to forget our party, our injuries and our pride for the sake of our country. In her service, humiliation and danger and sacrifice and death are welcome to us. Wherever we are required we shall be present, indifferent as to whether our post be humble or exalted. Whoever leads on we shall follow—insisting only that we shall go forward—forward, though graves were to yawn and gibbets to frown across his path.

In answer to a woman who heckled: 'You're a moral force man', Dillon said if the citizens of Dublin decided to form a national guard he would join them.

He was chairman of the Trades and Citizens Committee which issued a statement to the people of Dublin: 'It appears to us (to speak familiarly) that we have the game in our own hands if we will play it with boldness and with prudence. Seeing the disposition now universally prevalent towards a union of the national party—seeing the disturbances which are breaking in rapid succession in England and Scotland—seeing, moreover, the almost inevitable necessity of an immediate European war—it is impossible to arrive at any other conclusion than this, that if we are not too headlong, or too timid, we shall shiver this oppressive yoke to pieces within this very year.'[16]

This address condemned the food riots in British cities, while praising the respect shown by the citizens of Paris for property and for religion. Nevertheless, next day John O'Connell urged the people 'to repulse and defeat the continuous efforts being made by newspaper scribblers and others to weaken in your minds the teachings of my beloved father'.

The Young Irelanders used ambivalent language because they walked the tightrope familiar to political leaders of trying to rouse national fervour while controlling the masses. Their greatest display of 'public force' so far was a meeting held on 15 March—attended by 3,000, including an estimated 1,000 O'Connellites—to congratulate the French.[17] Dillon, who presided, said he wished to allay the fears of John O'Connell and Lord Clarendon, who knew 'he could not get a more favourable opportunity than a street riot to crush that rising spirit of resistance, which he views with alarm'.

Dillon challenged the viceroy to charge them with incitement: 'But no jury, fairly selected from the citizens of Dublin would, with the calamities which the usurped power of England has brought on the country, in their view, pronounce at his bidding that it is not the right and duty of Irishmen to struggle now and for ever for the overthrow of that desolating power.' O'Brien and Meagher were charged with making seditious speeches at this meeting, but were granted bail and subsequently acquitted.

O'Brien began by reading from an Irish-American address of prophetic sunburstry to the confederation:

> The time for slumber and inaction has passed away, and the morning of a bright regeneration is breaking through the darkness that enshrouds our country—the wrongs of centuries cry aloud for vengeance. ... The movement has begun in America—the free people of this republic, ever ready to rush to the aid of Ireland, are again arousing to action. ... Retribution may be delayed for a short period, but we feel that it is not the less certain, and our great aim and object will be to keep these feelings alive in the hearts of Irishmen and the friends of Ireland, that in the proper time they may be prepared for the regeneration of that misgoverned land.

He was convinced that, 'if events be favourable abroad', they could win the restoration of an Irish parliament within twelve months. Under present circumstances 'it would be consummate rashness to attempt to bring this question to issue by an appeal to arms'; nevertheless, O'Brien added, every Irishman should be ready to die for his country's freedom.

He pointed out that more Irish had died during the Famine than fell on battlefields in the Napoleonic wars: 'They calmly surrendered their spirits to their maker, with unexampled fortitude.' O'Brien was a sincere, brave, if weak, leader who, while prepared to sacrifice his own life, confessed to 'the utmost possible horror of engaging my countrymen in a fruitless and unsuccessful rebellion. I would implore you by the memory of past failures not to allow yourselves to be led away by any rash act, or any act of indiscretion on your parts, but to proceed in a regular and constitutional course for the attainment of your liberties.'

O'Brien went on to urge fraternisation with British soldiers—one-third of whom were then Irish; with the constabulary: 'a noble foundation for a national force' (John O'Connell considered three-quarters of its officers were 'embittered Orangemen'); with the several million British people favourable to repeal; and with France, although 'it is not on foreign aid the people of Ireland should depend but upon themselves.' He harangued his audience about taking a temperance pledge for a year, reminding them that he had resolved in 1844 to abstain from intoxicating liquor until the Union was repealed. (Not surprisingly, drinking had increased during the social disintegration of the Famine: Ireland paid £1 million a year in liquor duties.)

O'Brien said that until now he had considered it his duty to discourage any form of military activity as it might prompt 'misguided peasantry' to murder. In proposing an address of the Irish Confederation to the French republic, however, he declared that the situation had been transformed and urged the formation of a national guard. He told the French: 'We have firmly resolved that this ancient kingdom shall once again be free and independent. In imitation of your example we propose to exhaust all the resources of constitutional action before we resort to other efforts for redress.'

O'Brien, Meagher and Edward Hollywood were appointed to present the address in Paris. Hollywood, a Dublin silk weaver, was included in the delegation as a gesture to the new democratic spirit.

Meagher received a standing ovation in the course of a speech in which he proposed that a repeal deputation be sent to London.

> Should the demand be refused, let the Irish deputies pack up their court dresses—as Benjamin Franklin did when repulsed from the court of George III and let them, then and there, make solemn oath that when they next demand an admission to the throne room of St James's, it shall be through the accredited ambassador of the Irish republic. ... If the throne stands as a barrier between the Irish people and their supreme right—then loyalty will be a crime, and obedience to the executive will be treason to the country. I say calmly, seriously and deliberately—it will then be our duty to fight. ... When the world is in arms—when the silence which for two and thirty years has reigned upon the plain of Waterloo is at last broken, then be prepared to grasp your freedom with an armed

hand, and hold with the same. ... If I am rash it was Rome, it was Palermo, it was Paris that made me rash. ... Taught by the examples of Italy, of France, of Sicily, the citizens of Ireland shall at last unite. ... If the government of Ireland insist upon being a government of dragoons and bombardiers, of detectives and light infantry—then up with the barricades and invoke the god of battles. Should we succeed—oh! think of the joy, the ecstasy, the glory of this old Irish nation, which in that hour will grow young and strong again. Should we fail—the country will not be worse than it is now—the sword of famine is less sparing than the bayonet of the soldier.

The confederates planned to redeem the ignominy of the Clontarf capitulation with an aggregate meeting on St Patrick's Day. Organised under the umbrella of Dillon's citizens committee, it was postponed for three days in the (vain) hope of involving the Repeal Association. Despite threatening military preparations—troops occupied the main buildings of Dublin on 17 March—between 10,000 and 20,000 people attended the open-air meeting near the North Wall. The organisers contented themselves with voting an address to the people of France, which was to be brought to Paris by Dillon, O'Gorman and a bricklayer named Bartholomew Redmond.[18]

Dillon, who had drafted a petition to Queen Victoria, was 'suffering under a dangerous illness' at the time, and the address was read in his absence by Patrick O'Donoghue, a solicitor's clerk later to be convicted of treason:

Amongst civilised communities there exists no parallel to the condition of this your majesty's kingdom of Ireland. A population perishing of hunger in the midst of fertility and, year after year, beholding the food which their hands have raised, wafted from their shores. An aristocracy of degraded character and ruined fortunes—merchants and farmers insolvent—artisans unemployed and destitute—all society hurrying rapidly towards a dark gulf of pauperism and anarchy. And considering that in all lands except their own our people are not inferior to others in the various pursuits of civilised life, we are compelled to attribute their present calamities not to any inherent vice of theirs but to the political and social institutions under which they live. ...

It has been avowed and settled policy of your majesty's English ministers to bestow unfair advantages on certain classes amongst us, with a view to interest them in the continuance of this Union.

> Landlords have been subsidised by oppressive laws against their tenants, and Protestants by the revenues of the established church; and thus the peace and concord of our people have been deliberately and wickedly destroyed, that there might exist upon Irish soil a native garrison for the maintenance of British power. … We have resolved that our efforts for the restoration of a native parliament to this kingdom shall cease only with our success or our destruction.

They were willing to acknowledge the queen as head of an Irish state but, ultimately, 'the freedom of our country and the welfare of its people are of more importance in our estimation than the security of the throne'.[19]

Meagher, who had addressed a joint Confederate-Chartist meeting in Manchester on St Patrick's night, attended by 15,000 men, declared:

> We have been guilty of sad injustice in our abuse of the English democracy. The democrats of England are brave, intelligent, noble fellows and they will stand by you in the worst extremity. Let the government shed one drop of blood in Ireland, and the sky that spans the shores of England will scare them with the signs of a desperate retribution. Manchester, Liverpool—every great town in the manufacturing districts—will answer the fire that deals destruction upon the Irish people. Let the capitalists, the money changers, the merchants look to it.[20]

In the spring of 1848 the confederates began to appreciate the potential importance of the Irish in England and the Chartist movement. France was the connecting link. The Paris revolution and its enthusiastic reception by Irish nationalists and by English radicals frightened the British authorities. The London *Weekly Dispatch* claimed the Young Irelanders were trying to organise the Irish in Britain 'to be prepared to create a diversion in their favour whenever their purposes are ripe for execution'.[21]

The resurgence of Chartism seemed to provide repealers with a powerful ally. While there were direct links between Confederates and Chartists, the main value of the English radicals was seen not as formal allies but for the threat they posed to the British government.[22] Combined Chartist and Confederate meetings were held in the north of England. The Chartist barrister, Ernest Jones, announced that a third and last petition on behalf of the unrepresented classes would be presented to Westminster on 10 April, accompanied by a procession of 200,000.

Lamartine, although sympathetic to the Irish, had set himself against providing any effective help because of the necessity to maintain Anglo-French relations. Russell told Clarendon 'with great satisfaction' on 29 February that the British ambassador, the Marquis of Normanby, 'has had a visit from a person in the confidence of the ruling power in France to apprise him that the government meant peace and would not disturb the territorial arrangements of Europe'.[23]

Nevertheless, Lamartine alarmed the British government with a speech on St Patrick's Day referring to Ireland's 'soon-hoped-for constitutional independence', and by accepting an Irish flag from Irish residents in Paris. The French leader, who had been under pressure from his left wing, quickly issued a disclaimer saying the Second Republic recognised only one national flag for the United Kingdom.

Normanby was particularly incensed by the 'rebel flag' as an acknowledgment of Irish nationality. He reported to the foreign secretary, Lord Palmerston, that he had told Lamartine the flag incident 'was likely to cause the worst impression on England, and if repeated I would not answer for its effect upon relations between the two countries.' The British government accepted Lamartine's explanation about the flag but made an official protest over his speech. Palmerston warned that if the republic continued giving 'direct encouragement to political agitation within the United Kingdom … a cry will soon arise in this country for the withdrawal of our embassy from Paris'.[24]

Diplomatic pressure was intensified when a deputation of confederates, led by O'Brien, left for Paris on 22 March. Their mission was to extend fraternal greetings and to gain a declaration of French support for the Irish cause. The British cabinet was told, however, they were going to Paris 'to concert plans with Ledru-Rollin for the invasion of Ireland if she can exhibit the requisite "nationality".' Clarendon appealed to Normanby: 'You must endeavour to defeat them'[25] and Palmerston told Lamartine: 'We take for granted' that any communication with the Young Irelanders 'will be declined as inconsistent with the friendly relations which the present government wishes to establish between the two countries.'

One of the principal aims of the French leader was to forge good relations with Britain. He thought the monarchical powers might try to overthrow his shaky government, but calculated there was little chance of a hostile coalition being formed without British support. He was determined, therefore, not to give 'l'aristocratie anglaise le prétexte de forcer le cabinet anglais à une croisade contre la République'.[26]

The revolutionary rhetoric which had so alarmed the British government, and raised the expectations of the Irish, was intended mainly for domestic consumption. The wider demands of French foreign policy overruled support for Ireland. Forced to choose between Irish sentiment and British goodwill, Lamartine declared that France was at peace with the United Kingdom 'as a whole'.[27]

He gave Normanby a preview of his reply to the Irish, which the ambassador passed on with the observation: 'nothing can be more satisfactory.' Normanby assured Clarendon that Lamartine 'is said to have given the Irish deputation a good slap in the face'. Two days later the ambassador confirmed to Palmerston that the French leader had 'kept his promise to me' by declining to promote the repeal cause. Clarendon had extracts from Lamartine's speech translated and placarded throughout Ireland.[28]

'It has quite sobered the Irish', Elizabeth Smith, a Highland lady living in County Wicklow, wrote in her diary.[29] 'Whether the calm will last, who can say. The misery is great, the struggle is universal, the discontent widespread. In the country parts little mischief is dreaded. The larger towns may be turbulent and God help the rabble if they rise, for the government is in earnest.'

Dillon missed the trip to Paris due to illness. He may also have thought that the Irish delegation was already sufficiently large. On 3 April, besides the congratulations of the Irish Confederation, addresses were presented to Lamartine by O'Gorman from the citizens of Dublin, by Meagher on behalf of the repealers of Manchester, and by a representative of Irish nationalists in Liverpool.

The most significant outcome of the Paris mission was the inspiration it provided for the Irish tricolour. While in the French capital, O'Brien reported, each member of the deputation placed 'upon his breast the emblem of Irish union', thus 'uniting the orange with the green in connection with the tricolour of France'.[30]

Meagher brought a tricolour of green, white and orange back to Dublin and presented it to the Irish people as a symbol of 'new life'. Mitchel declared: 'I hope to see that flag one day waving as our national banner.' O'Brien said in Limerick: 'Henceforth that flag will be the Irish tricolour, as a sign that the Protestants of the north and the Catholics of the south will unite in demanding the rights of their country.'

Meagher's tricolour was displayed beside a green flag from a window of the council room of the Irish Confederation,[31] when a procession formed to escort him to stand trial for sedition in May. It was still in position the following day as crowds assembled to celebrate his acquittal and protest at the arrest of Mitchel. Dillon marched at the head of the John Philpot Curran Club (named after the barrister who defended most of the United Irishmen).

After the delegation had set out for France Dillon wrote an important outline of policy to supporters in Tipperary from Druid Lodge, 'whither I have been driven by a slight attack of illness'.[32] He despaired of 'making any good use of this great opportunity *if all the Young and Old Ireland divisions be not obliterated.* This should be the first thought in the mind of every patriot now.'

The co-operation of the Catholic clergy would make the movement irresistible:

> ... their attacks upon us ought to be easily forgiven. They were led to believe us the enemies of religion and the friends of anarchy; and while they conscientiously believed us to be such, it was their duty to denounce us. Their hatred of English oppression has undergone no diminution, and that sacred sentiment should reunite us all at this momentous time. I have dwelt upon this necessity of union with the Old Irelanders, and especially the priests, because I think all depends on it. If we advance without having thoroughly consolidated this union, it is my belief that in twelve months we should be at the close of an unsuccessful insurrection, and in the commencement of another century of aggravated servitude.

Preparations for a national council should go ahead, while 'every man should furnish himself with a weapon. ... Give us a 100 men in Dublin representing the wishes and confidence of the people; give us with that 100,000 men possessed of guns or pikes, and whatever is asked for by such a council will be granted without "one drop of blood". It is, after all, the surest and the only way to effect a "bloodless moral force revolution".'

He counselled against precipitate action:

> Any chance which time may bring must be in our favour. There are seeds of woe in Europe and America which a few months may ripen. The Chartists are making extensive preparations in England, and they will be soon in a position to create important diversion in our favour. The abundance of food which the harvest will bring, will give our people fresh strength and spirits for any exertion, moral or physical. These are advantages which must not be lost

through our impatience. Let the summer be spent in perfecting those two projects of a national council and a national guard, and by September we shall be able to say, 'an Irish parliament of else—'.

He developed his ideas in a letter to the confederation in April. It was read in his absence by John O'Hagan as Dillon was 'now labouring under severe illness':[33]

> There is a large portion—probably a majority—of those who are prepared to assist in any rational effort for the restoration of our legislative rights who are not willing to declare for an Irish republic. All such should clearly understand and that the object of the confederation is *not* the establishment of an Irish republic, but simply the legislative independence of Ireland. A native parliament, representing the will and sustained by the arms of the Irish people, is the end of our association; and, that once obtained, I, for one, would consider the term of my service *as a Confederate* fully completed.
>
> I would also suggest that our speakers should afford no pretext for disunion by the use of any language that may possibly be construed into incitement to immediate insurrection. It will clearly be more useful that *all* the repealers of Ireland should unite in some bold *measures* than that *we* should utter bold *words*. Besides aggressive insurrection is not our policy. We ask for a national council to deliberate upon the necessities of the country; and that measure can, in my opinion, be devised and carried out so as not to contravene any law. We further most earnestly recommend to the people that they should be provided with arms, in order that they may be in a position to defend themselves against any aggression that may be made upon them. The right to *self-defence* is acknowledged and insisted on by all repealers; and the plain, practical conclusion from this is—that the people should have arms wherewith to defend themselves. As to the question whether the government or the people should be the *first* to strike, I consider it altogether immaterial; for it is plainly in the power of the *united* repeal party to place the government in that position, that it must *strike* or *surrender*.
>
> By thus exhibiting a generous disinterestedness regarding the influence and the fate of our own party, and by tempering our determination with prudence, we shall cement that union which must be the precursor of victory. As to the Catholic clergy, they

should be convinced that religion has nothing to dread from us, but everything to hope from repeal. For my part, I cannot believe that *they* will be wanting to any wise and bold effort for Irish liberty. They are (if possible) more deeply interested in the over-throw of British power than any other class in the community. ... For the priest, whose heart is wrung by the daily contemplation of the miseries produced by English legislation ... the parliament and press of England have no reward but ferocious threats and brutal calumnies. ...

An opportunity now presents itself to that body to place their country and their religion for ever beyond the reach of the bitter enemies of both. But they may be assured that whining suppli-cation is an inadequate to that end, as ill-concerted insurrection. Their language and their conduct must be equal to the glorious time in which we live.

While the oppressed nations of Europe 'are liberated from foreign masters, Ireland shall not be suffered to pine and starve'.

Dillon's impassioned appeal to the clergy was a recognition that their support was a prerequisite for any popular movement. In his desire to unite Old and Young Ireland, however, he overlooked the extent to which the countryside had been debilitated by hunger. He also failed to see that circumstances were different from 1782, when Irish Protestants had gained legislative independence by the threat of force.

Mitchel told the same meeting with his flawed sense of history:

If Ireland were now united as in '82 and had her citizen army arrayed, each battalion under its own banner and emblems—my place in that army should be where the orange and purple were waving—but until those Protestants declared for Ireland and against England—until their colours are seen on the right side, the green is the colour for me. And I should like to know what quarrel the Protestant democracy of Ulster have with us (for I speak not of their gentry at all)? What is their great demand at this moment? Is it not security for their tenant-right? Against whom do they want this security? Is it against their brother farmers in the south? No: it is against their own Orange landlords, leaders and grand masters. Now, we want the democracy of the north to make common cause with the democracy of the south, and secure national freedom and tenant-right both together. I would far rather see 5,000 northern Protestants joining this confederation, than hear of 50,000 French-men whom somebody surmises to be ready to come here at our bidding. Indeed, I was sorry to see the enthusiasm with which you hailed the vague promise of possible aid from France, as if Irishmen were well content to let Frenchmen, or Americans, or anybody else, do for them what they ought to be doing for themselves.

Mitchel spoke as Lamartine was administering his rebuff to the Irish delegation.

Meanwhile, 'Eva of the *Nation*' (Mary Anne Kelly, of Headford, County Galway, a cousin of Dillon, who would shelter him after the rising) warbled:

> ... 'Twere sweet to die for you, Éire
> 'Twere sweet to die for you;
> And 'tis what in my heart I mean,
> If living will not do.[34]

Death from 'famine fever' was the reality of many. Between Scarriff and Toomgrany, County Clare, there were eight workhouses 'which might be better designated slaughter houses' because the average mortality was ten people a day; 'they are crammed to suffocation—four in fever in one bed. The healthy man is compelled to sleep with the fever patient, and the beds are literally heaps of manure'; there was no medicine and in one house the parish priest had found a putrefying corpse in a room with patients.[35]

Father Kenyon asked his parishioners in Templederry, County Tipperary, if they were ready to die for Ireland: 'Do you fear—you starved and whipped and lashed wretches—do you fear death?'

In a poem entitled 'Courage' Jane Francesca Elgee ('Speranza')— the future Lady Wilde—urged:

> Lift up your pale faces ye children of sorrow,
> The night passes on to a glorious tomorrow ...
> For the will of a nation what foe dare withstand?
> Then patriots, heroes, strike. God for our land.

'One rather grave incident in these thickening times'—the diarist, Elizabeth Smith, observed—'is a meeting of Protestant repealers in Dublin, tradesmen and professional men of the middle classes, calm, clear, steady men of business, thoroughly in earnest and not in the least excited. Men who six months ago treated repeal as the wildest of all crazy things. There really seems to be nothing else left for us.'[36] The poet, Samuel Ferguson, flirted briefly with nationalism when he spoke at a meeting of the Protestant Repeal Association in May.

A Chartist convention met in London during the build-up to the 10 April demonstration. Its vapourising, reported fully in the press, hardened opinion against the aims of the working-class movement and convinced men of property that phyical force was being planned. The convention issued a statement:

> Irishmen resident in London, on the part of the democrats in England we extend to you the warm hand of fraternisation; your principles are ours, and our principles shall be yours. Remember the aphorisms that union is strength and division is weakness; centuries of bitter experience prove to you the truth of the latter; let us now cordially endeavour to test the virtue of the former. Look to your fatherland, the most degraded in the scale of nations. Behold it bleeding at every pore under the horrible lashings of class misrule. What an awful spectacle is Ireland, after forty-seven years of the vaunted Union. Her trade ruined, her agriculture paralysed, her people scattered over the four quarters of the globe, and her green fields in the twelve months just past made the dreary graveyards of 1,000,000 of famished human beings. Irishmen, if you love your country, if you detest these monstrous atrocities, unite in heart and soul with those who will struggle with you to exterminate the hell-engendered cause of your country's degradation—beggary and slavery.[37]

It is doubtful if this eloquent polemic, placarded extensively throughout London, was understood by many among the hordes of Irish Famine refugees. Middle-class hysteria continued to mount, however, propertied Englishmen being obsessed with Jacobinism. Queen Victoria and her family left for the Isle of Wight on 8 April.

There was an unprecedented mobilisation of the respectable on 10 April: more than 7,000 military, 1,200 enrolled pensioners, 4,000 police and 85,000 special constables. Among the 100,000 converging on Kennington Common was a group with a banner proclaiming: 'Ireland for the Irish'. But the whig ministers, having absorbed the lessons of Paris, refused to allow a mass demonstration to accompany the Chartist petition to Westminster. Feargus O'Connor, suffering from a disease later to prove fatal and set on avoiding a bloody conflict in which he knew defeat would be certain, abandoned the march. He told the assembled multitude to disperse, while he and the executive delivered the petition in three cabs.

At 2 p.m. the government telegraphed Victoria that the meeting had dispersed quietly. Prince Albert crowed: 'We had our revolution yesterday and it ended in smoke'—although he would write in June: 'We have Chartist riots every night. ... In a single night the police broke the heads of three to four hundred people with their truncheons.'[38] Palmerston commented: 'Things passed off beautifully here yesterday but the snake is scotched not killed.'

Professor John Saville concludes: 'The Irish were, perhaps, decisive: with the very large Irish communities in Britain, there could be no complacency in Whitehall while Ireland remained in a state of turmoil.' It emerged, furthermore, that the main centres of Chartist unrest were the towns and regions where the concentration of Irish communities was most evident: London, Bradford and West Yorkshire, Manchester and its surrounding towns, and Liverpool. The failure of the third charter petition in London did not deter Chartist and Irish nationalists in Lancashire; thirty to forty confederate clubs were organised in Liverpool under the leadership of Terence Bellew MacManus. Speeches at the numerous joint meetings became increasingly violent.

> What happened in London, and almost certainly in parts of the industrial north, is that there developed over the next few months the embryo of an illegal movement, the growth of which was real enough but in its details is still shadowy. On the ground itself the scale of demonstrations and meetings increased until the mass arrests of summer brought the whole movement throughout the country to an end by September.[39]

The traditional view that the British state rode the waves of Chartism and Irish disaffection with triumphant ease has been modified by recent historical inquiry.[40] Nevertheless, it is difficult to avoid comparing the fate of the Chartist agitation, following the anti-climax on Kennington Common, with that of the repeal movement after O'Connell called of the Clontarf meeting.

Ultimately, the 'working compact' between Irish nationalists and English radicals was broken by the physical force of the state, which always held the initiative over its confused, if potentially formidable, opponents. The principal thrust of the Chartist and Confederate movements was constitutional mass action, but neither ruled out the possible necessity of violence. The leadership of both organisations failed to consummate the alliance declared at the Free Trade hall in Manchester on 17 March 1848. On the other hand, Dublin Castle and Whitehall remained determined to put down any conspiracy to win 'the charter of England and the repeal of the Union'.[41]

Lord Clarendon congratulated Grey, the home secretary, on 11 April; there was dismay in Dublin as 'great expectations had been formed here of the Chartist meeting in London, and the most villainous intentions were to have been carried into effect or attempted if that meeting had led to an outbreak'. On the eve of the Kennington Common demonstration street fighting had broken out between soldiers of two regiments stationed in Dublin. The 'repeal soldiers' were transferred hastily to the north. Before they marched Prince George of Cambridge inspected two foot companies and told Clarendon 'he never saw much a mutinous and sullen set of fellows—he expected they would knock him down.'[42]

Such incidents strained ministerial nerves and raised nationalist hopes. The lord lieutenant continued to send alarming and alarmist reports about the state of Ireland.

On the evening of 10 April the Crown and Government Security Bill, which became known as the Treason Felony Act, was introduced in the House of Commons. The home secretary explained that while it applied to the whole of the United Kingdom it was particularly relevant to Ireland, where the law was 'utterly inapplicable' to meet the growing problem of treasonable expression.

Smith O'Brien, on his way home from France, delivered his last speech in Westminster. A hostile parliament refused to listen to his constitutional demand for repeal. He warned that if Irish claims for a separate legislature were ignored 'during the present year, you will have to encounter the chance of a republic in Ireland'. He denied being a traitor to the crown and to having sought troops from France, but accepted responsibility for encouraging the Irish to arm and welcomed aid from the Chartists. He declared: 'If it is treason to profess disloyalty to this house and to the government of Ireland by the parliament of Great Britain—if that be treason, I avow the treason. It shall be the study of my life to overthrow the dominion of this parliament over Ireland.'[43]

Dillon reacted to the new act by asserting that, the more aggressive the government became, the more strenuously would he advise the people to arm:

> The Union must perish, or the people of Ireland must perish. Already the Union had deprived this country, by emigration or death, of one million of her people. Its appetite was still unsatiated—its jaws were still open for another million—and it must be got rid of or the people must die. The majority of the advocates of repeal wished to obtain their rights peaceably, and

without any disturbance of social order; but whether the Union was repealed peaceably or not depended mainly upon the government of England. The people of Ireland were determined to obtain their rights, peaceably if they could; but if, by an unconstitutional measure of British government, they were driven to defend their rights by arms, he declared openly and advisedly, that the place of every true man in this country would be in the midst of the people.[44]

By such arguments did the Young Irelanders politicise the Famine suffering and advance a putative nation. For Dillon the suspension of habeas corpus would be the ultimate provocation.

The establishment hoped that under the new law 'audacious broilers ... will soon retire to either Botany Bay or obscurity'. John Mitchel was the first to be silenced (albeit temporarily). He had already left the confederation. In Limerick on 29 April O'Brien was struck by a stone which the O'Connellite mob had intended for Mitchel (O'Brien disliked sharing a platform with Mitchel, whose ideas he viewed as 'criminal folly'; his resignation from the confederation was averted only by the withdrawal of Mitchel and his disciple, Devin Reilly).[45]

O'Brien spent several days in Druid Lodge recovering from injuries and preparing for his sedition trial.[46] He and Meagher, defended brilliantly by Isaac Butt, were acquitted. 'Mr Meagher was acquitted by one dissentient juryman. Mr Smith O'Brien by two. Out and out repealers with strong constitutions, R[oman] Catholics too, who would not give in.'[47]

Mitchel, however, would not be allowed to escape. The jury was so blatantly packed that out of 3,000 Catholics on the jury list not one was selected.[48] At a protest meeting against jury packing Dillon demanded a fair trial. He warned Clarendon's law officers, 'if it not be too late, against perpetrating any foul violence against John Mitchel. I am one of those who desire that no hostility, no spirit of animosity should survive this struggle in which we are engaged; and it is therefore I would implore of them not to perpetrate an outrage that never, never will be forgotten'.

He continued 'in his usual gravity of tone': 'Let no man depart from that meeting under the impression that they could counsel him to commit a crime against the laws of God. ... No sinful expression should escape their lips. They should not mistake it as their counsel that they should have recourse to acts of violence. O'Brien, Mitchel and Meagher, or himself, might be sacrificed—but let them, provided the cause prosper.'[49]

When Dillon and Meagher visited him in Newgate prison, Mitchel would recall, 'they were both eager for a decent chance of throwing their lives away.'[50] He hoped his conviction would precipitate a rescue attempt by the Dublin clubs and thus ignite the country. With Clarendon's nerves 'in a condition of diseased sensibility', the city garrison was increased to 10,000 troops. Against them were thirty Confederate clubs numbering, at an optimistic estimate, between 6,000 and 10,000 men, almost totally unarmed. Outside the capital the situation was worse, with only four clubs in Kilkenny; scarcely eighty clubs existed in the whole of Ireland and the confederates had no organisation in the countryside.

On inspection of the Dublin clubs, Meagher and O'Gorman advised against military confrontation. Dillon and O'Brien were convinced that a premature rising would be disastrous. They intended to be in a position to rise in the autumn, if necessary.[51]

Dillon had the unenviable task of proposing the resolution, carried unanimously: 'That it is the fixed conviction of the council that any outbreak or violation of the peace on the occasion of the trial of Mr Mitchel would be in the highest degree mischievous, if not fatal to the repeal cause, and that we therefore earnestly impress upon our fellow citizens the necessity of abstaining at this moment from any collision with the authorities.' The leaders believed they were standing between the hearts of the people and the bayonets of the government.

Mitchel's deportation had a catalytic effect. The outcome of his trial was a foregone conclusion as the sheriff packed the jury and neither Mitchel nor his counsel denied he had advocated revolution in the pages of the *United Irishman*. But the manner of conviction and the severity of the sentence—fourteen years' transportation—aroused widespread indignation and helped to close the ranks of the repeal movement.

Within an hour of being sentenced Mitchel was chained and taken by warship to Spike Island, a convict depot off Cobh, to be transported to Bermuda. Such was the speed of his removal from Dublin that his brother, William, failed to see him before departure. The police ransacked his home. Dillon subscribed £10 to a fund for Jane Mitchel, who had urged the confederates not to allow her husband to be taken away without a fight. John Martin immediately launched the *Irish Felon* in succession to the *United Irishmen*, while the *Irish Tribune* was started by two medical students, Kevin Izod O'Doherty and Richard D'Alton Williams.

According to Duffy, only now did a formal conspiracy get underway to prepare for an insurrection after the harvest and 'before the year closed'.[52] He wrote in the *Nation* that the first convicted felon was borne away 'amid unarmed citizens, from whom fell only tears and curses'.[53]

Europe and America 'will ask if '48 was only another '43, a thousand times more boastful and more false'.

Duffy considered a rising in May would have been a 'fatal error' because 'men cannot fight without food' and 'a systematic effort to put Ireland in an attitude of defence has scarcely more than begun. ... We must know no pause and no rest till Ireland is in a position to offer the *ultima ratio* to England. She understands no other argument.'

The fate of Mitchel had repercussions in Britain, too, where the Irish played a major role in the revived Chartist agitation. Duffy now admired the thousands of 'strong sons of labour congregated in various places in and near London' to express solidarity with Mitchel and 'abhorrence of his destroyers'; 15,000 met in Oldham; 7,000 assembled in Manchester; the demonstrations culminated in a London procession estimated at 50,000, and for the first time that year the metropolitan police were issued with cutlasses—some of which had a serrated edge on one side.[54]

The perspicacious Mrs Smith concluded: 'These confederates though noisy enough are really weak as a party.' She wrote that the asthmatic Mitchel had left his native land forever, as little hopes were entertained of 'a frail frame bearing up under a mind harassed both by grief and excitation'.[55]

The 1848 Rising

*Dillon—O'Gorman—good and brave men, but not sufficiently
desperate. ... A poor extemporised abortion of a rising in
Tipperary, headed by Smith O'Brien. There appears to have been
no money or provisions to keep a band of people together two days.*
JOHN MITCHEL, *JAIL JOURNAL*

The Young Irelanders were thinkers and dreamers rather than men of
action. In July 1848, however, during the euphoric year of revolutions,
they embarked on an ill-timed insurrection. Their plans, such as they were,
involved a rising in the autumn, but the government's suspension of habeas
corpus made a humiliating submission or a premature revolt unavoidable.

The uprising, in itself an insignificant affray, later assumed symbolic
importance. When their hour of destiny arrived a fatal paralysis overcame
those men of the pen. But their courage would live in the minds of the
people, and the Young Ireland tradition contributed to the evolution of the
Irish nation.[1]

Britain had the force to keep Ireland in the United Kingdom, if not the
will or machinery to feed her. The parish priest of Ballingarry, County
Tipperary, observed that a rising would not have been attempted if the
government was as anxious to prevent the Famine as to put down
rebellion.[2] By August there were 35,000 troops in Ireland, with naval
support off the southern coast.[3]

Dillon was at the centre of secret and public activities which culminated
not only in the break up of Young Ireland, but also in the disintegration of
the repeal movement. On 11 July he was a secretary to the inaugural
meeting of the Irish League—the belated move by Young and Old Ireland
to restore 'the queen, lords and commons by the fusion of Irish men in a
course of action at once constitutional and decided'. Eleven days later, as
the suspension of constitutional guarantees of personal liberty was
announced, he went with Meagher to O'Brien and persuaded him to head
the rising. According to Duffy, Dillon's 'decision' was the only one open

to men of honour, and O'Brien 'agreed that they must fight and accepted generally the programme of Dillon'.[4]

Meagher wrote (in 1849 while awaiting transportation) that Dillon had proposed going to O'Brien and, in case he 'conceived the time had come for making a stand, we should throw ourselves into Kilkenny, call the people to arms, barricade the streets and proclaim the separation of the countries'; the Dublin Club leaders had decided against making the capital headquarters of the insurrection because its garrison was increased to 11,000 men.[5]

The Young Irelanders were incorrigibly inept revolutionaries. Their extraordinary lack of foresight was conceded by O'Brien. Having gone to visit a friend in Ballinkeele, County Wexford, the first he heard about the suspension of habeas corpus was when Dillon and Meagher arrived.

> They told him warrants for their arrests were already in the hands of the authorities, that they got away as fast as they could and came to him to proceed to Kilkenny and with the aid they were sure to get there to raise the standard of revolt. ... He remonstrated with them on the hopelessness of such a struggle but they were satisfied the country was ready to fight and if W. Smith O'Brien did not place himself at their head all the blame would rest on his head. After some hesitation O'Brien said if they were prepared to fight 'it shall never be said I was the cause of their failure'. He then asked Dillon and Meagher what arrangements they had made with the clubs in Dublin before leaving. They had made none. He asked them what arrangements they had made about money. They had only a few shillings between them and thus equipped they took the field.[6]

In Kilkenny Dillon offered to attempt to capture the garrison if 500 armed men would follow him, but only about fifty could be found.[7] While none showed a 'more perfect contempt' for his life than Dillon, his enthusiasm ended in flight, disillusionment and a determination to withdraw from public life. Although one of the ablest of the Young Irelanders, he despaired easily.

After Mitchel's deportation representatives of the Young Ireland factions met secretly to plan for an uprising in September. Father Kenyon, John Martin and Devin Reilly represented the extreme wing; Duffy, Dillon and a third man, probably John O'Hagan, represented the moderates.[8] (Duffy wrote in the 1880s when O'Hagan was chief judicial commissioner of Gladstone's land commission and it would have been injudicious to name him as a '48 conspirator.)

The Young Irelanders had little enthusiasm for conspiracy and Duffy admitted they hesitated too long: '... if treason is to prosper it must not be spoken a day before it is acted'. O'Brien, 'nervously anxious about the safety of his own class', was not invited to join the conspiracy although he knew of its activities.[9] Three men were sent to enlist aid in the United States and France. William Mitchel went to America. Dillon selected the other US agent, Martin O'Flaherty, a friend who had been John Mitchel's solicitor.[10]

On their arrival in New York an Irish Directory was formed. Its members included: Horace Greeley, founder of the *New York Tribune*, whose mother was of Scots-Irish descent; Charles O'Conor, a wealthy Irish-American lawyer and the son of a United Irishman; and Robert Emmet, also a lawyer and nephew of the patriot executed in 1803. At a meeting of the Friends of Ireland on 5 June Greeley read an address to Britain calling for Irish self-government.

Duffy wrote later about Irish-America: 'The Irish of all classes gave freely from their earnings, and it was then there commenced to flow another stream which was never run dry.' The directory raised £10,000 and an agent was despatched to Ireland with £1,000, to be told by O'Hagan the money had arrived too late. Part of it was used to defend the political prisoners.[11]

At the same time John O'Connell intimated to O'Brien that he was finally ready for reconciliation. A joint repeal address was issued on 5 May (Dillon's 34th birthday) signed, *inter alia*, by Dr John Miley (who had been the Liberator's chaplain), O'Connell, O'Brien and Dillon. The negotiations which followed lasted fourteen days in the *Freeman's Journal* office. It was agreed that, subject to ratification by both sides, the Irish Confederation and the Repeal Association should be dissolved; the confederate clubs would remain as the nucleus of a national guard.[12] The reunion of repealers was brought to an ambiguous conclusion with the formation of the Irish League, which came too late to achieve anything of importance.

Sir Colman O'Loghlen drew up eight principles for the new organisation. At the request of the clubs, rules excluding 'place-begging and sectarian discussions' were added.[13] O'Connell, fearing that Meagher could commit him to violence, resurrected his father's peace resolutions. Dillon suggested as a compromise that, while neither side had abandoned its beliefs, no individual or newspaper should be authorised to interpret the principles of the Irish League. Moral and physical force were therefore not mentioned in the agreement.[14]

The council of the confederation adjourned *sine die* on 21 June. Dillon provided a financial statement which showed that receipts totalled only £916, £150 of which the council donated to Jane Mitchel. Nonetheless, he asserted: 'They had established a principle which he thought of exceeding great value, namely, that every man in Ireland had a right to have a weapon' to defy the prime minister when Lord John Russell 'tells the people of Ireland that he will resist their will by force and rule their country by force'.[15] On this note, irrelevant to a starving nation, the confederation expired. John O'Connell announced that he could never join the new body and departed prudently for a continental holiday, having first ordered Conciliation Hall to be shut up and barricaded; Duffy was later to say: 'that day's work was the most unfortunate and disastrous in his mischievous career. It alarmed the timid and gave the corrupt a pretence for spreading doubt and confusion.'[16] Moreover, it deprived the league of the O'Connell name.

In Paris the dream of a social and democratic republic ended with a left-wing rising against the government. During the bloodstained 'June days' the parliamentary government was driven into the arms of reaction as Louis Napoléon Bonaparte gained control. Archbishop Denis Auguste Affré was shot dead while crossing a blockade in an effort to negotiate a truce. According to Duffy this event influenced the fate of Ireland as decisively as the flight of Louis Philippe; the archbishop's death 'not only disgusted the clergy, but alarmed and alienated the middle class throughout Europe'.[17] (Significantly, an engraving of Affré was used as frontispiece of the 1849 Irish Catholic directory.) In Rome the reign of liberalism ended when 'red' republicans encroached on Pius IX's temporal possessions.

The taint of Jacobinism, added to the bugbear of infidelity, ensured the absence of clerical support for Young Ireland. Furthermore, a papal rescript had been issued on 5 February 1848, after intense British pressure, instructing the Irish priesthood to avoid politics. Accordingly, the priests were a moderating force in 1848.

At the end of June Edward Trevelyan heard that enrolment in the clubs was spreading 'fast and unchecked'. Like Clarendon he favoured the suspension of habeas corpus: 'Above all let us take and keep the lead *while there is yet time.*'[18] By July the clubs numbered 150, representing nearly 50,000 men[19]—figures which proved to be wildly exaggerated.

The contradiction between revolutionary and constitutional methods was resolved for the Young Irelanders when the government made another attempt to silence agitation. Firstly, Duffy, Martin and O'Doherty, proprietors of the *Nation, Felon* and *Tribune*, were arrested and charged with publishing treasonable articles. Meagher, Doheny and McGee were also detained but were granted bail. Police seized the issue of the *Nation* in which Duffy had written:

> The Irish peasantry must not return to con-acre and turnip-tops, even for a year; neither must they be any longer left at the mercy of the man-trap poor laws and destructive land laws. Either these criminal and unchristian institutions and edicts must be destroyed, or new ranks of this religious, loving, long-suffering people must be swallowed in the vortex of a new Famine. ... We are fast nearing the point of time and circumstance when resistance must begin. ... There are many hours in all lives when temporising is guilt, and here would be one of them. Every wind that ripples over this tender corn, or sighs through yon bearded barley, carries as many stings as a hive. If there be power in Ireland to save the lives of its inhabitants—and if there is not we could have made it—those who perished last year stand today accusing us before God. ... To doubt—to hesitate—now, is whetting daggers for hearts of our own flesh and blood. For behold the enemy lies in wait for our next harvest as for the past.[20]

By the middle of July police and military reports showed that members of the clubs were drilling openly and buying arms. Dillon and O'Gorman inspected clubs in Trim, County Meath. The lord lieutenant 'proclaimed' Dublin, directing all holders of unlicensed weapons to surrender them to the police.

At a conference of club delegates, Joseph Brenan, a fiery young man from Cork, proposed they should wait no longer but start the insurrection at once. Dillon said they should conceal their guns and offer passive resistance to the proclamation. His amendment, supported by O'Brien, was adopted by a small majority.

Dillon presided at a meeting of Dublin club representatives on 21 July at which he, Meagher, O'Gorman, McGee and Reilly were elected to an executive council. Lalor, the most radical thinker present, said each of the five selected should undertake to start the rising by 8 August. Meagher pledged to do everything in his power to rise even before date. Dillon declared he would do likewise.[21]

The Young Irelanders were taken unawares next day when Russell introduced a bill to suspend habeas corpus in Ireland until 1 March 1849. This draconian step was taken after reports of a semi-military demonstration on Slievenamon, County Tipperary, attended by 50,000; at this event Meagher, wearing his 'splendid tricolour sash', urged the people to hold the harvest, while Doheny said: 'We intend to realise the true gospel which was preached by John Mitchel.'[22]

The prime minister told the House of Commons the safety of the empire required that an 'incipient insurrection' in Ireland be stopped.[23] Feargus O'Connor, the Chartist MP, predicted this measure would hasten the rupture between Ireland and England; having goaded the Irish people into rebellion, the government now proposed to punish them. On the other hand, Sir Lucius O'Brien, Smith O'Brien's brother, voted for the bill, 'being strongly impressed with the necessity of these proceedings being put an end to for the sake of the poor fellows who are sure to be involved in great sufferings by their continuance'.

It was passed, almost undebated, and received the royal assent three days later. The final blow came with a proclamation declaring that membership of the clubs was illegal.[24] At the same time troops were encamped near towns to overawe the inhabitants.

Russell also considered another stratagem, in a letter to the viceroy: 'A nice point will be determined how far you will avail yourself of the offers of the Orangemen to arm and form volunteer corps—the spirit of religious hatred is very bad, but you cannot let your throats be cut to avoid religious animosity. A more serious point is whether a display of Protestant zeal may not drive many Catholics into the rebel ranks. It is for you to decide'; on reflection he added that arming 'the Protestants might disquiet not only English Catholics but the 8,000 Catholics in the army in Ireland'.[25]

The frightened lord lieutenant had already concluded: '... in any real danger we have only the Protestants to rely on.'[26] But in the event the need to mobilise the Orangemen, as had been done in 1798, did not arise.[27]

The burghers of Liverpool were so alarmed that they asked to have the habeas corpus suspension bill extended to their city, where Irish Catholics numbered 100,000 out of a total population of 375,000, and magistrates believed confederate clubs could arm two to four thousand men.[28] Events in Ireland would, however, complete their demoralisation.

The few leaders available in Dublin met hurriedly to consider the options: arrest, flight or insurrection. Submission to arrest would be construed as an abandonment of the cause; escape was also rejected at this stage; Dillon proposed joining O'Brien in County Wexford and, if he agreed, to make a stand in Kilkenny—the seventeenth century Confederate seat of government. The south-east was regarded as the strongest centre of support outside Dublin.[29] The chief burden of responsibility fell on Dillon as the senior member of the executive. He was thirty four; O'Gorman, who had gone to rouse Clare and Limerick, was not yet thirty; Meagher and Reilly were both twenty five; McGee was only twenty three.

McGee was sent to Scotland on the basis of a report that several hundred Irishmen there were prepared to come home to fight, and that they also had a supply or arms and ammunition.[30] On hearing that a decisive blow had been struck in Ireland, he was to seize a vessel and cross to the north-west with his diversionary force. Dillon even suggested that they land in Killala, headquarters of the French expedition fifty years before. 'This project may now appear a monstrously absurd one', Meagher wrote in 1849; but at the time it was estimated the Glasgow Irish numbered several thousand, that Chartism was 'panting for an outbreak' and that the city lay 'almost wholly defenceless'.[31]

On 22 July 1848 Meagher encountered Dillon and his brother-in-law, Charles Hart, in a covered car in Merrion Square. Before leaving Dublin they visited Dillon's house in Great Charles Street. He gave some money to his housekeeper, threw clothes into a bag and drank a glass of wine with Meagher to the success of their venture. They then went to Killiney, where Adelaide spent much time with her family in Druid Lodge. On the Kingstown train their fellow passengers discussed the suspension of habeas corpus. One man said the whigs were infernally slow to act but they had finally given the Young Ireland scoundrels enough rope to hang themselves.

Meagher's narrative continues: 'I nudged Dillon at the conclusion of these consoling observations. He threw a quiet, humoursome look at the loyal subject with the red whiskers and gambouge complexion, and burst out laughing. He was joined by other gentlemen and two or three ladies, who recognised us but little suspected, I should say, the errand we were on.' They dined with William O'Hara at Druid Lodge. Dillon's wife informed him later she did not shed one tear on 'parting with you, as I thought for life'. They kissed good-bye in his room; 'when I looked after you from the window and met your eyes', she wrote, 'all my love, all my heart and soul spoke to you'. John would remember Adelaide's 'earnest parting look' throughout his wanderings: 'an expression in which affection and pride and sorrow were all mixed up together'.[32]

Dillon and Meagher joined the stage coach in Loughlinstown, County Dublin, and reached Enniscorthy at five the following morning. While awaiting a jaunting car to take them to Ballinkeele, Meagher read to Dillon from Lalor's valedictory message in the *Irish Felon*:

> It is never the mass of a people that forms its real and efficient might. It is the men by whom that mass is moved and managed. All the great acts of history have been done by a very few men. Take half a dozen names out of any revolution upon record, and what would have been the result? ... Let us fight in September, if we may—but sooner, it we must. Meanwhile, however, remember this—that somewhere and somehow and by somebody a beginning must be made. Who strikes the first blow for Ireland? Who draws first blood for Ireland? Who wins a wreath that will be green for ever?[33]

O'Brien was awakened at 6 a.m. to be told that Dillon and Meagher wished to speak to him urgently. He 'asked us what we proposed to do', Meagher wrote.[34] 'The suspension of the Habeas Corpus Act was an event, he conceived, which should excite, as it would assuredly justify, every Irishman in taking up arms against the government—at all events, he felt it to be our duty to make the experiment.' O'Brien thus espoused the rôle of rebel leader—his final step in a progression, during twenty years as an MP, from tory to nationalist.

They returned to Enniscorthy in time for Dillon and Meagher to attend Sunday Mass. Afterwards, the three addressed a meeting in the town, which still echoed with memories of the fighting in '98. Dillon said he understood Wexford men kept their arms and their powder dry, and asserted that the time had come when they would be called on to use them.[35] A young priest said the people were unprepared for war but they would resist any attempt to arrest O'Brien.[36]

The three leaders left by car for Graiguenamanagh where the veteran rebel, General Thomas Cloney, blessed their undertaking. The people were told to prepared for the expected rising in Kilkenny and were urged by Dillon to prevent O'Brien's arrest. It rained heavily on the way to Kilkenny. The trio stopped occasionally for shelter, and the famished peasantry left them in no doubt about the lack of revolutionary fervour. They halted to inspect the antiquities in Gowran. This charming interlude shows that seldom can an insurrection have been conducted with more idealism and less realism.

In Kilkenny they went to the confederate leader, Dr Robert Cane. Their first shock was to learn there were not 17,000 club members, as misprinted in the newspapers, but 1,700.[37] The Dublin leadership had been led to expect up to 5,000 armed confederates in Kilkenny; their real strength was about 600 men, less than one-sixth of whom possessed guns.[38] The British garrison in the town had been increased to 1,000 infantry, with two troops of cavalry and light artillery. Cane was adamant that without additional support no worthwhile stand could be made in Kilkenny. (In 1849, perhaps finding his forte, he became first treasurer of the Kilkenny Archaeological Society.) Accordingly, on Monday O'Brien's entourage set out for the neighbouring towns. In Callan they were welcomed by a large crowd and the temperance band. Hundreds of 'fine young fellows' grasped them by the hands and girls 'with flashing black eyes' embraced them, according to the flamboyant Meagher. A party of the 8th Royal Irish Hussars listened to the speeches with 'deep interest and satisfaction'. Dillon thought the look on a corporal's face 'betrayed the gallant treason of his heart'.

At Nine-Mile-House they halted to changed horses and were told it was a pity the rising had not taken place 'five years ago when Mr O'Connell had the people and the priests at their head'. The parish priests were now entirely against the insurrectionary movement. O'Brien, Dillon and Meagher dined in a public house on bread, butter, eggs and milk, with their hostess exclaiming: 'Sure it was a pity and a shame to see such gentlemen taking such fare, and they having their own comfortable homes.'

On the road to Carrick-on-Suir they met John O'Mahony, a Gaelic chieftain and scholar who filled them with 'joyous confidence', but they rejected his advice to start the insurrection that night in Carrick, where Meagher beheld

> a torrent of human beings ... eyes red with rage and desperation, starting and flashing upwards through the billows of the flood; long tresses of hair disordered, drenched and tangled—streaming in the roaring wind of voices and, as in a shipwreck, rising and falling with the foam; wild, half-stifled, passionate, frantic prayers of hope; invocations in sobs and thrilling wailings and piercing cries, to the God of heaven, his saints and the Virgin Mary; challenges to the foe; curses on the red flag; scornful, exulting, delirious defiances of death. ... It was the revolution, if we had accepted it.[39]

He added lamely: 'Why it was not accepted, I fear I cannot with sufficient accuracy explain.'

O'Brien proved incapable of initiating hostilities. The local leaders persuaded him that any attempt to rise in Carrick would be drowned in blood, whereas Dillon believed the town should have been seized and held with the support of Tipperary and Waterford. There were about 3,000 confederates in Carrick, armed mainly with pikes, and 300 rifles and muskets.[40] Ranged against them, however, were 10,000 troops and armed police, and five warships lay at anchor in Waterford harbour.[41] In that city shopkeepers were eager to become special constables, with Meagher's father third to be sworn in.[42] In Clonmel the mayor enrolled ninety three special constables, who apprehended nobody more subversive than two boys stealing apples.[43] Farce and tragedy were never far apart during '48. On 2 August a mutiny broke out in Clonmel jail. It was not quelled till the turnkeys had bayoneted eight prisoners, killing two of them.[44]

By midweek the clergy had grown alarmed that the reinforcements pouring into the country would, if given an opportunity, re-enact the atrocities of '98. The spiritual leaders of the common people believed the rising had no chance of success, and so wherever O'Brien went priests perorated about the hopelessness of fighting without food or arms. As each town the leaders visited refused to strike the first blow, they were forced to fall back on the countryside, which was untouched by the clubs network. Crowds of hungry men, women and children greeted them, but scattered before clerical admonition.

Charles Kickham—destined to become a Fenian leader and writer, most notably of *Knocknagow*—turned out in Mullinahone with a freshly-made pike. He knew O'Brien from his portrait but did not recognise Dillon: 'A tall gentleman dressed in black, and having a plaid scarf tied sashwise over his shoulder, relieved me from my embarrassment by saying, with a winning smile, "I am Mr Dillon". I shook hands with him, remarking that we had never before seen any of our leading patriots in that secluded place. They turned back towards the town. O'Brien seemed to me to be like a man in a dream; while Dillon look calm and bright and earnest.'[45]

O'Brien commanded Kickham to ring the chapel bell. He desired, Kickham's narrative continued, 'that as many men as possible should come in armed; and messages were at once sent to different parts of the parish with orders to that effect. I asked Dillon—who expressed great satisfaction at finding so much of a military spirit among us—to come with me some distance along the different roads and point out the best places to erect barricades. He spoke to the farmers whom we met on the way and urged them to procure arms.'

According to an official report, however, 'substantial farmers' were hostile to the movement.[46] The parish priest foiled O'Brien's attempt to disarm five policemen, and later surrendered seven rifles and one pistol to Dublin Castle.

In Mullinahone the leaders stayed at the home of Thomas Wright, a TCD student, who told a crowd he 'hoped things would pass off without violence, and that the government would see the necessity of doing what would better the condition of the people'. Dillon's speech was cheered several times.[47]

Dillon was 'greatly amused', Kickham wrote, by the scene at a forge where men were clamouring for pikes.

> Before midnight the material for a splendid brigade had answered to the summons of Smith O'Brien. It was computed that from 6,000 men, armed with fowling-pieces, impromptu pikes and pitchforks, were drawn up and kept at rudimentary drill that night along the streets and the roads leading to the little town of Mullinahone. They were ready to face death beyond all question. A few barricades were thrown up, but O'Brien forbade the felling of trees across the roads without the permission of the owners of the estates upon which they grew. One poor Protestant gentleman granted this permission, but remarked ruefully that the trees on the other side of the road, which belonged to a magistrate, were spared. The boys felt the force of this appeal so strongly, that only a few of the least valuable of his trees were cut down. As the morning advanced the little army began to melt away. They saw no fighting to be done—no work of any kind; and had no idea where breakfast was to be had, except under their own roofs.[48]

Father Fitzgerald, the Ballingarry priest, wrote later that O'Brien's failure to feed his ragged army 'gave a death-blow to the entire movement'.[49] O'Brien, for his part, would blame clerical interference for his ignominious defeat. The leaders spent the week of the insurrection in a dilatory and cumulatively demoralising manner. Even the weather— 'damp and heavy'—was against them. From Mullinahone they went to Ballingarry. On being met by a party from that colliery district, 'Dillon desired that Mullinahone men to turn back', as preventing O'Brien's arrest was his only clear strategy. Kickham shook hands with Dillon and

O'Brien, 'who looked happy and dreamy smoking a cigar'. On Wednesday they entered Ballingarry at the head of 500 men. This force was reduced to fifty as local priests told the people they were rushing to destruction.[50] Meanwhile, O'Brien's 'staff' was increased by the arrival of: P.J. Smyth, Patrick O'Donoghue, James Cantwell, James Stephens, Reilly and Bellew MacManus. (MacManus had been unable to find 200 armed men among the clubs in Liverpool for his plan of storming Chester Castle, seizing its arsenal and sailing to Wexford in three steamers which he had chartered.)[51]

In Ballingarry, MacManus found Dillon with O'Brien and about a dozen followers:

> A large force had assembled the day before, but O'Brien sent them home with orders to appear the next morning, provisioned for two days. They never returned. On Thursday morning we rang the chapel bells and collected all the men we could. We paraded and drilled them, showed them how to form, charge, etc. Between 12 and 1 o'clock we marched to Mullinahone at the head of about 150 slashing fellows, tolerably armed and in high glee. Dillon walked at their head. When we neared the village I was ordered forward to purchase all the bread I could find, and I can speak confidently of the numbers as I paid for 160 men's shares and had a few left. During their hasty meal the parish priest got among them, and when we were ready to march we found a third of our men disaffected, and in a few minutes they dispersed.[52]

The rebels had their closest approximation to a victory in Killenaule. On being told that a troop of cavalry was on its way to arrest O'Brien, Dillon shouted: 'Up with the barricades'.[53] The dragoons—the Royal Irish Hussars already encountered in Callan—were evidently not hostile. While Stephens covered their commanding officer, Charles Joseph Longmore, with a rifle, Dillon mounted the barricade and asked it he had a warrant for the arrest of O'Brien.

Captain Longmore would describe Dillon as 'rather tall and sallow, respectably dressed but without arms' (elsewhere he wore a belt with a brace of pistols). The captain denied that he had any warrant and said they were merely passing through the village.[54] Stephens— co-founder of the Fenian movement with John O'Mahony—recalled: 'This explanation satisfied Dillon. A passage was immediately opened through the barricade and we allowed them to move off unmolested. On beholding the sympathetic countenance of the soldiers, as they rode by, I could not help being disposed to think that most of them would, under no great pressure, throw off their uniforms and fight for Ireland.'[55]

The crowd cheered as Dillon, a proclaimed traitor with a reward of £300 on his head, escorted the captain and his men out of Killenaule. He would be rebuked by Mitchel and John Devoy for not having precipitated hostilities, but according to MacManus, who was present, he acted with reckless bravery.[56] To engage a troop of forty five fully-equipped cavalry with one rifle and two muskets would have amounted to suicide. (A hidden casualty was an insurgent maimed by the dragoons when they returned the next day.)[57]

On 28 July the confederates held a council of war at Ballingarry. Meagher left a pen picture of the scene which greeted his arrival for the meeting:

> Approaching still nearer a shout was given—then another and then a third—the pikes, scythes and bayonets being thrust upward in the murky air, amid the waving of hats and green branches, and the discharge of pistols. ... Smith O'Brien stood with folded arms a little in advance of the crowd, looking as immutable and serene as usual. Dillon, with a large blue military cloak thrown over his shoulders, smiled quietly and picturesquely alongside him, his mild, dark, handsome features contrasting with the plainer and sterner aspect of O'Brien.[58]

The conference lasted only an hour and a quarter. Dejection reigned, according to Stephens, 'and every man appeared to be struggling with all the force of his soul against an overpowering despair.' The majority favoured going into hiding until the harvest. But O'Brien, refusing to become 'a fugitive where my forefathers' once ruled, persisted in his vague plan of appealing to the people 'till we gather enough support to enable us to take the field.[59]

Dillon wanted to fall back on Kilkenny, seize a large house and issue a proclamation of independence; his next proposal, to march on Limerick and 'fight or die', was also rejected. He then suggested going to his native Mayo 'and raising the people there. O'Brien smiled a smile of joy, shook Dillon's hand warmly and said "go". Somebody else made a similar proposal for his district and our leader gave a similar answer'.[60] O'Gorman's rebel encampment in the hills above Abbeyfeale, County Limerick, 'dispersed in sullen despair'.[61]

On his way westward Dillon made a final appeal to Father Kenyon, who despite all his bombast refused to come to O'Brien's aid. Kenyon had promised to call out twenty parishes, but when the time for action arrived he was unwilling to lead his parishioners into a hopeless insurrection. He had told an earlier deputation that he considered it ridiculous to conduct a revolution in the chivalrous fashion insisted on by O'Brien.[62]

Moreover, Kenyon, who had been suspended by his bishop the previous May, had submitted the following month and promised in effect to withdraw from the movement. Duffy would comment with understandable bitterness: 'It was but three weeks since he had been a party to transactions for which he and his comrades were liable to be hanged. There were missionaries in New York committing treason with his consent and concurrence, and he made this new and conflicting compact without communicating a tittle of it to the men with whom he was acting.'[63]

Kenyon received Dillon's delegation with coldness and irony. 'Fight? Yes, of course he would fight if the people showed themselves prepared for revolution: but it was not becoming for a priest to begin a bootless struggle.' He would not even allow his chapel bell to be rung, and could only suggest they 'raise a green flag on a pole anywhere in the district and see how many would rally round'.[64]

Dillon considered him eccentric, while 'Kenyon had no great admiration for Dillon. He even (contrary to general opinion) thought him flighty, or fitful and unreliable.'[65] Duffy observed: 'Either Father Kenyon was not able to read the most transparent of human faces on which the creator has written candour and integrity in luminous traits, or having done Dillon a great wrong he destested him.'[66]

Kenyon had been opposed to the dissolution of the confederation, a policy which Dillon helped to implement. According to Doheny, who was close to him in temperament, the fire-eating parish priest of Templederry retired from politics in June in protest at the reconciliation with the O'Connellites.[67]

When O'Brien refused to commandeer private property, Dillon had pointed out that it was 'an act of fatuity to engage in such a movement, and utterly impossible to prolong if for any time, without resorting to the usual expedient of making the property of the country support those who were battling for the interests and independence of their country'.[68]

At one stage O'Brien told his followers to disperse and come back in the morning with provisions for at least four days, recommending 'oatmeal bread and hard eggs'. Dillon 'next addressed the meeting, but at once perceived that his words found no response in the hearts of his hearers, nor was he altogether unprepared for such a result, when he recollected that most of those he was then addressing were prompted to join the movement solely in the hope of being fed. Indeed to anyone it must have appeared little less than solemn mockery of their wants to tell a people living on a daily allowance of a pound of Indian meal to return on the following day bringing with them, every man, four days' provisions.'[69]

O'Brien spent the last evening in Ballingarry writing his most radical statement: a letter to the directors of the mining company threatening to nationalise the collieries. He acknowledged 'the noble and courageous protection' which the people had given him. 'In case he should find that the mining company endeavours to distress the people by withholding wages and other means, Mr O'Brien will instruct the colliers to occupy and work the mines on their own account and in case the Irish revolution should succeed, the property of the mining company will be confiscated as national property.'[70]

The *Times* reported Dillon has been killed in Ballingarry, embellishing a rumour that he lay wounded.[71] In fact he had departed for the west before the final débâcle. At 1.30 on 29 July forty-six policemen commanded by Sub-inspector Thomas Trant passed through Ballingarry on their way to Boulagh Commons.[72] As they approached Farrenrory the crowd around O'Brien rushed towards them. The police took refuge in Widow McCormack's two-storey dwelling, which is still known as the 'war house'. Chorusing 'The British grenadiers', they broke the furniture and placed the house in a state of defence.[73] When MacManus started a fire at the rear of the building, Mrs McCormack appeared in a state of frenzy about her five children who were still inside. O'Brien, 'with great peril to himself', accompanied her to a window to parley with the police. While they were talking stone-throwing began, and O'Brien narrowly escaped martyrdom as the police retaliated with their carbines. They fired 230 rounds in the course of an hour, killing two insurgents and wounding others severely.

MacManus and Stephens with about twenty men returned the fire; 'but owing to the windows being barricaded so high our shots took no effect', MacManus wrote subsequently to Dillon. 'Immediately after a second volley was fired, the bullets knocking a splinter off the gate struck me in the leg and upset me. This is what gave rise to the report of your being wounded, as I was mistaken for John Dillon all through.'[74]

The rebels' ammunition was quickly spent. MacManus then advised O'Brien to fall back on the village and attempt to rally their dispirited forces. 'But he declared that an "O'Brien never turned his back on the enemy". In fact he became desperately determined and stood in the midst of the fire without any purpose.'

At this stage Father Fitzgerald rode up, accompanied by another priest and Constable John Carroll, who had been sent from Kilkenny to instruct Trant to await reinforcements. Fitzgerald recalled: 'Here we first met Mr O'Brien and the party who had just retreated from the house. All were indignant that the police had fired on the people without provocation, and were anxious to go up again to the house. I was asked if I would go with them, and when I refused Mr O'Brien asked what would I advise them to do, and said that he would act as I would recommend. ...'75

The priest reckoned that if the siege was renewed the police 'would very probably all be killed ... and, as a consequence, that martial law would be proclaimed throughout the kingdom'. O'Brien said the police could go free if they handed over their weapons. Fitzgerald agreed to take this message to Trant, who refused to surrender and pointed out that they had Mrs McCormack's children as hostages.76 If the police had not used the children as a shield, MacManus would have smoked them out and the insurrection might have ended in less of a fiasco.

Fitzgerald advised O'Brien to abandon any notion of resuming the attack. The priest spent nearly two hours restraining the people. O'Brien was reluctant to leave the field, but as a military commander he resembled Don Quixote more than his forbear, Brian Boru. He vacillated until eventually MacManus and Stephens led him away on Constable Carroll's horse, before reinforcements closed in. Later, wandering about, he met Carroll. O'Brien told him he did not want any bloodshed, returned the horse and departed.77 The rising of 1848 was over.

O'Brien was arrested at Thurles railway station on 5 August, having bought a second-class ticket for Limerick. The English railway guard who claimed the £500 reward for his capture had to leave the town for his own safety.78 The leaders were not betrayed despite the wretched condition of the people, and the warning of the under-secretary, Thomas Redington, that anyone 'who shall afford them the means to escape, or who shall aid in their disguises, or who shall mislead those who are in search of them, or who shall harbour or shelter them in their dwellings, or otherwise, are themselves guilty of the crime of high treason and will be dealt with accordingly'.

MacManus, the most determined of the leaders, lit a fire on Keeper Hill, on the Tipperary-Limerick border, 'with the vague thought that it might startle the people with the belief that all was not yet over'.[79] But he had already found they were unarmed and that much of their courage was starved out of them.[80]

On 30 August MacManus was arrested on board an emigrant ship in Cork. Meagher and O'Donoghue surrendered on 13 August, the former claiming arrogantly that the people were 'not up to the mark'.[81] 'Meagher of the sword' would find adequate scope for his martial ardour at Antietam and other battlefields of the American civil war.

McGee returned to Sligo where he established communications with Ribbonmen, hitherto anathema to the Young Irelanders. This agrarian secret society, which had a fertile imagination, promised 2,000 fighting men if the south rose. On receiving news of O'Brien's arrest McGee escaped to the US.[82]

The *Times* correspondent commented on the arrest of Fintan Lalor: 'To this man is Ireland mainly indebted for her present condition. He it was, by his own admission, who first instilled into the mind of John Mitchell [*sic*] those notions of republicanism and communism for which he paid the penalty of his liberty.'[83] Lalor was released due to ill-health but attempted further armed resistance before his death in December 1849.

There were 118 arrests during 1845-9 on suspicion of treasonable practices. The *Freeman's Journal* reported that twenty one rebel suspects arrived in Dublin 'very wretched and half-famished looking creatures and appeared to be from eighteen to twenty four years of age'.[84] Father Fitzgerald would recall: 'Prisoners were sent in shoals to Dublin and detained there a long time; and though there were no executions, whole families were left mourning and desolate, for many died in captivity and exile, others perished from long concealment in bogs and mountains.'[85]

After the collapse of the rising fear turned to derision in official circles. More ominously, Ireland became a victim of compassion fatigue. The British press turned a face of brass towards the misery of the Irish poor, whom it depicted as racially inept, lawless and violent. The filthy, diseased, starving people flooding into Britain confirmed this image.

In August it was announced that the potato crop had failed again. Lord John Russell warned Lord Clarendon: 'The course of English benevolence is frozen by insult, calumny and rebellion'; Edward Twistleton, chief commissioner of the Irish poor law, resigned in March 1849; Clarendon told Russell: 'He thinks the destitution here is so horrible, and the indifference of the House of Commons to it is so manifest, that he is an unfit agent of a policy which must be one of extermination'; the *Times* said the insurrection had exhausted compassion for Ireland.[86]

In retrospect, O'Brien wrote that he envisaged six months of 'honourable warfare' (Dillon had told the people that if they armed and protected O'Brien, Ireland would be free in six months).[87] O'Brien asserted that in Mullinahone, 'if it had not been for the interference of the Roman Catholic clergyman of that parish, I should have found myself in command of a large armed force. ... But they were completely paralysed by the operation of spiritual influences. The same men who had showed the utmost ardour in the evening were upon the following morning after listening to the exhortations of the priest, if not indisposed, at least utterly unfit for action.'

He had hoped to surround himself, not with a hungry mob, but with 'men sufficiently independent in their circumstances to be able to maintain themselves for a short time upon their own resources'. In Ballingarry O'Brien said 'he desired all married men who had families to remain at home, and all poor labouring men to continue at their labour—and stated he desired no man to join him who could not bring with him three days' provisions of bread or biscuit—that he desired society to be preserved. ... Mr Dillon also addressed the people much to the same effect.' Observing their followers on the road to Boulagh Commons, he said to John O'Mahony: 'Look at the ragamuffins, think of our venturing our lives for such a miserable set.' O'Mahony added: 'But neither Dillon nor I were then calm enough to remember the 2,000 men that escorted him and his companions from Mullinahone to Ballingarry, and guarded them there for two days until they were tired out and disgusted by a meaningless parade that had all the danger, but none of the adventures or glory of actual war'.[88]

In Newgate Duffy was joined by a prisoner who informed him: 'The towns bade us try the rural districts; in the rural districts the farmers would not give up their arms, and the labourers had none; the priests opposed us, and the clubs sent us about one per cent of their number to our aid.'[89]

O'Brien maintained:

> Had our instructions been obeyed, had even a portion of those who professed their readiness to fight taken the field—had even a few of the Catholic clergy placed themselves at the head of the people and any success been obtained which would have given confidence to those who were waiting for encouragement, it is impossible to say what might not have been the result of our undertaking. Enough occurred during a few days to show what might have been done if every man pledged to the cause had thrown himself into the conflict with unhesitating devotion. Four or five resolute men,

aided by a motley crowd of peasants, only a few of whom were armed with weapons of any kind, were enabled at the barricade of Killenaule to arrest the progress of a troop of cavalry; and if an actual conflict had taken place the result would probably have been favourable to the insurgents. At Farrenrory 47 policemen fled from a few hundred colliers, of whom not more than 60 or 70 were armed; and I am persuaded that if the police had not been saved by the intervention of two priests, they might have been compelled to surrender by the application of fire to the building which they occupied.

According to resident magistrates, popular sentiment in Munster regretted the rising had failed and was irritated by the clergy's opposition to the rebels.[90] The *Tipperary Vindicator* concluded: 'Were it not for the energetic exertions and the vast influence of the Catholic clergy throughout every portion of the archdiocese of Cashel, as well as in those parts of the diocese of Killaloe where disturbance has been apprehended, we have no doubt but that a sanguinary collision should have taken place between tens of thousands of the people, and whatever force the government might bring against them.'[91]

O'Brien presaged the words of the 1916 leader, Thomas MacDonagh: 'There is always a chance of success for brave men who challenge fortune.' Ultimately, however, he admitted to having 'totally miscalculated the energies of the Irish people'.[92] In 1848 the people were debilitated by hunger and defeated mentally.

Dillon initially blamed the failure on others: 'If any considerable portion of the Irish people had acted as we did, the result, I think, would have been different.' Furthermore, 'the poor fellows who were immediately around us would no doubt have fought will[ingly] if they had arms. But what is to be said of the clubs of Kilkenny, Cashel, Clonmel, Waterford, etc., etc. Not one of them came near us. Up to the last they would hear of nothing but *blood*, and threatened to assassinate anyone who spoke a moderate word, and when the hour came they hid themselves in their houses'.[93]

On reflection he would say: 'We failed and I am afraid we deserved it.'[94] According to his wife's memoir, he wrote an account of the rising 'but it unfortunately fell into strange hands and was burned. He never afterwards could be induced to rewrite his impressions of the attempted insurrection, or even to speak freely of it.' A letter written to Adelaide while Dillon was still a fugitive has survived. This 'history', quoted below, records graphically his opinions and adventures after the rising. It describes how he was sheltered by a clerical network organised by Anthony O'Regan, president of St Jarlath's College, Tuam, County Galway (later to become third bishop of Chicago)[95]. Father O'Regan, who had been a prefect when Dillon was a student in Maynooth, 'liked him and never forgot him'. In general the priests, although opposed to insurrection, sympathised with the vanquished rebels.

Meanwhile, the police searched for Dillon in Kilkenny and in Druid Lodge, where his sister-in-law, Pauline Hart, asked courageously for a warrant.[96] A strong force raided the Kelly home, near Portumna, after he had stayed there.[97] The Aran dispensary reported to Dublin Castle that people had been going to Inishmaan and Inisheer 'without any apparent business'. His hiding place on Inishmaan became known as 'Leach John Dillon'.[98] He wrote to his wife on 30 August 1848 from a presbytery in Ahascragh, County Galway (where coincidentally the demesne of the Clonbrock Dillons was situated):[99]

> My last letter was written in St Jarlath's College, Tuam, on last Friday week since which day I have been living very much at my ease in the house of an old friend—the Revd Thos. O'Connor. I must not forget to tell you that this man has placed me under deep obligations to him. Although our previous knowledge of one another was not very intimate, and we had lost sight of one another for a very long time, he at once consented to receive me into his house, and has since omitted nothing to render my abode with him safe and comfortable.
>
> I parted with O'Brien on Friday evening (28 July) and drove towards Thurles on an outside car, accompanied by Cantwell. About one o'clock at night we arrived at a farmer's house, where Cantwell awakened a patriotic young lady by tapping at her bedroom window, and she was not slow in providing us with tea and a bed. Next morning I started on a car and proceeded through Thurles in the direction of Killaloe, hoping that I might fall in with a steamer there that would take me on to Portumna.
>
> I passed by several police barracks and on one occasion as I was passing a police station which stood at a crossroad, not knowing what side to turn, I called a policeman and asked him the way. He had a paper in his hand which looked very like the proclamation offering a reward for my arrest, for it had arrived that very day in the country. However, my audacity lulled his

suspicions, if he had any, and I passed on. Arrived in Killaloe I found that no steamer would pass that day to Portumna, so I was obliged to get a fresh car and go by the road. I reached Eva's house near Portumna about seven or eight in the evening and slept there that night.

Up to this time my intention was to make my way into my own native district and made such preparations as would enable me to render effective aid, when the towns upon which we calculated would break into insurrection. However, on learning that a reward was offered for my apprehension, I saw that it would be impossible to remain for a day in my own county where I was well known, and accordingly I decided on going into the county of Clare.

I shaved my whiskers and put on a broad-leafed hat and thus metamorphosed I was pronounced by Eva to be a finished priest. After a very long journey I arrived on Sunday night at a small town called Kilfenora and slept there in a little inn which was very much to my taste—except in one particular, viz, that it is just opposite the police barrack. However, I departed next morning without any interruption and proceeded to the house of a priest whose name is Ryder, and who lives at a place called Ballyvaughan and there I spent another night.

Next day I went to Kinvara accompanied by Ryder's curate, and having spent Tuesday and Wednesday night with Mr Arthur, the parish priest of that place, I hired a room in a little cottage on the seashore about four miles from the little town of Kinvara. Here I spent four days in the character of an invalid priest seeking health at the seaside. Arthur came to see me every day. He is kind-hearted and very patriotic, but a little cowardly.

He has an awful idea of the power of a policeman and he confessed to me that his blood was almost frozen by terror when he read the proclamation denouncing the penalties of high treason against anyone that should harbour or help any of the outlaws. On Sunday, the 6th, I got a letter from him written under the influence of this terror, informing me that I had been traced—that Ryder's house had been searched for me—and recommending me to shift my quarters without delay. On Sunday night he came to me accompanied by a neighbouring parish priest whose name is Kelly, and who took a very warm interest in my safety, as also by his own curate (another Mr Kelly) who was so drunk that he fell about a dozen times while we were walking about on the road.

They hired a boat at Kinvara to take me into Aran on the following morning, and accordingly I set sail on Monday morning by daybreak and landed at about 2 o'c. p.m. on the southern island which they call Inisheer. During the passage I had an over-whelming fit of sea-sickness. I lay on the bottom of the boat and there I heard the boatmen remark that they were running a fine race against the cutter. This cutter is a small vessel in the service of her majesty and is always cruising about the bay to prevent smuggling. You may imagine that I did not court her society, and would have very willingly relinquished the honour of running a race with her. However, she insisted on bearing me company and on touching the shore I saw her at a distance of about 500 yards.

On the island of Inisheer the people are so unaccustomed to visitors that when a stranger arrives they all gather around him and escort him from the shore to whatever house he chooses to stop at; and accordingly I found myself surrounded by a crowd of at least fifty persons the moment I touched the shore. As all this passed under the immediate observation of the people on board the cutter, I fully expected that some men would immediately be sent on shore to arrest me, and I am still at a loss to know why this was not done, unless it was owing to a secret leaning towards rebellion in the mind of the captain which I believe does exist there.

At all events I knew I could not remain with any safety in a place which I had entered so publicly, and I determined on leaving it before day the following morning unless I was taken in the meantime.

I lay down on my cloak—the bed-clothes being scandalously dirty—and after a few hours' sleep I started in a canoe (that is a small boat made of canvas) for Inishmaan which is the middle of the three islands of Aran.

Here I took up my abode at the house of a man named Pat Maher. All this time you must know I passed for a priest, and so successful was I in my imposition that my host at Inisheer supplicated me to 'make a gospel' for his daughter, whereupon I was obliged to say that 'I was not a finished priest *all out*'.

I had been a few hours sitting in my room in Inishmaan when my landlord, Pat Maher, came in and said that a boy had just come over from Inisheer to say that there were police and coastguards searching the island for some person or other. I said that I was the person for whom they were searching, and explained to him the cause for which they were in pursuit of me. While we were consulting on the best means of baffling my pursuers, we saw from the window the cutter putting in at a spot which was about a mile from the house.

I sallied forth in quest of a hiding place accompanied by a young fellow, who brought me to a wild spot near the brink of the sea; and here I took my station in a triangular little nook formed by three huge rocks and open overhead. I remained here during four or five hours, during which time I read [John] Milner's *End of religious controversy* with great attention and composure. *En passant*, let me tell you that I have conceived from it a very high opinion of Milner's logical and literary powers.

The only inconvenience I suffered in my hiding place was from the cold. As for uneasiness I did not either then or at any other time suffer much from it. My determination was to endeavour by all means in my power to escape and, if I failed, to meet my fate with resignation. And I can truly say that any anxiety I have felt has been exclusively on account of others, but chiefly on account of one who is dearer to me than the whole world.

During all this time I had not heard one word about *you*, and dismal conjectures were constantly forcing themselves on my mind. Do you remember the little present you gave me the first interview we ever had? This little memorial which I have never parted with has been a great source of consolation; I have it this moment near my heart where I will guard it safe.

To return to my den. After I had been there for several hours, they came to apprise me that a party of police and coastguards had visited several of the houses and, after making inquiries and warning the people of the consequences of sheltering any outlaw, had quietly departed. Their search was not rigorous—probably because they knew it would hardly be successful. After this I found it necessary to use precautions against surprise, which rendered my abode in Aran the very reverse of comfortable. I never went to bed at night, but spent the whole or the greater part of the night in the open air, and slept during the day.

You must not fret about this, because it all passed over without having affected my health in the slightest degree. Indeed I am quite sure that you never saw me in so good health as I am at this moment. On Friday (the 18th) I was awakened from my midday sleep and a paper was put in my hand, on which I found a few lines in Latin. They informed me that three priests, who had been in search of me for several days, were waiting in the island of Inisheer and wished me to go to them.

I lost no time in complying with this request and found on my arrival the Revd Anthony O'Regan accompanied to two other priests. The romantic manner in which he was induced to go in search of me, you have heard (or *will* hear) from some other source; so I will not make it a portion of this *history*. On his advice I left Aran with him, and shortly after daybreak on Saturday morning we arrived at Salthill—a bathing place within a mile or two of Galway. I lay up here in a small lodge during the entire of that day and after nightfall I walked through the town of Galway—meeting on my way big Tom White, the barrister, into whose face I looked very steadily. Yet I think the brute did not know me.

On the other side of the town a gig was waiting which took me to a place called Claregalway, where I remained one night in the house of the Revd Mr Hosty. On the following night I went to the house of a neighbouring priest, named Dwyer, with whom I remained until Wednesday. Both those last-named priests were very selfish and very cowardly, and it was with much satisfaction on both sides that they and I parted.

However, there were worse priests to be found as appears from what follows. While I was remaining with Dwyer, O'Regan (who has been all through both fearless and unremitting in his efforts on my behalf) made a journey to this place where I am now staying, to ascertain whether the place was such as suit my purposes, and whether O'Connor [would] incur the risk attendant on receiving me into this house. He returned after an absence of three days with the intelligence that O'Connor was willing and that place seemed made for concealment.

I was impatient to get away from O'Dwyer's and proposed that we should leave it that same evening (Wednesday). I had heard something of a priest called Duggan, who was a very ardent patriot and made himself remarkable in that neighbourhood for his advocacy of war-principles. I proposed that we should spend that night with him (he lived six miles off) and that we should go on to Tuam on the following night. Accordingly, we sallied forth from Dwyer's at about 10 o'c. at night purposing to walk to Duggan's. Before we had advanced a mile it began to rain most furiously and by the time we had reached the house our clothes were saturated with wet. The priest was in bed, but O'Regan who was very intimate with him went into his bedroom and opened the object of our visit—whereupon this fearless patriot replied that he would on no account expose himself to the danger of harbouring me.

O'Regan spent a long time endeavouring to alter his determination, but to no purpose and finally we were obliged to sally forth again and walk into Tuam—about eight or ten miles more—while the rain never ceased to pour upon us. We consoled ourselves as we went along by the reflection that we would not exchange with the scoundrel who could do so base an act.

On arriving in Tuam about three in the morning we succeeded in getting into the presbytery—a large house in which Dr

MacHale's curates reside; and having remained there all that day, we shifted at night to St Jarlath's College, of which O'Regan is the president.

On the following (Friday) night we started for this place in a gig, and arrived here at daybreak on Saturday morning. About an hour before I started from Tuam McGan arrived there from Galway, and I learned from him with inexpressible delight that you were well, and were bearing all those trying reverses with more firmness than I could dare to hope for.

Saturday, 2 September: I am just a fortnight here this day during which time I have improved considerably in appearance. My health has been all through very good, and I have done nothing but sleep, eat and read. O'Connor has done everything in his power to render my sojourn with him as pleasant as possible, and I would be positively happy if a shadow did not sometimes steal across my mind on account of those I left at Druid Lodge on this day six weeks. Do you know I cannot help reflecting that I have been the cause of much trouble to your Mamma and Poll, and this afflicts me for I love them both.

As for *you*, I do not think of you in *that* way. *Your* trouble is my own trouble, and besides I know it never occurs to you to regret being my wife. Well, if I escape 'I will make a good *husband* yet', and will make amends to Poll and your Mamma for all the suffering I have caused them. If I do not, although you may *weep*, you shall have no cause to *blush*, for me. *In any case never doubt for a moment the constancy of my love.*

I suppose McGan has told you ere this of our prospect of escape. On Wednesday last I sent O'Connor's curate into Galway to ascertain finally and exactly the arrangements; and if he will bring back satisfactory tidings, it is probable I will have this tomorrow. Galway is about twenty eight from this. Half this distance I will accomplish on an outside car accompanied by O'Connor, and O'Regan will be my companion for the remainder. You may imagine that it is rather a ticklish operation this of driving through a country where I am at least partially known; but I expect to accomplish it in perfect safety with the aid of a clerical coat and stock, and a pair of glasses. ...

I may state this much of my future intentions in case I shall escape—that I regard my career as a patriot as almost closed; and that my energies and talents henceforth shall be devoted to duties of another class. *This I would not say to anyone but you.* If you should ever receive an American letter from me it shall contain a good deal on this subject.

I shall also defer to a time when I speak with more certainty what I have to say about your own future destiny. It would not be my wish by any means that you should leave Ireland before next summer. Sweet as your society is to me your *life* is more precious still, and nothing must be done that could at all endanger your safety. For this reason I would rather you remain with your Mamma for several months to come.

In the meantime I will be making matters ready for your reception. Think what I shall feel when I get the first glimpse of you after so long an absence. I sometimes wish that your Mamma and the whole family would come away and leave this forlorn country for ever. I know they never can be happy in it and I think they would be happy in America. Besides I do not believe there is anyone in Ireland worthy of having Poll for a wife and Charles never can do any good here. However, I fear there may be selfishness at the bottom of this desire so I will say no more about it.

McGan told me Charles and Mr O'Hara had gone somewhere avoiding an arrest. This must have rendered your condition much more forlorn. I sometimes feel so anxious about you all that I am half disposed to allow myself to be taken like O'Brien and Meagher. By the way did they not behave very softly in that business. Meagher appeared to think that he was bound in honour to remain to be taken. Now I consider that a man *is bound* to do the best he can to save himself, when he can do no more; and accordingly I am determined that an English minister shall never hang or (what would be scarcely less painful) pardon me, if I can.

In asking you to write to me, in case I escape, I forgot to warn you against writing until I shall have been two or perhaps three weeks gone. You know if the government became aware of my departure they would write to have the ship boarded by a steamer before it would reach the shore—so that nothing should be done which would lead to a discovery. ...

I am writing all this on the supposition that I shall escape, of which result I am far from being certain. Dolan has arrived with the intelligence that the preparations are progressing satisfactorily. The vessel sails on Friday next instead of Tuesday, so that I shall not leave this until Wednesday or Thursday. I shall write whatever occurs to me in the meantime.

Wednesday: Since I wrote the last lines, O'Connor has been in Tuam arranging with O'Regan all the details of my journey to Galway. They are all pretty confident of success. I also think the chances are in my favour, but I am fully prepared for a different result. We leave this tomorrow between 1-2 o'c. About 11 tomorrow night I am to get on board a fishing boat, in which I shall remain until the following night, and then (if possible) get on board the ship. Poor O'Regan is moving heaven and earth to ensure success. He has all the priests and nuns within his reach saying Masses and novenas for some object, of the nature of which they are entirely ignorant.

Now I am going to conclude this monster letter with a few practical directions. And first of all take care of yourself *for my sake*. It would be a matter of very little consequence whether I escaped or were taken if I had not a prospect of seeing you again; for, deprived of you, I would rather be dead. Let not these reverses weight too heavily on your mind. If ever I felt disposed to despondency, I thought of the time when *you* were lying in fever and when I was hourly in apprehension for your life, and when I often said that I did not care what misfortune shall befall me if *your* life were spared.

As I told you before I never fret on my own account, but I am sometimes sad when I think of what you and your Mamma and Poll must have suffered, to say nothing of my own poor people who are so devoted to me. The fate of O'Brien and Meagher is also a source of deep regret, If I had these two with about a dozen others in the same ship with me, I would depart with a light heart with a prospect of never setting foot on Irish soil again.

As for *the people* I have lost all faith in them. They are treacherous and cowardly, and if Ireland is ever destined to be free, her freedom must be the gift of strangers. It is in this connection I said my career as a patriot was almost closed. After what we have witnessed I think it would be madness to hope for any manly effort on the part of the Irish people; and the attempt to emancipate by foreign agency, a people who have not the spirit to raise an arm in their own defence, appears to me rather quixotic. All these are *secret* thoughts but no thought of mine is a secret from you. ...

Dillon acknowledged from the safety of New York that but for the 'devoted and heroic conduct' of Father O'Regan he would be on his way to Van Diemen's Land. 'Looking back at those scenes', he reflected further, 'I have often wondered how much of the bitterness of suffering and affliction vanishes when you put the cup bravely to your lips.'[100]

Exile

*Do bhí sean-fhear as Glínn Mheáin a rugav agus a tógav i
nGlínn Mheáin dá ínseacht dom, agus is fada an aimsir ó
choin, gur amach do charraig i nGlínn Mheáin a tógav athair
Sheáin Í Dhuilleáin i gcurrach—sin é athair an fhir a
nglaomuist Honest John Dillon air—agus gur imi sé as sin go
ndeagha sé ar bórd soithig, pé an áit ar imi sé d'imi sé i
gculaithe sagairt. Agus do bhí sagart i mBailí Bhocháin a
dtugaidíst Father Ryder air, agus is é a chulaithe sin a bhí air
[go ndeagha] sé isteach ar ché New York, más ann a landáil sé.*
LEABHAIR STIOFÁIN UÍ EALAOIRE[1]

On 11 September 1848 a brig, the *Gem* of London, hove to in Galway
Bay to take a 'Father Hughes' on board.[2] Dillon had been rowed in a
currach from a pre-famine fishing village on the north Clare coast
disguised as a priest. As the ship set sail it was hailed by a custom-house
boat. Dillon thought the game was lost. When the boat came alongside
and an officer was about to step aboard, a man on deck touched him on
the arm and spoke his name. 'Yes', he replied, 'my name is John Dillon—I
give myself up.' The man said: 'Hush, I am P.J. Smyth, all is right, that
boat has nothing to do with you.' Dillon had mistaken Smyth, who was
escaping dressed like an emigrant in a frieze coat, for a detective.

Autumn gales blew the vessel so far off course that Dillon feared he
might be joining Mitchel in Bermuda penal colony—'transported at my
own expense'. Towards the end of the voyage to New York he revealed
his identity inadvertently. The captain, glad to have a clergyman on board,
had invited him to his table. One day during heavy seas the brig lurched,
flinging a hot joint into Dillon's lap. 'His reverence' swore. The captain
laughed and said he 'thought so before'.[3]

Adelaide wrote on 19 September:

My darling sweetest love, this day I heard you are safe. ... So dear are you to me, so highly do I value the treasure of your love, that I think it very, very cheaply purchased by all I have suffered these eight sad weeks. And tho' even I were to lose you now—and with you all my earthly happiness—still I would a thousand times rather have been your own little wife than if I could have led the most brilliant, apparently happy, life this world affords. ... Religion has always been to me not merely a duty with which I complied from a conviction of truth and right, but a necessity of my heart and soul—a source of sweetest happiness, comfort and strength. Your heart, darling, was my earthly resting place and the bosom of Almighty God my heavenly home, where I turned when I was sorrowful and lonely; and found comfort, for I knew it was the same love that had given me you and all my former happiness, that now sent me this trial and grief and I felt a firm confidence that whether He gave me joy or sorrow, it must be beneficial for you and me, for we were in the hands of One who loved us with infinite tenderness.

Another source of consolation was 'the calm happy consciousness of having fulfilled your duty and done all that a brave man could do—it was this thought which chiefly supported me in all my sorrow. You know, John, I always told you I never would have loved you as I do if it were not that I can feel so proud, so entirely satisfied with you. ... I am happy that you have acted as you have done—for the sake of Ireland, for the sake of your own honour. ...'

Adelaide intended visiting 'poor darling Meagher and O'Brien' in Richmond jail until she learned the state prisoners had been transferred to Clonmel for trial at a special commission. It made her reflect: 'Can I ever be grateful enough for your escape.'

William O'Hara, Adelaide's uncle, had fled to France for the duration of the crisis. On the way home he read in an English newspaper of Dillon's escape. O'Hara told his sister that he was mistaken for Dillon's father-in-law by the *Standard* 'and that I had intended to spare neither money nor interest to procure him a seat in parliament. So you see we are of more importance in the world that we thought ourselves and are rising rather than sinking'.[4] As Liam O'Flaherty would observe in his historical novel, *Famine*, 'it is a great thing to be related to a man that had the courage to strike a blow.'

Charles Hart, Adelaide's brother, left Druid Lodge in tears on 28 July, the day Dublin Castle outlawed Dillon. He avoided the attentions of a detective in Killiney railway station as he bought a ticket for Kingstown, where he boarded the Holyhead steamer. Hart travelled from Liverpool to New York, where he awaited Dillon in the company of Martin O'Flaherty and William Mitchel. He spent the time sightseeing, studying and writing a journal.[5]

In Brooklyn Hart met Young Ireland refugees who were disposed 'to turn their "martyrdom" to some account in this country—in other words, to abuse the sympathy of the American people'. At Mass he noticed the 'vulgarity and almost rudeness of well-dressed Irish people. Originally poor and degraded, dress and a little prosperity can not make people refined all at once'.

Hart observed the 'more energetic men of the [Young Ireland] party', such as James Cantwell, had escaped—evidence that the people were 'willing at least to thwart the government'.

Dillon wrote to Adelaide on 30 October:

> Dearest love, we have *at length* come to anchor inside Sandy Hook about twenty miles from New York where we may possibly have to wait till tomorrow for a breeze to take us up. Yesterday morning we got the first sight of land, a most grateful sight after seven dreary weeks. In the course of the day a pilot came on board and brought us some papers which contained the Irish news up to 9 October. Sad news. O'Brien sentenced to death and the cowards around him sobbing like women or running to beg that his life might be spared. However, I was quite prepared for it. I revolved the matter a thousand times in my mind during the voyage and I could see no possible termination except that which has occurred. What his fate is to be those papers do not say, but on that point either I have no doubt. He will not be executed, but will be doomed to a severer fate, and the government will be thanked by 'the people and the faithful clergy' for sparing his life. I have reason to be grateful to God for being rescued from the grasp of such an enemy; but I am still more grateful for being separated from a people amongst whom I could not longer live without a constant loathing.

He presumed correctly that Michael Doheny and Richard O'Gorman had escaped, and ended his first American letter by expressing anxiety about Adelaide, who was five months pregnant, and looking forward to 'devouring' her letters which had been sent to New York friends, Susan and Edward Bill.

On 31 October Hart returned to his lodgings. 'In a few minutes', he recorded, 'in walked John wonderfully well considering all he had gone thro'—looked very weather beaten and thin.'

By the Lord Lieutenant General and General Governor of Ireland.

A PROCLAMATION.

CLARENDON.

WHEREAS We have received Information that *Thomas Francis Meagher, John B. Dillon,* and *Michael Doheny,* have been guilty of Treasonable Practices:

Now We, the Lord Lieutenant, being determined to bring the said *Thomas Francis Meagher, John B. Dillon,* and *Michael Doheny* to Justice, Do hereby offer a Reward of

THREE HUNDRED POUNDS

to any Person or Persons who shall secure and deliver up to safe custody the Person of any one of them, the said *Thomas Francis Meagher, John B. Dillon,* and *Michael Doheny :*

And We do hereby strictly charge and command all Justices of the Peace, Mayors, Sheriffs, Bailiffs, Constables, and all other Her Majesty's loyal Subjects, to use their utmost diligence in apprehending the said *Thomas Francis Meagher, John B. Dillon,* and *Michael Doheny.*

Given at Her Majesty's Castle of *Dublin,* this 28th Day of *July,* 1848.

By His Excellency's Command,

T. N. REDINGTON.

Printed by GEORGE and JOHN GRIERSON, Printers to the Queen's Most Excellent Majesty.

1   Dublin Castle proclamation seeking John Blake Dillon and companions in 1848

2   Adelaide Dillon *c*.1864

3 John Blake Dillon *c*.1851

5   John Mitchel (1815-75)

4   John O'Hagan (1822-90)

6   John Edward Pigot (1822-71)

7   John Martin (1812-75)

8   Thomas Francis Meagher (1823-67)

9   Charles Gavan Duffy (1816-1903)

10   Richard O'Gorman, junior (1826-95)

11   William Smith O'Brien *c*.1860

12   John Blake Dillon in 1866

13 Leach Dillon, Inis Meáin, Aran Islands, 1952: James Dillon with his son, John Blake, and wife, Maura. Forbears of the three islanders in the background sheltered John Blake Dillon in 1848 (photograph: T. Andrica)

After being sentenced to death O'Brien sent the following lines to Meagher:

> Never despair, let the feeble in spirit
> bow like the willow that stoops to the blast.
> Droop not in peril, 'tis manhood's true merit
> nobly to struggle and hope to the last.
> When by sunshine of fortune forsaken
> faint sinks the heart of the feeble with fear
> stand like the oak of the forest—unshaken
> never despair, boys, oh never despair ...

In the course of his speech from the dock in Clonmel courthouse, Meagher declared: 'For this country, I can now do not more than bid her hope. To lift her up—to make her a benefactress to humanity, instead of being, as she is, the meanest beggar in the world—to this end, to restore her native powers and ancient constitution—this has been my ambition, and this ambition has been my crime. Judged by the law of England, I know, this crime entails the penalty of death. But the history of Ireland explains this crime, and justifies it.'[6]

This was a splendid exit by the man who brought the tricolour to Ireland. In a letter to Adelaide on 14 November Dillon commented: 'You are quite correct in your estimate of Meagher's speech. It was superior, vastly superior, to Tone's or Emmet's or anything perhaps ever delivered on such an occasion. It appears to me that the judges, truculent as they are, were ashamed of the duty they had to discharge. ... I did not clearly understand why O'Brien did not avail himself of that opportunity for vindicating his conduct, but I presume he was induced to keep silent lest anything he might say should injure others who remained to be tried.'

During his wanderings Dillon himself thought about what he would have said if confronted by Judge Francis Blackburne 'and his black cap.

> I intended to discuss the foundations of the duty of allegiance and to show that, as far as the Irish people were concerned, that duty had no existence—and with that view I would have entered into a full justification of the attempted insurrection. I think someone should have done this. A good and clear argument delivered on such an occasion would have met with universal attention. But one and all they acquitted themselves like brave men and how much more pleased and proud ought one feel to have his name associated

with such a gallant band than to be classed amongst the base and venal scoundrels, who subsist upon the dishonour of their country and the miseries of its most wretched people. When I think of my present position I congratulate myself not so much on having escaped the vengeance of the British government, as on being rescued for ever from the contaminating society of its slaves.

Besides O'Brien and Meagher, Bellew MacManus and Patrick O'Donoghue were also sentenced to be hanged, but as Dillon foresaw, there would be no executions: Lord Clarendon decided they would only provide nationalist Ireland with martyrs,[7] and the sentences were commuted to transportation for life. Special legislation had to be passed to facilitate what the British government considered an act of mercy. O'Brien was prepared for death but unwilling to accept the indignity of transportation.[8]

Gavan Duffy was tried five times. Professor Murray, of Maynooth, still making amends for having attacked the *Nation*, secured 40,000 signatures to a remonstrance to the lord lieutenant.[9] Father Mathew broke his pledge of political neutrality by acting as a character witness, describing Duffy as 'a man of the highest integrity and principle.'[10]

Isaac Butt said he could defend everything except the *Nation's* leading article entitled 'Jacta alea est' ('The die is cast')—one of the articles written during Duffy's imprisonment by 'Speranza', who had inflamed the government if not the populace. When Duffy was being questioned about them in court, the future Lady Wilde stood up and declared: 'I, and I alone, am the culprit, if culprit there be.'[11]

The government eventually dropped Duffy's prosecution. He was released in April 1849, 'chaperoned' Carlyle around Ireland during the summer, and resumed publication of the *Nation* in September. He would probably have been convicted except that, on the basis of an incriminating document found in O'Brien's portmanteau, the indictment against him was changed from a charge of treason felony to high treason.[12] The other editors, John Martin and Kevin Izod O'Doherty, were each sentenced to ten years' transportation under the Treason Felony Act.

In New York Dillon lived 'very much retired, lest I should be confronted with a shoal of *exiles* who are swarming about this city endeavouring to make something of the misfortunes of their country'.

Well-wishers flocked to his boarding house in Brooklyn. 'A poor boy named Madden who had been at Ballingarry with Smith O'Brien arrived here with his brother', Hart wrote.[13]

> He is a fine boy, gives a very consistent probable account of this affair, at which John Dillon was not present, and proves S. O'B. to have acted with determination and skill according to his resources. He had men employed piling hay against the rear of the house in which the police were, and those who had guns covering them by firing in at the windows which overlooked the rear, when Mr Fitzgerald and two or three other priests came up and by the most violent moral and physical exertions drove away the people who were firing and then the more easily those who were carrying the hay.

Hart concluded, in justification of the 'late attempt' in Ireland, 'that it was now or never—that any spirit which remained in the country would be starved out of it in one more famine, and all confidence in the leaders lost'.[14]

The need for a scapegoat in defeat is a recurrent theme in history. The Young Irelanders blamed the clergy and the people for their failure. There was much criticism of O'Brien on both sides of the Atlantic. Dillon, however, remained aloof from the factions which grew up around the refugees, although he disliked Doheny and D'Arcy McGee, and championed Smith O'Brien. Doheny was engaged in writing about his adventures, which he published in 1849 as *The Felon's track*. According to the gossip which Dillon relayed to his wife, 'he spends his evenings in a public house reciting to an audience of *"rowdies"* his exploits and his hair-breath escapes'. Dillon, who spent his evenings reading, thought recent events in Ireland merited a dignified silence.

McGee had started a New York edition of the *Nation*. Dillon considered him an opportunist, who lacked 'good feeling ... has been puffing and publishing himself ... is trading upon the misfortunes of his country and his friends'. McGee eventually renounced the Irish cause. He moved to Canada, where he became one of the architects of confederation. He was assassinated by a Fenian sympathiser in 1868.

Doheny remained an Irish revolutionary. However, he attempted to 'fasten some charge of rashness upon O'Brien', Dillon informed Adelaide. 'Nothing can be baser than this. It is both false and ungenerous and I am resolved when a proper time arrives to vindicate O'Brien's character.' The Dublin correspondent of McGee's *Nation* wrote 'that Mr O'Brien did not make a good military leader'. This statement elicited Dillon's only public contribution to the post mortem on '48.

He wrote to the New York *Nation* on 11 December that if Hannibal or Napoleon had been in O'Brien's position

> neither of those great commanders, with such materials as he had and such co-operation as he received, could have achieved any more respectable result. At no time, to my certain knowledge, had Mr O'Brien an armed force that could be rationally expected to withstand a single company. About 30 rust-eaten fowling pieces, and some few auxiliary weapons of the most despicable description, constituted the most imposing array of arms exhibited throughout the whole 'campaign'. Of the many thousands of armed club-men (some of whom are probably now criticising Mr O'Brien's conduct very freely), those who 'followed him to the field' fell short of a dozen men.
>
> He was met repeatedly in the streets and opposed by priests, acting, I have no doubt, in strict accordance with the dictates of conscience. His orders and instructions were received by the people with respect—nay, sometimes with cheers, but they were *never obeyed*. I wish, sir, that for the benefit of others who may hereafter be placed in like circumstances, your correspondent would furnish us with some easy method of achieving a revolution with a handful of unarmed and disobedient peasants, opposed by a disciplined army of some 40,000 men.
>
> It will naturally be asked why did Mr O'Brien and his friends ever conceive the preposterous idea of resisting, with such contemptible resources, the power of the English government? But of his conduct in this respect, I submit, no fair judgment can be formed without a knowledge of the antecedent facts—of the representations which had been made and of the promises which never were fulfilled.

Dillon referred to the suspension of habeas corpus as tyrannical.

> The alternative before them was this—either to submit passively to imprisonment without trial, or resist. And the worst, perhaps, that can be said of them is that they chose ruin and exile and death, rather than suffer that right which lies at the bottom of all freedom to be violated in their persons. Of Mr O'Brien, individually, I can

say with perfect truth that, of all that party which acknowledged him for its head, he was ever the most reluctant to commit his country to the perils of a civil war—and that, once driven to resistance, he was of all the firmest and most fearless in maintaining the position he had assumed and the last to abandon it.

Your correspondent may possibly think he is rendering good service to Ireland by sacrificing the character of an individual, in order that the character of the country may be saved. But impartial men will hardly tolerate this. They will say that William Smith O'Brien has devoted 20 years of a spotless life to unceasing efforts for the good of his country, and that finally he has forfeited life itself for her sake; and they will conclude that it argues but little generosity in those for whom he has sacrificed so much to seek to rob him of that which he prizes above all that he has lost—the reputation of a brave and true man. Sincerely wishing that this may be the last time my name may appear in connection with the events referred to in this letter, I beg to subscribe myself, etc., John B. Dillon.

McGee recanted in the next issue of his paper: 'On reading over the paragraph in our correspondent's letter we do concur with Mr Dillon that it is unjust towards Smith O'Brien; but we must observe that few men—no man perhaps in or out of Ireland—had equal opportunities of knowing the truth with Mr Dillon.'

His encomium of O'Brien would be dismissed by John O'Leary, with some justification, as nonsense.[15] Nevertheless, Clarendon asserted: 'It is perfectly true that the insurrection was forced on before the preparations were complete and that accounts for its being of the paltry character described by Dillon, but that was no fault of the leaders. They meant to wait till the harvest was got in and the club organisation was completed throughout the country.'[16]

Adelaide reported, after a visit to Richmond prison, that O'Brien was 'quite delighted' with the letter. Dillon had already informed her (12 December): 'Of course I do not abuse the people' in public. However, 'I feel a decided conviction that this generation of Irishmen must remain slaves, and it is only throwing away one's life to endeavour to redeem them. ... I seldom express an opinion on the conduct of the people in the recent affair, but my notion is that a more shocking exhibition of national cowardice was never made.'

He continued (19 December):

Is it not disgusting to hear those ruffians talk about him now, who would not lift a hand to help him. We were there for a *week* almost within cannon shot of Kilkenny, Carrick, Clonmel, Cashel, etc., where the villains had been roaring like mad bulls—and not one man came from any of those towns to help us. Yes, there was one and only one [James Stephens]. I felt strongly to fall upon those cowardly scoundrels but you know I never *write* [publicly] in a passion and I said nothing except what I thought necessary to O'Brien's defence. His reputation was beginning to yield before these cowardly calumnies and the impression was spreading here that the failure of the movement was owing to his having opposed some bold counsels recommended by the rest of us. But my letter has set that matter finally at rest.

Dillon received a 'pressing offer' to join the staff of a Catholic newspaper in New York called the *Freeman's Journal*. He declined, explaining (he wrote to Adelaide on 26 December): 'that my intimate connection with public affairs up to this time arose rather from the melancholy state of the country in which I lived, than from my own natural inclination. And now that I happily found myself in a land where my mind would not be distracted by the continued contemplation of oppression and misery, there existed no motive sufficiently strong to conquer my natural preference for private and peaceful pursuits'.

The proprietor of the paper—James McMaster, a Presbyterian convert to Catholicism—said Bishop John Hughes had spoken of Dillon 'in very flattering terms'. He wanted to publish Dillon's letter, 'but I am determined to decline this offer too ... it would be generally regarded as an ingenious stuff—concocted between the editor and myself'. In refusing to become involved with journalism again the co-founder of the *Nation* commented that, although the editorial writing was not so good, 'as newspapers the American papers excel'.

One evening while Dillon was visiting the Emmet family Devin Reilly arrived, having escaped from Ireland. 'The poor fellow was dreadfully cut up'—so changed Dillon hardly recognised him. But they spent 'a glorious evening during which Reilly amused us by a comical recital of his adventures'.

Reilly launched a journal entitled the *People*. According to Dillon it was 'to be devoted to the cause of European republicanism. The idea of reviving the cry of Irish nationality is justly regarded as wild and mischievous. I am resolved to resist all temptations to engage in this or any other such speculation'. In his short-lived venture Reilly was assisted by

John McClenahan, formerly editor of the *Limerick Reporter*, who later
sub-edited Mitchel's New York *Citizen*. Reilly's brief but remarkable
journalistic career ended with his death in 1854, three weeks before his
thirtieth birthday. Mitchel wrote of his disciple in the *Jail Journal*: 'The
largest heart, the most daring spirit, the loftiest genius of all Irish rebels
in these latter days sleeps now in his American grave.'

While Dillon awaited news of the birth of their first child he was
'reconciled for the present to the state of *single blessedness*, hoping always
for a spring termination of it'. Next to feeling Adelaide's arms around his
neck 'the greatest enjoyment in this world was to read her letters'. He
wondered if they would ever be 'a cool sensible pair. I sincerely hope not.
The highest position that man ever aspired to would not compensate for
the joys that spring from this ardent love. ... Do you ever feel as if it was
too great happiness for mortals to enjoy?'

Life in the nineteenth century hung on a more fragile thread than today.
Childbirth was potentially life-threatening. Hence the preoccupation with
Adelaide's delicate health. 'It does seem to me', Dillon wrote, 'that you
are too beautiful and too good to be left to me. However, as I have said a
hundred times already, my trust is in God.'

As Christmas approached he reflected on his good fortune.

> ... when I think of the position which I *might* be in, I see in my
> present condition no cause for any feeling except gratitude and
> satisfaction. I have often fancied myself marched in and out of that
> cursed queen's bench, subjected to the gaze and the condolence of
> those stupid barristers, for whom I always entertained the most
> profound contempt—and *always thinking* of the darling who
> would be grieving at home on my account. I think it would be
> harder on me than any of them—but it is hard enough too on them,
> poor fellows.

In one of her letters Adelaide described a visit to Richmond, where the
state prisoners were treated as gentlemen by the Dublin corporation
authorities. Meagher had his cell 'settled with all his beautiful pictures—
books and carpeted and made as comfortable as possible. ... He looked
much better too, quite himself—not at all stupified as before—dear
glorious little fellow—it makes me more sorrowful than I can tell you to
see him locked up there in the power of this hateful English government.'[17]

On Christmas Day 1848 Dillon and Hart dined with a doctor and two priests. One was educated at Maynooth—'a regular Irish priest, rough, talkative and conceited but by no means devoid of talent and information, and I think moreover a good-natured fellow'. In another letter he told Adelaide about meeting a member of Congress and the Prussian envoy at a supper party. 'Exclusive to our own friends, I think it would be hard to make up such a party in Ireland—so intellectual, so unconstrained and so agreeable in every respect.'

Robert Emmet, 'a noble fellow' and the son of Thomas Addis Emmet, was a frequent visitor. On one occasion he was accompanied by the son of William MacNeven, who had been on the United Irish Directory with Emmet's father. Dillon was also visited by Dudley Persse, who unlike his conservative brothers in Roxborough, County Galway, had become a 'thorough republican'.

Dillon had been placed on the Irish Directory, a largely honorary position. He was 'a little overwhelmed by emigrants bringing introductory letters. But I have been able to serve a few and that is some compensation for the annoyance.'

A human bridge was being formed between Ireland and North America. According to the 1850 census, 26 per cent of the 513,485 people in New York city were Irish-born. Dillon assured Adelaide she would 'have numbers of very kind friends with warm Irish hearts and, in many instances, a rich Irish brogue. So that you will think you have only crossed the Shannon, instead of the Atlantic'. Moreover, unlike most emigrants, 'one short fortnight will take you (by steamer) to Ireland whenever you please.'

In New York Dillon observed only prosperity and energy, in contrast with the sloth and misery of those living under 'European despotism'. The people he came into contact with were less traumatised than the Famine refugees. During 'pedestrian excursions into the neighbourhood of this city' with friends, they considered 'how different is everything that we see here from all that we were in the habit of seeing at home. People may talk of the refinements of aristocratic society (which by the way are rather superficial than real) but no amount of refinement or elegance can compensate for the substantial comfort and the contentment which are universally diffused over society here.'

Even the climate, which relieved Dillon's pulmonary weakness, was 'immensely superior' to the damp Irish weather.

It was a grand thing, he enthused to Adelaide, to be surrounded by people unafraid to look a bailiff or a policeman in the eye. 'It is delightful too to think that this country must in less than twenty years to be the most powerful on the earth. In that time its population will be over fifty millions and its wealth and commerce will be beyond all calculation. For ourselves then, dearest, we have no cause to regret that our destiny is linked with that of the stripes and stars.'[18]

Emmet and other prominent lawyers were arranging to have him admitted to the New York bar. Dillon noted with approval that US lawyers wore neither wigs nor gowns. He was admitted at the state capital in Albany on 5 March 1849. The chief justice, Ira Harris, said 'the court had fully satisfied themselves as to Mr Dillon's capacity and character, and they considered that the circumstances which caused the present application to be made, warranted them in departing from the ordinary practice of admission.'

In reply Dillon stated that he had more than one reason to be thankful to the judges.

> It is valuable to me in as much as it restores to me that occupation which is most agreeable to my tastes and habits. It is perhaps more valuable in as much as it indicates your approbation of my conduct and your sympathy for that cause, in adhering to which I had forfeited my profession and my home. Nor is its value in this latter respect confined to me. It will be a consolation to my friends (who have been less fortunate—though more deserving than I have been) to learn that, in this favour conferred upon one of their associates, *their* principles and conduct have been stamped with approval by men whose character and positions entitled their verdict such weight.[19]

This letter amounted to a skilful propaganda exercise. Dillon was an imposing figure as he embarked on a new career. Over six feet tall, Mitchel considered him 'one of the finest and handsomest men in the world'; furthermore, 'of all our confraternity of '48 he was perhaps the most beloved, had most friends and fewest enemies.'[20] To an air of dignity he added the distinction of having eluded the British authorities.

John O'Hagan congratulated him from Dublin: 'Of all the men implicated in the late affairs there was *no one* who excited more interest among friends and foes than you; no one for whose escape more joy was expressed. That you have a great career before you and will not only be a happy man, but an eminent man in your new sphere I feel assured. Still you must keep your eye on Ireland. To serve her is your true mission.'[21]

An Observer in America

From ruined huts and holes come forth
Old men, and look on yonder sky.
The power divine is on the earth:
Give thanks to God before ye die.
And ye, oh children worn and weak,
Who care no more with flowers to play,
Lean on the grass your cold, thin cheek,
And those slight hands, and whispering, say.
Stern mother of a race unblest,
In promise kindly, cold in deed.
Take back, oh earth, into thy breast,
The children whom thou wilt not feed.

AUBREY DE VERE

Dillon's correspondence in 1849 reflects the broken spirit of the country which fuelled the Famine diaspora. His broad, speculative mind lacked consistency. He now believed Irish politicians 'ought to abandon all thoughts of a nationality which had no existence except in our dreams, and link the strength and fortunes of the country with those of the peaceful-progress party in England'. The path from Ballingarry was leading towards the National Association.

Adelaide opened the year with a graphic description of Ireland:

You cannot imagine how wretched and disgusting it has become—there is nothing here now genial to a *young* mind ... there is the one story eternally ringing in your years—ruin, beggary, want, the poor rates—no work to be had—no employment—everyone from the lord to the poorest farmer bankrupt and broken—and the land all lying uncultivated. Hopeless ruin indeed it seems and one feels at a loss to know how or where it will end. But worse—far worse—is the indescribable state of *moral* and political degradation. ... I have, as it were, grown *accustomed* to corruption, servility, cowardliness, want of principle, timidity and all the other slavish vices. ...

Later (15 May) she found it 'heart-sickening and depressing' to observe countrymen in the streets of Dublin: 'They are not like human beings at all.' Once respectable farmers were throwing up their land and emigrating. It was no longer possible for a person of feeling to live 'in such an atmosphere of slavery'. Nevertheless, a visit from 'Fahy the piper' to Druid Lodge proved there was some vitality left in the country. Adelaide 'knew the sounds of his pipes the moment he began to play under the window; we made him come up to the drawing room and play all the old tunes for us. The poor fellow was inquiring of course most affectionately after you ... and all the others'.

Dillon noted (29 March) that resources were being transferred from Meath to Rome but not to the west of Ireland: 'The same papers which contain those doleful accounts of destitution and suffering, announce with the greatest exultation the great banquet to Dr MacHale and the remittance of £1,000 to the pope from the single diocese of Meath.' Dillon was unfair in imputing lack of concern about the famine to MacHale, whom he disapproved of since the days of the colleges controversy. None the less, his criticism of the distribution of Irish wealth was apposite.

He himself attended a supper party around this time given by Bishop Hughes of New York. The other Young Irelanders invited were: O'Flaherty, Hart, Reilly and Smyth. Doheny gate-crashed the party, arriving drunk. Dillon regaled his wife:

> Sitting between the bishop on one side and Charles on the other— with both his elbows planted wide asunder on the table cloth, he shouted rather than talked after such a fashion that no voice could be heard but his own. Sometimes when he could get no-one to listen to him he would turn round and seizing the bishop by the arm would shout out some absurdity. He seemed particularly desirous to find someone to argue with him the great question of moral and physical force, but everybody judiciously declined the combat. There happened to be a Yankee convert of the name [Orestes] Brownson sitting opposite. He is a fellow of a good deal of ability and of enormous pretensions, and towards the end of the evening when Doheny was furiously drunk, he and this Yankee got into a deadly argument about the right of resistance. They abused one another very freely while all the rest of us, including the bishop, were falling off our chairs with laughing. We, that is

Chs., O'F. and myself, enjoyed it particularly because we knew
something of this Brownson, and were not sorry to see him in such
an unenviable plight. He is one of a small knot of fanatical
Catholics (consisting as far as I know of three persons in all) who
take particular delight in pronouncing sentence of damnation not
only upon heretics, but upon Catholics and even priests and
bishops who do not entertain the precise opinions which they
maintain. Brownson is the leader of this petty sect and my friend
McMaster (who is a little mad) and a shallow conceited priest of
the name Commins are his disciples. ... I never saw religion
present itself in such a repulsive form as it does in the creed of
those fanatics.

Hart recorded in his diary (24 February) that Doheny's performance,
'coupled with his unhandsome and false insinuations and statement about
S. O'B., have made us resolve not even to have pity on him for the future'.

Dillon's initial impression of Bishop Hughes was: 'by far the best
specimen of a Catholic churchman I have ever met'. Known as 'Dagger
John' due to his bellicosity, he became the first Catholic archbishop of
New York in 1850. Later Dillon decided that Hughes was a demagogue,
who 'is not for tolerating Protestantism or infidelity in Catholic countries.
This is bad, very bad.'[1] He saw that the advocates of ultramontane
Catholicism were provoking a backlash, which would find expression in
the Know-Nothing crusade against Irish immigrants. 'The bigotry of the
Catholic clique is truly disgusting and likely to prove highly injurious to
the Catholic interests in this country, where the idea of religious ascendancy is regarded with horror. It is a sad thing that a few madmen can
bring discredit and odium on an innocent community, for the Catholics at
large have no sympathy with them.'[2]

Adelaide thought the New York *Freeman's Journal* was 'an illiberal
stupid paper ... calculated to do an infinity of harm to Catholicity in
America'.

Dillon reported at one point during his American stay (22 February
1853), that the Catholic papers were moving 'in the direction of good
sound orthodox bigotry'. Soon everyone calling himself a Catholic would
be an object of suspicion. He feared another outbreak of church burning
in the US.

As his wife's confinement approached in February 1849, Dillon prayed
she would survive childbirth. 'I ask the request on the ground that you are

not less necessary to my happiness in a future world than in this—for I felt that I was every day growing better under the purifying influence of your love.'

On receiving a letter from his mother-in-law he disappeared into a tavern and read that, after a 'severe and dangerous' ordeal, Adelaide had given birth to a girl. She was christened Rose and known affectionately as Zoe. On learning that his wife was safe Dillon reflected gratefully: 'What must be the feeling of a man who is conscious that his children are in the hands of a foolish or a bad mother.'

In April Adelaide wrote sadly to announce that she would be unable to join him until the autumn. Her mother and delicate sister were on a Mediterranean cruise in the hope of restoring Pauline's health, and 'I could not possibly run off without even seeing them or bidding them good-bye'. It would then be mid-June and too risky to take her baby to humid New York. Dillon, who loved one person in the world 'so devotedly that all self-love disappears whenever her happiness or safety comes in question', had already written:

> I beg of you not to consider me at all. I have recovered all my philosophy since I have received such happy accounts of you; and if my pilgrimage should be protracted a few months longer, I will make myself happy by constantly thinking of its termination. I say this because I think if possible that you might wish to remain until September in order that yourself and Rose might have time to grow quite strong, and indeed perhaps this would be the best. In that case we would have four months more of this solitary existence, but we would live on hope and on the weekly letter, together with bright accounts which with God's blessing we are sure to receive from Poll.

Adelaide's letters revealed 'a passionate self-forgetting love that none but a deep soul ... could feel'.

In the spring he went on a trip up the Hudson river with Hart and O'Flaherty. They spent a day at the country seat of Charles O'Conor, 'one of the most beautiful spots in the world'. They visited West Point military academy which delighted Dillon, who examined the forts and spoke to cadets.

Before returning to Ireland, where he eventually became a solicitor, Hart met the widow of Tone in Washington two weeks prior to her death in 1849. Matilda Tone observed that Irish revolutionaries were apt to exaggerate the quantity of arms under their control.[3]

Dillon continued to view McGee and Doheny with patrician distaste. He wrote (14 May) that McGee was 'scheming and puffing as usual. Doheny loafing about and collecting money—growing very fat and red about the nose, and every day becoming more and more devoted to the *cause of his country*. For myself, the humblest of the band, I spent this (the first day) in my office which is situated on the third floor in 45 William Street—"more near to my income, fresh air and the gods".'

He complained to Duffy about McGee, who had set himself up 'as a sort of agent of yours in America' and persisted in criticising O'Brien, 'whose character I regard as a sacred trust deposited in my hands'.

In a private letter Dillon admonished McGee for being unjust 'towards a man whose great sacrifices and disinterested heroism go far to rescue his country from that contempt which the conduct of others is calculated to call down upon it. ...'[4] Regarding himself, 'I desire nothing more than that my connexion with Irish politics should be altogether forgotten.' McGee returned this insulting epistle after reading it. Dillon did not blame him but added pompously to his wife: 'both he and Doheny have done a great deal to destroy whatever character our party had in this country,' where 'no respectable man', such as O'Conor or Emmet, would speak to McGee.

Dillon, meanwhile, found it 'vastly pleasanter' sitting in his office awaiting clients in the American fashion than to be strolling around the Four Courts in Dublin soliciting work. 'I always regarded that habit of going to court whether one had business as most absurd and mischievous—but it is only one of a hundred absurd customs which paralyse all human energy in Ireland.'

On 12 March Meagher wrote a stirring letter from Richmond prison to Dillon, 'for I know you are too much inclined to despond when things go wrong'. He recalled:

> A few days previous to my arrest I saw that our proud and darling scheme was baffled. I saw that, by us at least, it was destined not to be worked out; but I felt that we could transmit it to the future, stamped with characters of truth, fidelity and honour. A cause such as our's derives its immortality from the devotion of its martyrs not less than from the genius of its champions; and next to a victory, a sacrifice conduces most to its progress and its glory. This was the condition which chained me to the soil and forbade me to escape, even when the hope of rallying the routed energies of the

country had completely vanished. Even then I saw there was one act more open to me to perform, and that was *to suffer for the cause.* Already I have done to some extent, and to a still greater extent am quite prepared to do so. ...

I still believe in the resurrection of our island, though 50,000 guards sit upon her sepulcre and the crown of England seals the entrance.

A nation divested of faith in its future was 'as sad a spectacle as the poor wretch in whose soul a consciousness of immortality has been extinguished'. Meagher admired the tenacity of the Jewish belief 'that the Temple will be one day rebuilt. ...'

He continued: 'No, Dillon, you must never give up the old cause—never lose faith in it. True—here upon the old, green sod nothing seems capable of doing done; but, beyond these shores, wherever two or more Irishmen are gathered together, much can be done. The bolt, at least, may be forged. Heaven will raise the storm in which it may be launched. Look at Poland. For many years her history has been a history of cruel failures. Yet her heart is as sound and fresh as ever. Cut to pieces as she has been, in every bleeding fragment she preserves her passionate, proud vitality. ...'

Meagher's letter, received through 'a private hand', failed to awaken any response in Dillon's breast. He assured Adelaide (14 May): 'I will believe in the resurrection of Irish nationality when I see dead men rising from their graves. Surely no one will be so absurd as to attempt to engage the Irish people again in pursuit of this *phantom.* I think I see a fair career before them, but the first step in it must be to blot out all recollection of the past. The prostration of the British aristocracy ought to be the single aim of all future efforts and in that effort the whole strength of the people of the three kingdoms should be united.'

In a letter of advice for Duffy after his acquittal, Dillon proposed a federal republic of Britain and Ireland.[5] He considered Duffy was 'in a better position than he has ever occupied ... all prejudice against him on the score of infidelity, etc., must have been entirely dissipated in the course of his trials'. Dillon argued: 'the tenants want the land—the landlords want the rents; but no-one ever cared about nationality except our own set. Repeal itself was sought by the mass of the people as a means to an end.' He concluded:

The old forms of society, the old laws and the old language have perished irrevocably. For these reasons I would, if I were Duffy,

abandon this ground of Celtic nationality and take my stand
henceforth upon the rights of man. A federal republic is what Great
Britain and Ireland want and if that object were judiciously pursued
it might perhaps be realised within 20 years. ... Here is a new
gospel of which Duffy might become a great apostle; and *London*
is the spot for him to erect his pulpit in. If he could only start a
great journal in London, he would have the whole democracy of
the three kingdoms in his hands in three years; and in this country
he would be the most popular of living men. From that centre he
could influence Irish opinion just as much, and he could brave Irish
prejudices with vastly greater independence. From that place, too,
his voice will be heard in foreign nations. In Ireland he must either
suppress his opinions on most important questions—education for
example—or he will become once more the persecuted mouth-
piece of a provincial party. Suppose (for another example) he were
called upon to express his opinion on the relation of the pope to
his subjects and suppose him to state his opinion truly (as he would
not fail to do) would he not have the whole Irish church upon his
back ...[?]

Finally, Dillon advised Duffy to 'shun all aristocratic alliances'.
Adelaide communicated her husband's views to Duffy, who copied the
letter to consider its contents further. In reply Duffy said he was not
interested in radicalism or republicanism but in Ireland: '... your pleasant
dream of a fraternal union of the imperial democracy addressed by a
journal in London does not realise itself in me.'[6] Yet Duffy accepted part
of Dillon's advice. On reviving the *Nation* he announced that he had lost
all faith in the landlords; he founded the Tenant League with Frederick
Lucas[7] and by 1852 had become MP for New Ross. Dillon transferred
American money for this election.[8] He revealed to Adelaide that harsh
things were said about the way Duffy had used every legal means to escape
conviction. Dillon recognised 'a strong dash of selfishness in his character,
but the good qualities preponderated so decidedly that I always sedulously
closed my eyes to this unamiable defect. ... Altho' he was *esteemed* by
many, I believe not one of his associates regarded him with so friendly a
feeling as I did except Davis'; in 1851 he considered Duffy 'immeasurably
the best man in Irish politics'.[9]

Dillon was right about one thing: Duffy clashed with Archbishop
Cullen—recently returned from Rome—who mistook him for an Irish
Mazzini. In the changed circumstances of the 1860s, however, Dillon and
Cullen would coalesce.

Meanwhile, Adelaide paid a farewell visit to the state prisoners, who were transported on 9 July 1849. She was indignant at O'Brien being sent to Van Diemen's Land 'with 250 common English convicts. And poor Meagher that I love so—such a glorious noble spirit—well the bloody old British empire has triumphed this time'. In Killiney Pauline Hart noted in her journal: 'Meagher, O'Brien and MacManus, our darling, darling glorious friends, left Ireland and sailed past the bay. One short year and Meagher was our intimate and almost daily visitor here. …'[10]

O'Brien, Meagher, MacManus and O'Donoghue reached Hobart on 27 October. They joined Martin, O'Doherty and Mitchel, who was transferred from Bermuda penal colony.

Before leaving Ireland Adelaide went to County Mayo for her mother-in-law's blessing. John was gratified that she visited his 'poor old mother … a truly good woman'. He had feared his mother 'would take it into her head that you were what she calls a fine lady, and in that case you would never be able to make any way with her.'

The arrival of 'Counsellor Dillon's wife' aroused Ballaghaderreen fleetingly from its lethargy. However, she wrote, 'it would make you sorrowful, dear love, if you could see the country now. Of course you read the accounts of it in the newspapers but it is very sad to be actually among them and to see their suffering.'

Dillon, writing in a melancholy but analytical mood about his native place, congratulated her (26 June) on having 'seen the lowest point to which humanity can be reduced'. He associated 'nearly all the sweet memories' of his life with Druid Lodge. On being told of his sister Jane's unhappy marriage he declared (16 July):

> I shudder at the thought of what men and women are brought to in that country. I have never known a single case in which a man *loved* the girl he was married to. This holy union has become amongst that degraded people a mere traffic, and it is invariably negotiated in the same spirit as men purchase an ox or a horse. And would you believe it, Ady, that I have heard Dean [Bernard] Durcan … maintaining that these cold prudential marriages are more in accordance with religion than those which are prompted by love. … But what can be more significant of debasement than this ignorance of the meaning of *true* love. … Latterly it has become *so hard to live* in Ireland that every fine feeling of our

nature was lost in the absorbing pursuit of the means of sub-
sistence.

Adelaide reported from Ballina (23 June) that she had 'battles royal
with the priests here (including your friend, Mr Durcan) about Rome and
the pope—not one of them will take the true honest view of it'. In February
a republic had been proclaimed in Rome and Pius IX was driven out.
Adelaide, whose ideas were far ahead of her time, thought the Catholic
Church should lead the struggle for human freedom. Instead, she conceded
it would be natural for a young Italian to '*revolt* from that religion, the
ministers of which were leagued with the deadliest enemies of his
country—or an Irishman disgusted with the priesthood here. Yet I would
rather attribute the degeneracy of the clergy to our slavery, than our slavery
to our religion. ... It grieves me very much that the ministers of our religion
so often act in a way calculated to alienate the minds of those who cannot
discern between a religion and its priesthood.' She loved and was deeply
interested in the church 'because I so earnestly believe in its *truth*, and it
grieves me then to see it perverted and clouded by the representations of
bigots and fools'. (Adelaide was to find a kindred spirit in John Henry
Newman, first rector of the Catholic University in Dublin.)
    Mazzini became the first effective head of the Roman republic, before
it was crushed by French troops on 3 July 1849. Pio Nono's return led to
a vain attempt to retain possession of the papal states. Dillon considered
the pope had identified himself with 'the conspirators who are plotting
against the liberties of mankind'.[11] He informed his wife (17 July) that he
was critical of the church 'as a political system' and because of

> the spirit which now pervades the entire of its priesthood through-
> out the world. I believe there is no place in which they are not
> opposed to liberty and it must be so while the church is at all
> associated with politics. While the popedom is a temporal power
> it is quite impossible that its interests can be separated from the
> interests of other powers. And when the pope takes part in the
> struggle between liberty and despotism the chances are that he will
> 'stand by his order'. I never could understand why the happiness
> and freedom of millions should be made secondary to, and
> dependent upon, the interests and intrigues of that petty Italian
> state. You say if Catholicity be true it must be reconciled with the
> freedom and happiness of man. But my notion is that if the
> church—that is to say the pope, the bishops and the priests—must
> be leagued as it is now with despots and murderers, Catholicity

has gone out of it and we must seek for it elsewhere. Christ did not come into this world to put fetters upon men's limbs or thoughts, nor was it his custom to ally himself with powerful oppressors and to trample the weak and humble in the dust.

Shortly afterwards Dillon wrote saying he hoped she had not been shocked by his anti-clerical outburst. He would not speak so strongly of the priests 'if they merely advocated *principles* which I believed to be false and mischievous—for in that case they might be right and I wrong. But when they associate themselves for any purpose with such scoundrels as Dillon Browne,[12] Louis-Napoleon, etc., I have no hesitation in pronouncing them scoundrels themselves. I am sure St Paul would rather his followers were limited to 100 than spread his religion through the earth by such agency.'

He also hoped Adelaide was not too upset by the 'shameful exhibitions' of loyalty during the British royal visit in August. At a time when windows to view Queen Victoria and Prince Albert were hired out at six guineas each in Dublin, Dillon wrote: 'I take it for granted that you will all remain quietly at Druid Lodge during her stay, and that if she should pass through Merrion street you will have the house shut up as closely as if you expected an attack. I would not allow on any account a single soul to appear at the windows.' He added: 'If I were in Ireland now I would not look at politics. Nothing but the immediate prospect of rebellion could have induced me to remain an agitator.'[13]

In New York he fled from the Independence Day celebrations (and a cholera epidemic) to Glencove—'a decidedly handsome spot' on Long Island, then thirty miles from the city. There he was joined by Richard O'Gorman, whose escape from Ireland had been scarcely less dramatic than his own. (After the attempted rising O'Gorman walked through County Limerick and crossed the Shannon to west Clare, where he was sheltered by the legendary Father Michael Meehan. A month later he was put on board a ship bound for Constantinople and he eventually made his way to New York.)

Dillon reported innocently to his wife that O'Gorman and himself were enjoying themselves in Glencove. A friend of Mazzini had introduced them to ladies as 'two distinguished patriots'. Nevertheless, he tried to spend some hours alone each day. 'Though somehow it never occurs to me that anything could weaken our love, I cannot help feeling proud and happy in the reflection that I have been in thought and act thoroughly true and constant to you.'

As Dillon contemplated their forthcoming 'rapturous meeting', he promised to remain an untypical Victorian husband:

> I was so distracted by politics ever since our marriage that I never could devote much of my time to your happiness. But henceforth I will be blest in the thought that every hour will be spent in making you happy. Whenever I am not at work I will be always *with you*. I am quite resolved to set my face against all amusements which you cannot share with me—such as gentlemen's parties, etc, things which are very common here—and we will have such beautiful chats together in the evenings and such delightful rambles. As regards the latter we shall be immensely better off here than we used to be in Dublin. You could hardly find any country walk more agreeable than some of the streets in Brooklyn on an autumn evening.

In September Adelaide arrived with Rose, chaperoned by her mother, sister and uncle. The Dillons set up house on Long Island where a son, William, was born in 1850. Dillon and O'Gorman, meanwhile, laid the foundations of a successful law partnership. John's vision of domestic bliss was clouded by his wife's ill-health, however, which was compounded by the death of Pauline Hart at the age of twenty. In May 1851 he sent Adelaide home to Ireland for the birth of their third child.

Alone Again

My poor love, we have been rather harshly dealt with by
fortune in this respect: At the end of the first five years of our
married life we shan't have been half that time together. Well
this comes of getting into scrapes, political and other. ... We
must only remember that we are not the universe and that its
wheels must go round even though they bruise us occasionally.
JOHN TO ADELAIDE DILLON

The Dillons were to be separated by the Atlantic for more than two years. The main problem was Adelaide's poor health. She suffered from a prolonged illness after the birth of her second son, the future John Dillon, on 4 September 1851. Prior to the birth, her husband had written: '... you are the only thing I care to live for and the possibility of being deprived of you is enough to fill me with terror.'

Afterwards he proposed an embargo on *accouchements*. He blamed her pregnancies for 'that horrible disease' (neuralgia, as it turned out) and wondered 'whether I ought ever to expose you to the same peril and suffering again. ... I could be as happy as I deserve to be by being near you every evening and getting a kiss going to bed.'

Sickness played an inordinate role in their lives, even by Victorian standards. At first Dillon did not realise the seriousness of his wife's illness, or understand her delay in returning to him, but in September 1852 he wrote to Mrs Hart: 'May God favour your efforts in preserving her.' During that autumn his heart 'used to grow cold when the steamer was announced'. Emotionally preoccupied with Adelaide, his moods were dictated by reports of her health.

Adelaide wrote (5 May 1852): 'I am quite sure that happiness, or at least peace of mind, has more to do with health than most people (mamma, for example) imagine.' She recalled that Matilda Tone, 'one of the bravest women [who] ever lived', also became delicate while separated from her husband but recovered when Tone rejoined her.

A year later Dillon wrote to his mother-in-law, agreeing to meet the family in Europe on condition 'that I shall not be sent back to America alone. Ady has frequently written to me that she believed a little mental contentment would do her more good than all the doctors could effect. I believe this to be quite true, and therefore nothing will induce me to consent to any further prolongation of our separation. In those nervous diseases, more than any other, I should say that repose and contentment should be secured at any cost, and I fear she has had very little of either for the last twelve months.'

While Dillon relished the hustle of New York, his wife never really accepted being away from Ireland. Moreover, Adelaide's family was reluctant to part with her after the death of Pauline in America. Dillon's 'widowhood' lasted accordingly for two years during which his principal consolation was a weekly letter.

'The day you left was to me a most miserable day', he wrote to Adelaide in June 1851. He paid off the cook and maid and sat alone for a long time in their rented home. With O'Gorman he moved into a house in Brooklyn with a small stock of furniture and the assistance 'of an old rip' of a housekeeper, who was constantly complaining. 'In this way my transition from the married to the single state was effected, not without some feelings which I would as soon not experience again. ... Kiss poor little Zoe for me and don't let her forget me if you can.'

At that stage they hoped to be reunited the following spring. 'It will not seem quite so long when once I begin to get letters.' He missed her during Sunday excursions: '... the only real pleasure I know in your absence is thinking of you in connexion with things that I see.' Gazing at her daguerreotype, he was convinced 'that we both were to be together for ever—having but one spirit and one existence.'

To console himself he read Schlegel's *Philosophy of History*[1]—a favourite book of Adelaide's—and Carlyle's *Cromwell*.

He was involved with O'Gorman and Dudley Persse in a project to establish a steam packet service between New York and Galway. They failed, which was not surprising as the transatlantic packet station commission reported in 1851 that the selection of an Irish port would be prejudicial to Britain.[2] It recommended Liverpool, while the Galway harbour commissioners remained split. Adelaide commented (30 June): 'It seem really as if there were a fate over everything connected with Ireland—or rather there is *England* over her, who will allow nothing that could possibly conduce to Ireland's prosperity.'

She moved from Merrion street to convalesce in a rented house in Dundrum near the Dublin mountains. Her mother took Rose to William Wilde, the ophthalmic surgeon and antiquary, around the time of his marriage to 'Speranza' in 1851. He made a blister on the child's arm, which—to her concerned father—seemed 'a roundabout way of curing a sore eye. To tell you the truth I am afraid Wilde is just as anxious to produce an impression on the *spectators* as to cure the *patient* ...'

On learning of the birth of his second son, Dillon wrote (24 September): 'Although an Irishman he has already evinced a very considerate disposition. By the way, I am quite in the dark as to his name, but I leave that in your hands altogether.' Dillon celebrated the birth by attending a concert given by Catherine Hayes, the 'Swan of Erin', who had arrived in the same vessel as O'Gorman's parents. 'Her singing of the "Harp that once", etc., was most affecting and moved me very much, though I had made up my mind before she began that said harp and the '"knights and ladies bright" were all a delusion.' He met the Irish soprano through the O'Gormans and 'rather liked her manner. Her mother ... talked with a good Limerick brogue.' But he found her 'quite jealous' of the Swedish soprano, Jenny Lind. When Hayes took her impressario to court later, Dillon's firm appeared for the defendant and collected a fee of $250.

Dillon attended a performance by the raffish Lola Montez, also Limerick-born, who was touring the US with her play about Bavaria. 'So thoroughly disgusting a person I have not seen for twelve months' was his verdict. A less *risqué* pastime was playing draughts with Richard O'Gorman, senior. They argued about politics, too, 'I insisting that England, bad as she is, ought to be supported against [the] Russians ... and he swearing that the devil ought to be supported against England'.

Old Mrs O'Gorman indulged occasionally 'in a mournful retrospect regarding the accommodation which Kingstown afforded in the way of churches and priests'. Finding American society uncongenial, she returned to Dun Laoghaire with her husband after ten months. Before leaving, Dillon had to surrender to her application of a mustard plaster on his chest to cure a cough during the 'fearful winter' of 1851-2.

Regarding 'the future hope of mankind', he wrote (18 July 1851), 'there is *much* to find fault with here, but elsewhere *everything* is rotten'. He visited a Fourierite commune in New Jersey. Inspired by the French writer, François Fourier, forty-one *phalanges* or socialist communities were founded in the US during the 1840s. Dillon's 'anticipations of the establishment were rather agreeably disappointed. I expected to find them all excessively grave and sombre, and everything done by strict rule. But it was quite otherwise. There is rather more than the average amount of gaiety and light-heartedness, and the utmost freedom of action consistent with propriety.'³ Property was held by the members of the community in shares. Wages were high and women received the same pay as men.

> One good effect of the system is very apparent and that is the entire good feeling between the members. There being no possibility of a collision in interests between any two of them, all causes of hatred are removed and they seem to regard one another as brothers and sisters. I am not at all satisfied that I individually would be as happy there as I would be in a snug quiet little house with no-one under the same roof but yourself and a few near friends. But still I admire those who are making the experiment and wish them success, if the system be calculated to put the poor human race, especially the poor labourer, in a better position.

As Christmas approached Dillon looked wistfully at toyshops—and thought of Adelaide and the children. He requested four copies of *Traits and stories of the Irish peasantry* by William Carleton, intending to present one of them to his hostess, Mrs Christian Sloane, a sister of Charles O'Conor.

Dillon bought a plot near the O'Conors and Sloanes at Fort Washington, on the north end of Manhattan, overlooking the Hudson river. The three-quarter acre site and house built on it for Adelaide cost £1,200.

He joined Persse and O'Gorman in the purchase of real estate and was involved with Christian Sloane, a stockbroker and financier, in a company to manufacture a type-setting machine invented by William Mitchel. He admitted that if Adelaide's 'sweet influence were entirely removed, I would become quite sordid and material—an object of contempt to myself.'

In 1852 he informed her: 'The rate at which our business is increasing leads me to hope that after this year, I shall be able to allow the interest of your money to accumulate, and have a very fair income to live on besides. In fact I begin latterly to think it quite possible that in 12 or 15 years I may be able to give up business either partially or entirely—and then we would travel for the sake of the children. There is a piece of castle building.'

Dillon had heard of MacManus's escape from Van Diemen's Land the previous July: 'He got off splendidly without breaking his parole which was a great point. I should not like to see any of them here on the condition of their breaking their parole. They never would be respected after.' From San Francisco MacManus wrote to Dillon—whom he knew mainly by reputation and as a trustee of the Irish Directory fund—proposing an armed expedition to free the remaining prisoners[4] and enclosing a copy of a letter he had written to Robert Tyler, an Irish sympathiser and son of the former US president, John Tyler.

MacManus claimed O'Brien wished for death and that Martin was in a similar state of mind and body. He continued:

> Mitchel is bearing his exile with more equanimity, and as his period is terminable he means to live it out and have another day in Ireland with *them* yet. Meagher is bearing up capitally but he is young, has drawn pretty largely upon his father and has taken to himself a young and beautiful wife and lives in the bush. O'Donoghue when I left was still undergoing the punishment of his crime (of visiting O'Brien). He was in close confinement at the penal station of Port Arthur, rejoicing in the grey garb of a felon and labouring in a gang of trebly convicted thieves and murderers.[5]

Committees were formed in various American cities to petition the US government to press Britain to pardon the Irish political prisoners. Dillon and Richard O'Gorman, senior, met President Millard Fillmore. Dillon reported to his wife that they 'had a good deal of conversation chiefly relating to the Galway project and to our friends in Van Diemen's Land'. He told the president he had discouraged the public campaign of behalf of the prisoners. Fillmore, however, did not hold out any hope of pressurising the British government: 'The president is a sensible but a small-minded man,' Dillon concluded. 'I fear the prisoners must remain where they are until England shall deem it for her interest to release them.'

On 22 January 1852 a delegation of 250 members of a pressure group called the 'Baltimore movement' met Fillmore. The president again declined to intervene in the internal affairs of the United Kingdom, being prepared to make only 'private and personal' representations on behalf of the Irish state prisoners. Nevertheless, the *American Celt*—edited by McGee in Boston—declared that the voice of Ireland was for the first time 'officially audible' in the White House.[6]

In February 1854 James Buchanan, US ambassador to Britain and future president, asked Lord Clarendon, then home secretary, about the possibility of pardoning the remaining prisoners.[7] On the eve of the Crimean war, for which Irish recruits were needed, Lord Palmerston announced that the government was advising the queen to pardon Smith O'Brien.[8]

Since experiencing 'the pain of separation from you', Dillon had written wrote to Adelaide (in April 1852), 'I have never regarded without a shudder the living death [of transportation] from which I have escaped. ...' On 28 May he reportedly excitedly

> My own sweet love, I have news to tell you that will astonish you, I guess. Yesterday about 1 o'c. Richd. and I were sitting together in the office when a stout military looking gent with a moustache walked in, and I was rather astonished by seeing Richd. suddenly start from his chair and seize the stranger by the hand and wring it in the most energetic way. I looked on for some time wondering who it could be that Richd. was so very intimate with and who was perfectly a stranger to me, when at last a certain never-to-be-forgotten chuckle made me also start up and seize—who do you think! *Meagher*. Here he is safe and looking admirably—in high spirits and free, without any obligation to his enemies or any stain upon his honour. ... Meagher is now out ... at our house. The news became public only this day and the city is quite in a ferment—extras flying through the street. My little offices have been hardly able to contain all the people who thronged them today asking 'is it true?' Just this moment a fellow came in with his eyes as red as two coals, having spent the last hour he says crying copiously.

That evening 7,000 well-wishers surged around O'Gorman's house in Brooklyn demanding a speech from Meagher. He was sent to Glencove, where they were joined by Father O'Regan, who had emigrated to take up a teaching post. In this company Dillon's 'Anglo-Saxon tendencies received a considerable check.'

Dillon and O'Brien exchanged letters at the end of 1852. Regarding the 'frothy talk' of their former comrades, O'Brien wrote:

> It is very easy to be belligerent in America in the cause of Ireland. Big talk and warlike demonstration when made under the protection of the flag of the US do not require the possession of much courage. But this sort of demeanour seems to me peculiarly unsuitable to a party who made a most inglorious failure—and who when the moment for action arrived found it expedient to retreat rather than fight. Perhaps they were compelled by an inevitable necessity to abstain from actual collision with the enemy, but considering that 20,000 men might easily have joined us when we

were in Tipperary and that not more than half a dozen actually
came to the scene of action, the less our friends in America say
about their disposition to fight the higher will they be estimated in
the opinion of all bystanders. I am rejoiced therefore to find that
you have discouraged all *bravado* on the part of the Young
Irelanders in America. It is quite right that they should as members
of the America militia learn the use of arms and military training.
Perhaps contingencies may hereafter arise which will enable them
to prove that they never were deficient in courage. But in the
meantime they cannot do better than imitate the example of you,
whose personal bravery is beyond all question, and say as little as
posssible about their ardour for combat.[9]

To his 'dear friend' Dillon replied: 'Considering that discomfited
revolutionists have ever been apt to quarrel with one another, our old
associates have been less pugnacious than might have been apprehended.'
Except for Meagher and O'Gorman, he did not see much of the other
Young Ireland refugees. 'They are still politicians and agitators, we are
sober and not unprosperous citizens. However, we have always preserved
a good understanding with them all save McGee, whose acquaintance we
have quietly and silently dropped.' To Dillon it seemed 'as if Ireland had
fallen back two centuries in the same number of years. No voices audible
save those of rabid bigotry on the one hand, and servile adulation on the
other. ... You will hardly be surprised that O'Gorman and myself, in view
of such facts, should regard the regeneration of Ireland as an object too
remote and difficult to excite in us any lively interest. In truth, no whig
feels more thoroughly convinced than I do at this moment that Ireland is
not at present capable of existing under a respectable government of her
own formation; and therefore (if we only had you and our other friends on
this American soil) I would see little to regret in the result of our efforts
in '48. If the queen had only shown some magnaminity in your regard, I
am not sure that she would have a more ardent well-wisher than myself.
Our private resentments should not blind us to the fact that England is the
only country (save this) where a man dare speak the truth. As between her
and Louis-Napoleon, if compelled to take *any* side, I should certainly be
the ally of our old enemy.'[10]

In the US he had found that, while all religions enjoyed 'perfect equality
before the law, in society it is far otherwise. In this latter respect, this
country may be said to be eminently Protestant, and the inconveniences
to which persons of strong Catholic convictions are subjected are neither
few nor inconsiderable.' But 'as for Richard and myself, we find no

difficulty in making ourselves quite at home in heretical society.'

The bearer of Dillon's letter to O'Brien also took an epistle to John Mitchel from his brother, William, who lived with his mother and two sisters near Dillon and O'Gorman 'and the happiest hours we spend are in their society'. A spare bed in Willie's room was reserved for Dillon, who stayed there as often as possible. He played whist with 'the old lady'.

Intellectually, Dillon was in revolt against the ultramontane church. He deplored the centralising tendency of the papacy and its identification with the forces of reaction. He attended a Hughes dinner on one occasion sorely against his will, and was disgusted at the bishop's 'calumny and demagogism' towards republicans in Europe. 'I long for a renewal of the struggle on the continent in order that we may be compelled to take sides. I feel degraded in being mixed up in any degree with this ultramontane despotic party. I was writhing last night while the bishop was uttering those calumnies, sweetened by a little flattery of the flunkeys who surrounded him.'[11]

Adelaide supported Mazzini, although she wished he would distinguish between 'the truths of Catholicity and the men who compose the church of Italy at the present day'.

Dillon's latest hero was Louis Kossuth, the Hungarian revolutionary subsequently lionised during tours of Britain and the US. Kossuth was one in a series of Europeans who passed meteor-like through America and then flared out. Hughes condemned him as an anti-Catholic humbug. Dillon and O'Gorman took the unusual step for them of publicly supporting a cause because 'it was assumed by everybody that the Irish *en masse* were bitter enemies of Kossuth ... and they were thoroughly detested therefor'. In a letter to the press Dillon claimed the Irish people had been taught to love the principle of civil and religious freedom and to strive for its universal triumph.[12]

He asked his *Doppelgänger*: 'What is this church going to become? It is *everywhere* doing *everything* that it ought not to do—and nothing that it ought. If a Kossuth—a man of highest intellectual and stainless character—appeals to the world on behalf of an oppressed country, by some strange fatality he is sure to be "an enemy of *the church*". If a Louis-Napoleon—a notoriously unprincipled villain—moved by selfish ambition overthrows a constitution which he has sworn to defend ... no doubt the pope will in due time give his benediction.'[13]

Louis-Napoleon's *coup d'etat* in December 1851 marked the triumph of reaction in Europe. The following year he became Napoleon III, emperor of the French. Dillon, who was a strong civil republican, believed he had strangled liberty in France.

He continued sounding off to Adelaide: 'When religion becomes a thing like that running about and begging every perjured profligate and murderer to protect it (eternal truth) from socialism, what honest man will care one fig whether it survive or perish. ... I have been urging on the friends of Kossuth here to form a universal peoples' league—a sort of holy alliance of peoples, or political church. Kossuth would make a good pope to begin with. ...'[14]

Like other highly intelligent people Dillon had some silly ideas.

> I sometimes feel a great weariness myself and think those months of separation are interminable. But then the daily occupation helps to pass the time and I very often think how sad you must be spending the whole day at home. I haven't entirely given up the hope of seeing you early in the summer. If that Clarendon were out of Ireland, I think his successor would hardly refuse. I would not ask their permission (even with so great an inducement) if I had not lost all sympathy with Irish rebellion. I would not tell it to many but really it is so—that if the separation of Ireland from England were to depend on my single vote, I could not say yes. I believe that by so doing, I would be hurling it back into medieval darkness and barbarism, and strengthening the arm of tyranny throughout Europe.[15]

He went on to refer to press rumours about invading the United Kingdom in conjunction with Napoleon. Dillon, free of fanaticism but capable of self-righteousness, lacked insight into the Irish-American underworld in which fantasy and hatred suppurated, as the annual rate of emigration from Ireland reached a climax at 250,000 people in 1851.[16]

He read with delight Adelaide's scolding 'about my present opinions of Ireland. It is likely enough I have gone into an extreme'. On the other hand, he thought (12 December 1852) Mitchel's view—that it was the duty of an Irishman to side with 'Czar Nicholas, Louis-Napoleon or the devil' against England—savoured of impiety and insanity. 'This exalting of transient nationalities above universal and external principles is a mean thing after all.' If Napoleon III invaded Ireland the result would be 'an ecclesiastical-military despotism. ... And then a censorship will be established and newspapers will be suppressed and so the liberation of Ireland will be finally and gloriously achieved. And as for the Godless colleges, not one stone of them will be left upon another.'

Dillon asked how John O'Hagan, soon to be appointed lecturer in political economy at Newman's University, could support the direction being taken by the Church. In an 'enormous letter' O'Hagan replied: '... deeply conscious as I am of the truths of the Catholic Church, and of the peace and blessing even upon earth that follow the faithful observance of her precepts, there is nothing I would not do to bring back to her any one, and above all a friend, who has left her.'[17] While admiring an article by O'Hagan about Carlyle in the *Dublin Review*, Dillon had claimed his intellect was enslaved by the formula 'that outside of the Catholic Church there is nothing but one black bottomless chaos of atheism.'

O'Hagan denied the charge, feared Dillon was relying too much on human reason and urged him to pray daily; he was judging the church 'by claims which she never asserted and a standard to which she never appealed. The church does not claim for her priests or her laymen as individuals, or the nations subject to her, any pre-eminence in science, art, literature or natural human attainments of any kind, or in what is commonly called civilisation. ... She simply claims to teach men to know God, love him and serve him (as the catechism says).' He asked what would St Paul, who was struck by the spiritual blindness of the Athenians, 'have thought of the popular Protestant argument which makes "civilisation" a test of religious truth'.

Dillon had said that 'saving souls' threatened to become a cant in Ireland and Italy. O'Hagan admonished him 'to consider the question in the light of saving your own soul, suspending for the present your consideration of the political and social action of the church upon the world'. Dillon retorted: 'Is it not wonderful that clear-headed men like J. O'Hagan would not see the folly of setting a church to lean upon such a shabby rotten crutch as Louis-Napoleon.'

Nevertheless, he entered the lenten season in a penitential spirit, confessing to Adelaide (8 March 1852): 'My observation about the lack of thought in writers on the church side is decidedly insolent, considering that I have taken no trouble about searching it out.' O'Hagan had recommended Pascal's *Pensées* and the Letters of St Paul as spiritual reading. Dillon started reading *Introduction to the devout life* by St Francis de Sales and St Augustine's *Confessions*.

He also undertook to read aloud to the O'Gormans each night from a book of Dr Newman's sermons annotated by Adelaide. Initially, he was not impressed with the sermons: 'Some of them present in a new and more decent dress ideas which have been familiar to my mind when I was in the habit of listening to certain shining lights in the west of Ireland—damned souls howling and struggling in the grasp of demons who smell of the charnel house and flames, etc., all which appears to me to be rather *pagan* in its aspect.' Subsequently, however, he came to 'a good hearty assault on flunkeyism, the worship of the base idols—*wealth* and *notoriety*'.

Dillon attended a lecture by Archbishop Hughes which he found much less objectionable than some of his recent effusions. He considered it 'a fair answer to the assertion that this is a Protestant country; but as a plea for toleration to Catholics it was insufficient.'

Dillon was in New York in 1852 for the first organised celebration of St Patrick's Day in that city. He spoke at a dinner of the Friendly Sons of St Patrick and became a vice-president of that exclusive society. The customary toast to the British monarchy was abandoned as it had become 'latterly a source of annoyance to the bulk of the Irish here'. Dillon was given credit for 'revolutionising' the society, having refused to attend the previous year on account of the toast to Victoria. He explained to his wife (23 March): 'Now on principle I haven't much objection to drink her majesty's health. As kings and queens go, I think she is the least objectionable specimen of the class. But I should not like to exhibit the slightest appearance of deserting my friends and therefore I was resolved to be absent this year too if the toast were not abandoned.' Dillon responded judiciously to the toast: 'Ireland—the land of our fathers'. He said the Irish searched history 'not for lessons for our future guidance, but for fuel to feed our animosities towards each other'.[18] Instead of listening to voices of genius and patriotism, such as Swift and Grattan, 'the people still brooded over the past and they stood scowling at one another from the opposite banks of the Boyne.' He claimed that 'thanks to the great and good men who founded this republic, the Irish exile is no longer a wanderer without a home. And if called to shed his blood in battle, he fights no more for ambitious or ungrateful despots, but for a country which adopts him amongst the most favoured of her sons'.

In July he enjoyed a week's solitiude at the unfashionable Long Island resort of Cold Spring, where the people were 'rude and the fare simple. The dinner of which I have just partaken consisted of clams and bacon, which approaches quite closely enough for my taste "to locusts and wild honey". On this point I have always been and I hope ever will be very easily satisfied.'

His holiday reading included *Religion in society* by Abbé Martinet (recommended by Hughes): 'It is written in a spirit of the most thorough pugnacity and I fear it was this as much as anything else that recommended it to the archbishop.' He looked forward to reading Dicken's latest novel, *Bleak House*, with Adelaide as it appeared in serial form on both sides of the Atlantic.

In September 1852 Dillon travelled 2,000 miles during a business trip, and crossed the Canadian border to have a better view of the Niagara Falls. On British soil he 'felt a little nervous lest some old detective should come up and claim acquaintance'. Back in New York he settled down to another winter without Adelaide. He generally dined with O'Gorman and Meagher, who was awaiting his Tasmanian wife, at a restaurant in Broadway where the Irish proprietor gave them special attention. Afterwards they sipped whiskey provided by Mrs O'Gorman. Dillon reported to Adelaide that he had grown overweight and was exercising in a gymnasium for an hour each evening.

Around this time he met William Makepeace Thackeray, the English novelist who had discovered that in Ireland 'there are two truths: the Catholic truth and the Protestant truth.' Dillon brought Mary Haslett Mitchel to hear Thackeray lecture on Alexander Pope. Meagher, who was also supplementing his income as a lecturer, accompanied them.

> As we were going into the church where he lectures, we heard some person running behind us and who should this be but Thackeray himself, who seeing Meagher very good naturedly ran after him to be introduced to him. He seems really a frank honest fellow. If you were here I would certainly make him spend an evening with us, but there is little use in thinking what might be done. You may perceive that I have not been leading a very lonely life, though I confess I would do so if I were guided only by my own inclination, but people are so pressing that there is no choice but to visit or fall out with them. ... Some weeks ago I was in a very sad state of mind, but thank God the world does not look so dark to me now.[19]

Thackeray had coined the sobriquet 'Meagher of the sword'. He found Meagher, Dillon and O'Gorman 'three as fine Irishmen as ever I met ... refugees and flourishing lawyers at New York'.[20] Dillon conquered his 'usual aversion to lion hunting' and visited Thackeray with O'Gorman. They organised a 'quiet dinner' during which Dillon asked him why he didn't come to live in the US, 'where we respect and honour men of genius and place them in high positions, instead of living in a country where a duke or marquis is thought more of than Shakespeare or Milton'. Thackeray riposted: 'Ah! my good fellow, I see how it is—*your* tail has been cut off.'

A few months later the Young Irelanders attended a lecture by Thackeray on 'What the humorous writers have done for the cause of benevolence and charity'. Afterwards he whispered in Dillon's ear: 'When shall we have another little dinner?'

He invited Dillon and O'Gorman to breakfast next morning. 'Thackeray came out in an old dressing gown and said he hoped we had no objection to eat with a Unitarian minister—and Mr Bellows would strive to get over any scruple he might entertain about sitting at the same table with a pair of rebels. Whereupon he agreed to set off one scruple against the other, and made ourselves exceedingly happy. I don't believe I spent so pleasant an hour since 22 May 1851'—the last day he had been in Adelaide's company, two days after her twenty-third birthday.

Thackeray observed that Meagher was 'at war with the priests'. Dillon told Adelaide (11 January 1853) that the 'low Catholic press in this country professing ultramontane principles ... began to growl and snarl at him suggesting that there were certain parts of his recent conduct not quite consistent with sound Catholic principles'. During his lecture tour Meagher had been shunned by the clergy. 'Everywhere he was received with open arms by the Americans and by such of his own countrymen as are not governed by priests.'

Mitchel would dismiss the editors of the Catholic press in America as 'spurious spawn: What cared they for the graves and pilgrims of Clonmacnois? ... They never drew a drop of milk from the warm breast of our beauteous motherland; never looked upon her mournful and noble face; never grew glad with the music of her voice in the mountains; never had a word, a smile of maternal recognition from her.'[21]

He was thinking particularly of McMaster, of the New York *Freeman's Journal*, who had 'a touch of Calvinism not yet sponged out of him'.[22] (Meagher horse-whipped McMaster after being accused by him of cowardice and breach of parole in Van Diemen's Land.)[23]

Dillon feared they were 'on the eve of a struggle in this country which will renew all the horrors of Young and Old Ireland'. He defended Meagher 'because I knew he was not what his assailants would make people believe him to be—a red republican and an anarchist. I certainly will not, if I can help it, relapse into the platitudes of Young Irelandism again.' At a soirée of the Thomas Francis Meagher Club, the *Irish-American* reported, Dillon, 'in a speech of supreme power and thorough determination, vindicated his friend … from the calumnies aimed at him, and coincided in every word and sentiment that fell from him touching the sacredness of the republican institutions of this country, and the damaging nature to society of the sectarian and intolerant spirit which was unhappily springing up, particularly among the Irishmen who found an asylum in this commonwealth'.

The report went on: 'As John B. Dillon said, so beautifully, at the Meagher ball supper, there is a middle place between the frozen region of monarchy and despotism, and the torrid zone of anarchy and red republicanism—those pleasant valleys of rational liberty and true republicanism— where philanthropists who love the freedom and happiness of mankind can abide in peace and security together.'[24]

Dillon wrote to O'Flaherty, who had returned to Ireland: 'Meagher has got into an ugly snarl with the priests which he ought to get out of as soon as he can. No good is to be done by fighting with them. I have good reason to believe that a majority of them would roast O'G. and myself before a slow fire because we are not faithful sons of the church going about and abusing Protestants like McGee.'[25]

Writing in a depressed mood to his wife (8 March 1853), Dillon said:

> I am perfectly aware of this that the priests as a body have done their best to injure the firm of Dillon and O'Gorman since we declined to become parties to the howl against Kossuth. This act of disobedience, coupled with our refusal to subscribe to the Catholic University,[26] has caused us to be regarded as very dangerous characters. While we are resolved to avoid all public controversy with them, we are not the less resolved to let them see by our acts, that we have not rebelled against tyranny at home to become the slaves of a more ignorant, more false and in every respect a baser despotism here.

Given to overstatement himself, Dillon had scant patience with his fellow-countrymen whose fundamentalism was born of insecurity.

Meagher received a 'hostile missive' from Archbishop Hughes, accusing him of disloyalty to the church. Dillon drafted a conciliatory reply which nevertheless averred: 'That a spirit of extreme intolerance does pervade a small but prominent section of American Catholics is unfortunately too true. And as this small band omit no opportunity of publicly exhibiting their bigotry in its most offensive form, it would not be an unnatural mistake in one less acquainted with Irish Catholic feeling than I am, to suppose that the entire Catholic community are tainted with the same intolerance.'[27]

The letter reminded Hughes: '... our fathers have contended and suffered *that all religions might be equal before the law*. The most illustrious bishops of the Irish church have upon their oaths denied and repudiated the doctrine that "heresy" should be "punished as a crime"— that doctrine which a few nameless writers seek now to impose on us as a test of the genuineness of our Catholicity. In expressing my hostility to this offensive bigotry I am uttering a sentiment which is daily uttered by thousands of good Catholics in the United States.'

He found it 'incomprehensible why the priests and bishops throughout this country have become such ferocious bigots. ... The name Catholic is fast becoming thoroughly hateful; and I should not be surprised if those church burning riots should be revived. For my part I can't blame the American people for any amount of bigotry they may exhibit towards a body of men who openly avow that if they ever get power they will punish and persecute all who honestly differ from them.'[28]

Dillon and his friends foresaw the consequences of a provocative Catholic press. But their voices were eclipsed by the Know-Nothing outbreak of nativism during 1854-5, when 'Dagger John' organised vigilantes to protect churches in his archdiocese. As usual it was the poor who suffered. The Anglo-Saxon spirit of the age was summed up in the slogan: 'No Irish need apply.'

Dillon met his wife in Europe during the summer of 1853 and went back to New York before her. In his first letter (23 October) he hinted at his eventual return to Ireland: '... between you and me ... while Richard and I are on as good terms as ever we were, there is not that sort of attraction on either side which would render a separation at all disagreeable.'

Michael Doheny made shrewd social observations in the course of a letter to O'Brien in 1858: 'I could have done very well if I devoted myself exclusively to my profession as Dillon and O'Gorman. But I was busy with the military and the old hope, and I now busy myself in endeavouring to reanimate the Gaelic. ... Meagher mixes with the world and enters into its feelings and aspirations. ... O'Gorman is reformed and loyal and sharp as a chisel and equally keen in his race for money. We meet and salute and that's all.'[29] Doheny's sole amusement consisted 'in reading and translating Gaelic ballads, and discussing them with O'Mahony twice a week or oftener'. John O'Mahony, who founded the Fenian Brotherhood in that year, 'seemed to care nothing for success in life, his whole mind being absorbed with one idea—rebellion in Ireland'.[30]

Dillon and Meagher also drifted apart. Dillon found his lectures about Ireland had become 'a mere piece of acting' and 'financial speculations; and I confess I am not sufficiently yankeeified to be reconciled to the notion of converting sham patriotism into dollars.'

Meagher made his peace with Hughes and persuaded him to officiate at his marriage to Elizabeth Townsend in November 1855. His first wife, Catherine Bennett, had died at her father-in-law's house in Waterford the previous year giving birth to a second son (the first died in Tasmania). Dillon did not bother to attend the wedding, regarding the second Mrs Meagher as 'a Fifth Avenue lass and nothing more'. Adelaide had considered Catherine, the daugher of 'a common English convict', unfit for Meagher.

The Dillons—'two very dear friends'—were among those who greeted John Mitchel in New York on 29 November 1853 after his escape from Van Diemen's Land. P.J. Smyth had been sent by the directory 'with abundant means' to rescue O'Brien and Mitchel 'or either of us, if both could not go'. Smyth, 'playing with the handle of the revolver in his coat', accompanied Mitchel to Bothwell police station in Tasmania where he withdrew his parole on 8 June. After several weeks 'on the run', he succeeded in leaving the island and boarding a ship in Sydney bound for San Francisco.[31]

On arrival in New York Mitchel launched the *Citizen* newspaper. His serialisation of the *Jail Journal* led to a controversy with Duffy, who counter-attacked in the Dublin *Nation*. Mitchel never forgave Duffy for not having started the rising when he was convicted in May 1848.

Although Dillon was among those who rallied to Mitchel's support, his letter began with a rebuke:

> I have not waited as you know for this occasion to express to you my opinion that the passages in your *Jail Journal* which reflect on Mr Duffy's conduct in 1848 are unjust, and that their publication was an uncalled-for aggression on your part. I desire to repeat this opinion now, lest in protesting against a portion of Mr Duffy's letter to you, I should be misunderstood as engaging in a controversy which has no attraction for any true friend either of Mr

Duffy or yourself. The passages in Mr Duffy's letter from which I would record my dispute is that in which he accuses you of having broken your parole in escaping from Van Diemen's Land. I have, I believe, a pretty accurate knowledge of the facts connected with your escape, and I am at a loss to find in those facts any foundation for the accusation in question; unless there be some code of honour yet unheard of by me, which makes a prisoner responsible for the cowardice, or disaffection, or venality, of his jailers. I was one among many thousands in this city who celebrated your escape by public rejoicings, and since then no new fact has come to my knowledge which causes me to regret the part I took in those rejoicings. It seems superfluous to add that there is one of your friends at least, who—not agreeing in all your opinions—does *not* "hang his head when your name is mentioned"; but who, on the contrary, is proud of your friendship, and would freely stake his life on your honour.[32]

Smyth returned to the Antipodes with £1,000 from the directory to rescue O'Brien. On arrival in Melbourne he learned that the remaining prisoners, including O'Brien, had been released conditionally. Smyth then took the liberty of engaging in a mining speculation with directory funds; after the gold-digging lots proved non-productive, he wrote: 'I have had rather a kind letter from Dillon in which he states that if I can dispose of those lots for £300, the directory will let me off.'[33] O'Brien, with his strict code of honour, continued to worry about repaying public money spent on an earlier rescue attempt. Dillon would assure him that no portion of the American fund had been 'specifically applied for the purpose of furthering your escape'.[34]

Nevertheless, O'Brien insisted on paying £500 in two instalments when he visited the US in 1859. On a receipt signed by (then) Judge Emmet, he added: 'This sum was paid by me in liquidation of an advance made by the Irish Directory in 1850-51 for paying expenses incurred by parties at Hobart ... to procure the means of escape from Maria Island.'[35]

In August 1854 the Dillon and Mitchel families spent their holidays together in Stonington, Connecticut. It was 'a place of intensely puritanical aspects', especially on Sundays: 'People go with a grim and mortified aspect to their various conventicles; march back again to their houses, where every window-blind is strictly closed.' Mitchel thought there would be a great commotion if a piano was heard in one of the wooden houses rattling out 'The wind that shakes the barley'. Some fellow guests praised him for attacking Hughes in the *Citizen*. Mitchel opened on their 'vulgar

Protestantism … in a manner which made Dillon laugh loud'.[36] (The archbishop's crozier proved mightier than the pen of Mitchel, who at the end of 1854 drifted southwards into the pro-slavery confederacy.)

In September Mrs Hart arrived in New York with 'Johnny'. Adelaide thought her son's brogue, acquired in Ballaghaderreen, 'the funniest thing I ever heard'. The Irish servants at Fort Washington were 'in perfect ecstasies of admiration' about the three-year-old boy.

In a letter to her brother announcing the birth of a daughter—christened Jane but also called Alice—Adelaide commented on the sudden death of her brother-in-law, Thomas: 'One meets so little of friendly and disinterested affection in this world that it is hard to lose so much of it as we do in him.'[37] During his tour with Carlyle, Duffy had consulted Thomas Dillon in Ballina about the feasibility of a tenant-right campaign.[38] John— who considered his brother, Val, 'a weak fellow'—said Tom's death 'deprives my projected visit to Ireland of a good deal of the pleasure to which I look forward'.

In June 1855 Dillon enjoyed a trip to Paris with Adelaide 'after seven years' contact with the hard and not graceful realities of American life'. They were joined by Duffy, who, having despaired of Irish politics, was emigrating to Australia. He recorded in his diary: 'Dillon looks vigorous and tranquil; he preserves the sweet serenity that distinguished him of old.' On Sunday Duffy and a companion agreed that the lady kneeling in front of them in church was the best dressed woman they had seen for a decade; it transpired that the lady was Adelaide.[39]

Dillon spend a few weeks in Ireland before returning to New York to wind up his business affairs. Adelaide remained at home for the birth of their fifth child, Thomas. While Dillon did not relish standing with his 'back to a pillar in the Four Courts waiting for briefs that will not come', he had decided that 'any amount of failure would be better than these ever-recurring separations'. He considered it 'no trifling thing … to appear for the first time in the hall of the courts with the wig and to receive the congratulations (or commiseration) of old associates. … I am as certain of remaining as I can be of anything in the future, but still I would have the bridge open behind and for that reason I again exhort all of you to remain silent on the subject.' He had a strong desire 'to prove to myself that I can do something in the world. But on the other hand, I have not grown less sensible (rather the contrary) of the fleeting and precarious character of life and its enjoyments.'

Back in New York, where he boarded with the O'Gormans for $10 a week, Dillon wrote (25 September): 'Financial considerations would

induce me to remain here but every other motive leads me to Ireland. ...
The fact is, my sweet love, that there is no motive whatever weighs so
much with me as the desire to see you happy and contented; and, although
I know you would come over with me contentedly enough, still you never
could be as happy here as in Ireland.' He hoped to make £3,000 profit in
disposing of his property and to return to Ireland in May 1856 and lead
'an idle (or rather a studious) life' during the summer.

> All this looks favourable to the fulfilment of your design to deprive
> this republic of one of its most useful and accomplished citizens.
> As for the possibility of my being happy in Ireland, etc.—you may
> make your mind easy on that head. No doubt the business part of
> my life would not be quite so agreeable, and the political atmos-
> phere of the Four Courts would not be grateful; but these dis-
> agreements would be vastly more than compensated by the
> domestic enjoyments in which I would absolutely revel after such
> long and frequent privations. In fact my feelings on this point may
> be summed up in one short sentence—I can be happy anywhere
> with you while God gives me health and a competence—and
> nowhere without you whatever other advantages I may have. And
> as to bringing you out here I begin to hate that operation
> exceedingly, so on the whole I have as good as made up my mind
> to try my luck on that side of the water: but still I wish to have my
> designs kept dark until I am prepared to act.[40]

Homecoming

... yet very few of all the crew can look back with so little
self-reproach as you. My judgment is that you were right all
through those 10 years, and that you are right now. Cela étant,
you may enjoy private life, and busy yourself with professional toils,
and send public duty to the devil; perhaps even, may come to wear
ermine and horse-hair—yet no, the line must be drawn somewhere.
MITCHEL TO DILLON (1857)

Dillon returned quietly to Dublin with the 'tacit assent' of the government.[1] In July 1856 Smith O'Brien came back to the 'sunken and spiritless city', although 10,000 people gathered at Cahirmoyle to welcome him home.[2]

John O'Hagan, always ready to encourage his friends, left the Uffizi gallery in Florence on 11 June to write to congratulate Adelaide on her husband's safe return: 'John is quite right to begin work at once. He should go [on] the summer circuit, and give every indication of planting himself finally and in earnest.'

But Dillon did not need such advice. He wrote to Adelaide from Sligo (13 June): 'I think that for the next few years I ought to shape my course exclusively with a view to the getting of business. My cough is nearly gone and I feel generally the better of the open-air life I have been leading.' He added: 'It is the greatest comfort imaginable to receive a letter from you as I do on arriving at each town. ... You may be quite certain that I do not love my darling less than when I was writing those love letters nine years ago.'

Thanking Adelaide for news of the Catholic University, O'Hagan had written: 'I quite agree with you. It is the only thing in Ireland I can look upon with pleasure or hope.' He suggested that Dillon visit Dr Newman, who had spoken to him at length about Dillon one evening' with the greatest interest'. (It is not known if the two men met, but Dillon later heeded Newman's valedictory advice as rector: 'Trust the church of God implicitly; even when your natural judgment would take a different course from hers, and would induce you to question her prudence and her correctness . . .'.)[3]

O'Brien retained considerable influence in constitutional nationalist circles.[4] Dillon assured him that if during the years of exile 'I felt a disposition to regret or be ashamed of my political doings, I always found encouragement and support in the reflection that (both in peace and in war) I was generally found following where you led the way.' Eight years' separation, O'Brien replied (3 November), had not diminished his esteem for Dillon; he invited him to visit 'our humble domicile' with Adelaide during the Christmas holidays. Two years later Dillon wrote: 'It would gratify me very much if I could avail myself of the kind invitation of yourself and Mrs O'Brien to visit Cahirmoyle. But I must not forget that I too pretend to be a patriot, and that my destiny is therefore to work hard for small rewards.' At this time, Dillon also resumed his friendship with John Martin, who married Mitchel's sister, Henrietta.

The Dillons owned 51 Fitzwilliam square west but regarded Druid Lodge as their real home. They loved Killiney and the sea near by. The boys' sailing exploits were regarded by people waiting at the railway station 'with mingled admiration and apprehension'.

In spite of Dillon's protestation that he would be satisfied holding Adelaide's hand, she gave birth to eight children; three of them were born after his homecoming: Henry (1857), Charles (1859) and Christina (1862). However, ill-health dogged the family. In May 1862 Thomas, aged six, and Charles died.

One day on entering his library in Druid Lodge Dillon found himself face to face with James Stephens, whom he had last met at the barricades in Killenaule.[5] Stephens had returned from France and wished to be engaged as a French tutor. According to Denieffe, William and John Dillon became Stephens's 'first pupils and through these he secured more pupils, which placed him in a position of comparative independence' (Dillon was reproached later by a loyalist judge for recommending the Fenian leader as tutor to his children).[6]

At the beginning of 1858, however, Dillon wrote apologetically to Stephens dispensing with his services. 'Our little girl, Zoe, was so much in need of general instruction in English, music, etc., that we have been obliged to employ a governess for her who does everything.' He praised Stephens's excellence as a tutor, adding significantly: 'But I fear indeed that you are not sufficiently in love with your present profession to be much gratified by this compliment.'[7]

Dillon—'perhaps intellectually the most eminent Young Irelander' in the country at that time—was the first person Stephens consulted about forming the IRB. He tried to obtain a letter of recommendation from him before setting out on a fund-raising mission to America. (On learning that he had not succeeded, Doheny predicted that Stephens would therefore receive nothing from the New York Directory.)

Dillon was convinced the Fenian conspiracy would fail. Nevertheless, he declined to publicly censure the Phoenix Society—the forerunner of the IRB—when O'Brien wrote a letter of condemnation to the *Nation*.[8]

While rejecting Fenianism, Dillon's reaction to an attack on O'Brien in the *Morning Post* ('Lord Palmerston's organ') showed that he was still a rebel at heart. At the personal level this 'course and brutal vituperation' could be laughed off as an effusion of English malice, he wrote.[9]

> But taking it (as it unquestionably is) as a correct expression of the feelings excited in England by an exhibition of patriotic sympathy towards Ireland, what are we to expect from a continuance of this connexion—rather let me say from a continuance of our subjection to such irreclaimable scoundrels[?] The brutality in question has fixed more firmly in my mind the conviction that the question between England and the Irish race is one of life and death. As a people there are only three things we can do. We must become English, or leave this island to the English, or drive the English out of it; and our choice amongst those courses must soon be made. I for one am resolved that no son of mine shall stand towards the state in the position in which I have stood and now stand.

Ultramontanism was quite as odious to Dillon as to O'Brien: 'To come nearer home; it we were independent and if any faction would dare to attempt a substitution of one kind of religious ascendancy for another, you would not be more prompt or more earnest in opposing such an attempt than I and (as far as I know) every man who has belonged to our party in old times.'

There was one point, Dillon continued, on which O'Brien differed from most of this former followers:

> You have some hopes of the Protestant gentry of Ireland. They (including myself) have none. ... It appears to me that they have made up their minds to stand or to fall with English power in this country; and what is left to us but to pray that they and it may perish

together. Need I say that I speak of them as a class and that the exceptions are all the more appreciated for the contrast they present. ... Which of us has ever loved you the less for being a Protestant landlord?

Dillon lived privately for a few years, devoting himself to his family and the law. Duffy wrote from Melbourne (15 April 1858), where he had been appointed agriculture minister for Victoria. He hoped Adelaide was restored to health. 'You merit that compensation for living in Ireland under the regime of Paul Cullen and William Keogh. There is, I am sorry to say, no place under the sky of heaven where I would live with so little satisfaction as in the dear old country.' In 1862 Dillon informed him: 'I rejoice that you are not here to witness the wreck of all the high hopes we have cherished. You, I think, could not exist here without being a public man, and being that you would be miserable.'[10] At one point, indeed, Dillon told Kevin O'Doherty (10 February 1861), who had returned to Australia with Eva Kelly as his bride, that he was thinking of emigrating to Sydney. 'I certainly do not feel at home here and am not likely to feel so until some change takes place, of which I see no immediate prospect. ... A couple of years must inform us what shape events are likely to take, and then if we cannot lead honest lives here we must look for some place on the globe where such a life may be led.'

A man of Dillon's reputation could not remain out of politics. G.H. Moore, restless since the demise of the independent Irish group at Westminster, consulted him about a project to form a volunteer force on the 1782 model. Dillon spoke to his Young Ireland friends and reported to Moore.[11]

In any plain straightforward action for getting rid of English power here you will have them with you I think to a man. ... What will come of it is another question, and that I think depends on whether there will be a war in which France and England shall be on opposite sides. If that contingency cannot be reasonably anti-cipated, my advice to the young men of Ireland would be—such of you as can live under English government stay and assimilate as fast as possible; such as cannot, go away and find a government to which you can be loyal.

During 1860-61 a petition calling for a vote by universal male suffrage on whether Ireland desired to maintain the union with Britain, had been organised in imitation of the successful plebiscites then taking place in Italian states and approved by the British government. The petition, signed by 430,000 Irishmen, was ignored. Dillon thought that campaign stood in the way of a new agitation. 'I wish there was an end to it', he told Moore.[12]

John Martin added: 'I hold it of great importance to the starting of a national movement that such men as John Dillon and John Pigot should come out in their proper names before the country and take their place under the national flag. ... The MacManus funeral has proved plain enought how ardent and deep-seated is the national sentiment in the masses of the people.' (The Fenian-managed obsequies of MacManus, who had died in San Francisco, culminated in a procession of 50,000 people in Dublin on 10 November 1861. Dillon attended the funeral in a carriage.)

But the men of 'social influence and of ability' hesitated in coming forward to lead the people. Dillon prepared a manifesto of Irish grievances which, O'Brien explained to Moore, 'may be presented to all mankind in justification of our efforts to obtain a domestic legislature'. He added: 'For obvious reasons J.B. Dillon does not wish his name to be spoken of in connection with this document unless it is likely to be effective.'[13]

Dillon's manifesto, a modified version of an address by Mitchel to the French people, does not appear to have achieved wider circulation than the proof copy marked 'strictly confidential' sent to Moore. It listed fourteen arguments in support of the premise 'that to be bound by laws made by an Irish legislature is the ancient, inalienable right of the Irish people'. In it Dillon asserted that Ireland, the poorest country in Europe, was subjected to much the same financial burdens as Britain, 'which is the richest'. While absentee landlords drained the country of £5 million annually in rents, 'Ireland is compelled also to maintain an extravagant church establishment for a sect which numbers about one-eighth of its population'. The great majority of the tillers of the soil lacked security of tenure. 'The improvements which they effect by their labour belong by law to their landlords, who for the most part are English in sympathy and origin,' and whose power 'is almost that of life and death'. The administration was entrusted to Englishmen, 'whose ignorance, incapacity and arrogance greatly aggravate the evils of our condition'.

Dillon concluded:

> History affords no parallel to the destruction of human life in Ireland. Within the last 20 years our country has lost about two and a half millions of its people, while during the same period the

population of England has increased by four millions. ...

A people who wear a yoke which they have the power to cast off may be deemed undeserving of pity. But a people who, disarmed, disorganised and in effect disfranchised, submit to irresistible force will have the sympathy of all who love freedom and hate injustice.

Fifteen months later P.J. Smyth wrote to Moore, who was a difficult man to work with: 'We are all here—Dillon, Pigot, Cantwell [who had also returned from the US] and others— anxious to meet you, and we believe that a few minutes conversation would remove all difficulties. There is a fine spirit going to waste in the country—men everywhere call aloud for organisation.'[14]

By then Dillon had been persuaded to accept nomination for a seat on Dublin municipal council. He was adopted unanimously at a caucus meeting to represent Wood Quay ward and elected on 14 February 1863. A.M. Sullivan, editor of the *Nation*, hailed his return to public life as an event of national importance. Dillon's 'polished manners, his high intelligence, his graceful eloquence, would render him an ornament in any assembly; his tried and proven patriotism perfects his character as a worthy representative of his countrymen in any field of action.'[15]

On St Patrick's Day he addressed a banquet of the 'nationalists of Dalkey, Bray and Kingstown'. Dillon said: 'This country with its mountains and rich fields and mineral wealth and teeming crops belonged, by the law of nature and the law of God', to the Irish people.[16] He spoke of the need for leadership and pointed out that the spirit of faction had always been the bane of Ireland; since his return he had not made the slightest attempt to re-enter political life, and considered 'himself above the suspicion of being animated by any desire to become a leader'. He asserted that 'he was a democrat and, like O'Connell, he could not understand how any man had a right to ride rough-shod over his fellow men'. Illustrating the cross-pollination between the revolutionary and constitutional traditions, he expressed the hope of living to see liberty, equality and fraternity prevailing in Ireland.

The next toast at the banquet was to 'our suffering sister, Poland'. During the Polish uprising against the tsar in 1863 a solidarity committee was formed in Dublin. Its members included Dr Cullen and Dillon, who was still self-conscious about working with people regarded as Catholic whigs. Responding to a lecture by O'Brien in the Rotunda, Dillon said 'he knew there were many who came there to testify their feelings in favour of Poland, who did not entertain the same feelings in regard to Ireland that he did, and he hoped he could, without giving offence, express a wish that rose in his breast whilst listening to the lecture, that Ireland were in a position to send to Poland not merely the expressions of her sympathy, not merely a few pounds, but a division of 10,000 men (loud applause and a voice—'We want them at home'), who on the plains of Poland would testify the merits of their national weapon—the pike.'[17] He apparently did not see any inconsistency in supporting the Polish insurgents, while discouraging Fenianism.

In Dublin city hall Dillon proposed that a committee be appointed to inquire into the taxation of Ireland. The *Nation* published his 'masterly statement, which for nearly two hours held the auditors fastbound in deep interest, wrapt attention and warm admiration'.[18] The background to Dillon's initiative was the failure of the harvest in the early 1860s, when emigration resumed at the rate of 100,000 a year. He stated: 'The wail of distress which, week after week, reaches this building from every quarter of the island—the untilled field, the crowded emigrant ship—all tell the sad tale of ruin.'

The condition of Ireland reminded him of the 'disastrous transformation' of Cyprus under three centuries of Turkish rule. Dillon asserted: 'He knew not whether Ireland was destined to be reduced by similar causes to similar ruin, but he knew it was the duty, as he hoped it was the desire, of every Irishman to avert that catastrophe; and it was especially incumbent on this council, representing as if did whatever was left of the wealth and intelligence of the metropolis of Ireland, to made some effort for the country in the dire extremity to which it was reduced.' His report to the municipal council—published subsequently with a preface by his son, William—concluded: 'Ireland owes no debt to Britain.'[19] On the contrary Alderman Dillon believed his country was grossly over-taxed. The following March he moved the adoption of a petition to the House of Commons on Irish taxation. He estimated that 'after supporting all our own establishments, including the army stationed in Ireland, the administration of justice, the constabulary—everything, in fact, from the viceregal establishment down to the police barrack, we remit to England every year … from £3.5 to £4 million sterling.'

Dillon declared that if he had 'honours to bestow, the highest should be awarded, not to princes or to peers, but rather to the skilful farmer, the enterprising merchant, the ingenious workman and the liberal employer'.

If Ireland had 'become no longer habitable to a people who love her and who leave her shores with poignant sorrow, it is not because her children are thriftless or indolent, or her skies inclement, or her green fields unfruitful, but because her wealth is carried away to be spent amongst strangers, who have rarely respected her misfortunes or sympathised with her distress.'

In January 1864 Dillon wrote to O'Brien:

> You will probably smile when I inform you that I have just this moment been writing out a form of agreement under which The O'Donoghue and John Martin are hiring portion of a house in D'Olier Street for the purposes of an association to be called the Irish National League—object to obtain a repeal of the union by influencing public opinion, etc. I think with our opinions that you and I can do nothing but look on at this experiment. For my part I don't believe in the possibility of repealing the union by anything else than round shot and rifle bullets, and therefore I cannot honestly encourage the people to expect it by an appeal to public opinion. J. Martin thinks me very wrong, but I can't help that. As far as I can see, I think this is a step in a wrong direction.[20]

The O'Donoghue was a grand-nephew of the Liberator and a popular MP at the time. Dillon was governed by reason, not emotion: 'There are some things which might be accomplished now if taken in hand vigorously.' The state church could be disestablished and a 'good measure got for the tenants, and a few small victories of this kind would inspire the peope with confidence in themselves and their leaders'.

In his declining years O'Brien was still prepared to tilt at windmills to vindicate the national honour. In 1862 (the year after his wife's death) he challenged the chief secretary, Sir Robert Peel (a son of the prime minister), to a duel for referring to the '48 insurgents as 'cabbage-garden heroes'. He grew increasingly despondent about family and public affairs, telling Dillon: 'I pity such men as you and a few others whom I believe to be sincerely desirous to do something for the country. In the meantime I think that you act wisely and patriotically in supporting every useful [? move] even though it proceeded from men in whom you place no confidence.'[21]

William Smith O'Brien died on 18 June 1864, while staying with his sister in Wales. A group of friends met in Dillon's house 'to devise some mode of testifying the affectionate respect so universally felt towards the departed patriot'.[22] They included: Richard O'Gorman, senior; R.R. Madden, the historian; John Martin, Smyth, Pigot, Martin O'Flaherty, James Cantwell, the redoubtable Father Kenyon, A.M. Sullivan and the lord mayor of Dublin, Peter Paul McSwiney.

As the votaries of O'Brien met in Fitzwilliam square, a Fenian assembly in the mechanics' hall discussed the obsequies with a view to emulating the MacManus demonstration. Any such ideas were abandoned when O'Brien's eldest son, Edward, who was a magistrate, requested a private funeral. Nevertheless, police estimated that 8,000 marched in Dublin behind the coffin, which was flanked by Martin, Cantwell, Sullivan and Dillon, who accompanied the body to County Limerick for interment.[23]

Martin wrote that O'Brien 'had been wishing for death, feeling that he had little to live for—nothing to do. The very last time I saw him (though he entertained John Dillon and me quite cheerfully, taking a glass of wine with us, which was not his habit), he said to me before we parted that "he had never had one hour's happiness since his wife's death".'[24]

Dillon's metamorphosis from church critic to Catholic politician is unclear. He had commented to his wife (23 April 1852): 'I regard the election of Dr Cullen in Dublin as a calamity to that unhappy country. This religious bigotry is now flaming so high on both sides, that it seems as if a European *religious* war were impending. ...' He was writing from New York in an atmosphere generated by Pio Nono, who had restored the Catholic dioceses in England and Wales and sent Cullen to Ireland as papal legate. In 1849, at the end of his Roman career, Cullen had seen the brief triumph of anti-clerical nationalism. This experience helped to form the deeply conservative mind which would declare during the Fenian emergency that famine was a lesser evil than revolution.[25] On the other hand, Cullen believed 'Mammon is the ruling power of England at present, and the safety and rights of the people are immolated to that idol';[26] while Irish revolutionary movements 'invariably have brought ruin and desolation in their train', O'Connell gained Catholic emancipation 'which would never have been extracted from our rulers by force' (or, Cullen might have added, without the threat of violence).

In his 1865 pastoral condemning Orangeism and Fenianism, Cullen said love of country 'is a virtue that ought to be cherished by all; and, in my opinion, those Irishmen who sneer at the place of their birth, or deny it, or who get their children educated in a spirit of hostility to their native land, are worthy of sovereign contempt and should be looked on as destitute of the best feelings of the human heart'.

Dillon and Cullen would find they had much in common. Meanwhile, the archbishop was remarkably successful in building up the ultra-montane church, with a concomitant growth in the confessional nature of Irish life. Politics were of secondary importance to Cullen, whose popularity never recovered from his failure to condemn those members of the independent Irish party who defected in the early 1850s. Having escaped from this arid political landscape, Dillon commented to Adelaide: 'I perceive the last change of ministry has thinned the ranks of the Irish brigade. Willie Keogh solicitor general! Thank heaven there is a place where honest men can live.' He added (18 January 1853): 'The strangest part of the comedy is poor Duffy's amazement at Keogh's profligacy.' Dillon went on to predict that the bishop of Elphin, George Browne, would continue to support Keogh after he accepted office.[27]

While the Eccesiastical Titles Act of 1851 assuaged an outbreak of 'no popery' in Britain, it heightened sectarian tensions in Ireland, where proselytising by evangelical groups had already inflamed passions. Events in Italy at the end of the decade further exacerbated the Irish religious divide, as Catholic Ireland sent men and money to defend the beleaguered papal states. (Dillon probably shared Mazzini's disillusionment with the *risorgimento*—'I thought I was awakening the soul of Italy and I see only the corpse before me'—especially when unification was achieved with the support of Emperor Napoleon and Lord Palmerston.)

It is clear, however, that back in Ireland he fell under the growing moral hegemony of the Catholic Church. His epistolary effusions had acted as a catharsis. Furthermore, on re-entering politics Dillon gravitated towards that 'faith and fatherland' perspective which was to have a fateful influence in shaping modern Ireland. Like most contemporaries he did not realise the country was being partitioned mentally.

In a far cry from the comprehensive nationalism of Young Ireland, he asserted (at a fund-raising meeting for the Augustinian church in John's Lane, Dublin, the foundation stone of which was laid by Dr Cullen on Easter Monday 1862): 'I, an Irish nationalist, know, and the enemies of Irish nationality also know it, that the cause of the Irish Catholic Church and the cause of the Irish Catholic people are one and indivisible.'

Dillon, who had long abandoned revolutionary politics, now regarded integrated education 'as radically false and mischievous',[28] and sent William to the Catholic University. He paid tribute to the Christian Brothers in whose schools 'the name of Ireland was not prohibited. ...

With every truth that they communicated to the young mind they impressed on it at the same time the lesson that all the knowledge which it
has, and all the knowledge it was capable of acquiring, formed but a drop
from the boundless ocean of eternal truth.'

Cullen saw Dillon as a figure of stability in a country threatened by
revolution, in conditions of near-famine and mass emigration. Dillon, on
the other hand, agreed with his amiable friend, John Martin: 'It is a
valuable thing for Ireland to have the Catholic bishops, even Dr Cullen,
committed to patriotic exertions.'[29] Martin wrote in January 1864: 'The
progress of denationalisation is very rapid at present. Emigration carries
off the best of each year's generation, and leaves a larger and larger
proportion of the spiritless, feeble, or corrupt, ready to be anglicised and
enslaved.'

On 8 August the foundation stone of the O'Connell monument was laid
in Dublin. An estimated eleven bishops, including Cullen, and 150 priests
marched while 300,000 people attended the ceremony. This display of
Catholic assertiveness prompted Belfast Orangemen to burn the Liberator
in effigy; in the ensuing riots eleven people were killed and 316 injured.[30]
Dillon was a leading member of the O'Connell monument committee. (His
political transition is suggested by the recollection that twenty years
previously he had contributed towards the cost of placing 'an inscribed
though humble flagstone' on Tone's grave.)[31] In contrast with whig
committee members, it was O'Connell the repealer whom he admired. At
a banquet that evening Dillon said he had found at the bottom of all
O'Connell's agitations 'one great principle—one great motive actuating
his conduct—one great ambition filling him, and that was that Ireland
should belong to Irishmen'. The essence of Irish patriotism was 'that the
rule of the stranger should cease ... that his bigotry should no longer insult
our convictions, and that his greed should no longer devour our substance.
In front of all our institutions, civil, military and ecclesiastical, that
shameful inscription might still be read, "This land belongs to England".
To erase this foul legend has been the object of the efforts of every genuine
patriot from Swift to O'Connell.'

In 1864 also, James Henthorn Todd's book on St Patrick, claiming the
national apostle as the founder of the Anglican Church of Ireland, was first
published. The adrenalin of the emergent Catholic middle class hardened
into a demand for disestablishment. Alderman McSwiney, a large Dublin
draper, sent a circular proposing an agitation to Cullen, who described the

established church as 'the source of all the evils of Ireland'. By October Cullen had been persuaded, apparently by Dillon, 'that something should be done to rescue this Catholic country from the position of political subjection and religious inferiority in which it now lies'.[32]

In November the veteran repealer, W.J. O'Neill Daunt, received a letter from Dillon announcing that a campaign 'for tenant right, disendowment of the state church and free education is contemplated by all the bishops and a large number of laymen'.[33]

Later that month Dillon spent three nights in Mount Melleray Abbey.[34] The circumstances of his pilgrimage to the Irish Catholic mecca on the slopes of the Knockmealdown mountains are intriguing. Adelaide and Rose were wintering in Malaga. Bishop Laurence Gillooly of Elphin, who became Dillon's political confidant, visited the monastery just before him. It is likely that both men consulted the abbot, Bruno Fitzpatrick, who was in the bishops' confidence and had addressed the national synod in Thurles convened by Cullen. Dillon was poised in the footsteps of O'Connell, who had also made a spiritual retreat in Mount Melleray, the first Cistercian foundation in Ireland after emancipation.

On returning to Dublin he decided with Cullen to circulate a requisition calling for an aggregate meeting to inaugurate the new association. At a meeting of the friends of St Brigid's orphanage in the pro-cathedral on 23 November, with the archbishop presiding, he denounced the Anglican establishment and proselytising, and stated that the organised power of the Irish (Catholic) people would soon be brought to bear on the question.[35]

The *Nation* considered the National Association had been virtually launched.[36] Gillooly told Dillon: 'I am glad to see your committee is beginning to act.'[37]

The association was founded on 29 December at a meeting attended by 5,000 in the Rotunda. As arranged by Dillon, Cullen in a keynote address proposed the first part of a resolution calling for disestablishment; having moved the second part, O'Neill Daunt noted ironically in his diary apropos the recently-published syllabus of errors: 'Was it not amusing that just as the pope's manifesto appeared affirming state-churchism, I, a staunch Catholic, speaking in the immediate presence and with the full approbation of the pope's Irish legate, the archbishop of Dublin, should publicly pray heaven that in no revolution of ages might the Catholic Church in Ireland be cursed with state support, or otherwise sustained than by voluntary principles? We are in no way bound by the pope's political notions.'

Dillon told the first general meeting: 'If the act of joining this asso-ciation involved anything like an abjuration of the faith in the right of

Ireland to control her own affairs in a legislature of her own, I should not be found in the position in which I now stand (cheers). I believe that we shall not impede, but materially aid, the progress of Ireland towards the ultimate goal of home legislation by removing those barriers which now keep apart the different sects and classes into which our people are divided.'[38]

He referred to the Anglican establishment as 'this monstrous institution'. (In a letter read to the aggregate meeting the radical MP, John Bright, had described it as a national insult.) Dillon considered it was 'a struggle for life between the Catholic people and the Protestant establishment; and all who love the people are bound to struggle for the overthrow of an institution whose preservation depends on their destruction. Let no man accuse me of bigotry for the utterance of this sentiment. ... I claim no advantage or superiority over any man. What I demand for the Catholic I am ready to demand and to struggle for on behalf of the Protestant—that is, full and perfect equality for all.'

Regarding the association's demand for denominational education, he asserted:

> I know there are many men of liberal minds who find it difficult to understand why we object to have Catholics and Protestants taught the elements of knowledge at the same school, by teachers who may be Catholics or Protestants as chance or the will of government officials may decide. I can all the better comprehend these views, because I once very firmly and very honestly entertained them myself, but it was at a time when I had no children to be educated; and I have certainly lived to learn that, of all the shallow notions which are often mistaken for liberality, there is none more shallow than that which mistakes mere teaching for education, and which would sacrifice the formation of the character to the cultivation and development of the intellect.

The archbishop of Cashel, Patrick Leahy, explained that the bishops had decided to enter the political arena because they were obliged to consider the welfare of their people, who were being swept away by emigration. It was probably Dillon's idea to extend the objects of the association, conceived as an agitation for disestablishment, to the land and education questions.[39]

In the Tipperary by-election of February 1865, the first test for this constitutional alternative to Fenianism, the association's candidate, Charles Moore, was opposed by the eccentric editor of the *Tipperary Advocate*, Peter Gill.

Dillon went down to support Moore and encountered a pro-Gill mob in Clonmel. He reported to Bishop Gillooly on 3 March:

> Many of the priests themselves half sympathised with the Fenian revolt against their own order, and the tory landlords gave all their influence to Gill with the avowed purpose of detaching the people from the priests and inflicting a death-blow on the influence of the latter. Under the circumstances, I resolved to throw myself into the meleé, and I spoke to the people not only at the hustings but wherever I could find a crowd. I also spent a couple of days driving through the county, visiting the priests and dissipating as far as I could all delusion respecting the true character of the contest.

Dillon's reflection on how times had changed since his mission as an insurgent chief is not recorded. Moore won the election although the unusually low poll indicated that the electorate as well as the clergy lacked enthusiasm for his candidacy.[40]

Archbishop MacHale would not join the association because of his estrangement from Cullen. Dillon met G.H. Moore by chance in Dublin and they agreed to approach the two prelates to see if a reconciliation could be effected. Moore visited Tuam and reported favourably to Dillon, who wrote hopefully to Cullen (enclosing a copy of Moore's letter): 'Such a reconciliation would be hailed by the country with genuine delight, and would certainly be of incalculable advantage to our association.'[41] Cullen apparently did nothing about the initiative of Dillon, who had expected to be contacting Moore again. Moore, concluding he had been exploited, turned against Dillon and towards the Fenian leadership.[42]

Dillon believed the relation between landlord and tenant was the cause of most of the evils of the country. In May-June 1865 he explained to a parliamentary committee the immediacy of the Irish sense of historic dispossession.[43] The seventeenth-century confiscations were still 'very recent' in Ireland, he contended. Irish landlord-tenant relations required exceptional legislation because in no other European country had the occupier less protection and fewer motives for improving the land. Also, the difference in religion between the people and their landlords tended 'to render the position of the occupier less secure and less pleasant'.[44]

Insecurity of tenure remained the principal reason for the backwardness of Irish agriculture. The situation had worsened since the Famine as many of the old landowners had been replaced by 'land jobbers'. Dillon considered sub-letting by middlemen to be the 'worst form of landlordism'. Other members of the committee asserted that previous legislative attempts had 'failed from the difficulty of giving to the tenant the right of improving his land against the will of the landlord'. Dillon said he did not think it followed that if landlords had been unyielding 'for so long a time that they should remain obstinate for ever'. He favoured the granting of thirty-one year leases but being a realist concluded his evidence by stating: 'Nothing is more likely to make the population of Ireland contented and loyal than a good measure, giving them compensation for their improvements'.[45]

At home Dillon tried to hold the association together. During a dispute about its rules agreement emerged from talks in Maynooth. Six bishops, including Cullen and MacHale, then met Dillon in a Dublin hotel and drew up amended rules, which were approved unanimously by a special committee. The spirit of conciliation was short-lived, however.

Back in his diocese MacHale wrote an uncompromising letter to be read at a banquet for Duffy, who had returned on a visit after ten years in Australia. Moore followed with a speech at the dinner in Dublin on 27 June which reopened old wounds.[46] Dillon, who presided, said he would have proposed a toast to the hierarchy without comment but for the previous speaker's 'eloquent invective' against Cullen.

> He looked back into the history of his country, and if the religion of their forefathers had come down to them unsullied and uncorrupted, if the moral elevation of their race had been preserved intact, he wished to know to what influence those great blessings were to be attributed. Where would they be that day but for the hierarchy and clergy of Ireland, and looking forward in the future, and putting aside vague generalities, what had they to rely upon if it was not the confidence and affection of the people for their hierarchy and clergy, and the intimate union between the two. Individuals amongst them may have gone wrong, but while he admitted that he would not be one to impute moral guilt.

Moore, unwilling to allow Dillon have the last word, interrupted him. But Duffy supported his old friend: 'There is substantial truth in all Mr

Moore has said regarding the past; but still I believe that if we maintain an Irish vendetta that knows no truce, we will go down to our graves without seeing anything accomplished for the Irish people. When I hear that John Dillon—in whose capacity and judgment I have a deep trust, and whose integrity I know to be beyond all controversy—took up the people's cause again, I rejoiced to hear it; and I confess, if I were living in Ireland, that this is the course I would feel bound to pursue.'[47] The issue of the *Nation* which carried this report, however, joined in the attack on 'Cullen's association'. Such was the state of disarray among constitutional nationalists on the eve of a general election.

Member for Tipperary

... the time is probably approaching when I must
definitely decide whether I am to devote the greater portion
of my time and thoughts to the service of the public,
or to the duties of my profession.
DILLON TO BISHOP GILLOOLY, 3 MARCH 1865

Dillon, with keen political insight, saw that the general election of July 1865 marked the beginning of a new order. The parliamentary following of John Bright was increased; and John Stuart Mill, the political philosopher, had been induced to emerge from retirement to support the radicals. The death in October of Lord Palmerston—who had equated tenant right with 'landlord wrong'—facilitated the emergence of Gladstonian liberalism (although Earl Russell succeeded initially as prime minister).

Free of the bitterness engendered by Irish politics in the 1850s, Dillon broke the mould dictated by the principle of independent opposition. He realised that the 'only chance of obtaining justice from parliament lay in an alliance with the "advanced liberals"' in Britain.[1] He admired Bright, who urged consistently that Irish unrest should be tackled in its causes rather that in its effects.

In 1849 Bright had reminded a complacent House of Commons:

> Hon. gentlemen turn with triumph to neighbouring countries and speak in glowing terms of our glorious constitution. It is true that abroad thrones and dynasties have been overturned, whilst in England peace has reigned undisturbed. But take all the lives that have been lost in the last 12 months in Europe amidst the convulsions that have occurred—take all the cessation of trade, destruction of industry, all the crushing of hopes and hearts, and they will not compare for an instant with the agonies which have been endured by the population of Ireland under your glorious constitution.

During the Fenian emergency of 1866, he declared that the majority of the Irish people would, if they could, 'unmoor the island from its fastenings in the deep and move it at least 2,000 miles to the west'. If they could shake off the authority of the imperial parliament they would gladly do so.

The *Daily News*, organ of the British liberal party, concluded that the Anglo-Irish ascendancy had outlived its usefulness. The social divisions which Britain's *divide et impera* strategy promoted in Ireland remained 'after they have ceased to be an aid and have become instead the chief hindrance to empire'.[2] The paper hoped condescendingly but with enlighted self-interest that

> hatred of foreign rule may in time be overcome by just and generous government. The instances are numerous in which under this treatment a conquered people has become heartily one with its subjugators. But few cases can be pointed to in which this result has been attained when the victorious power has employed as the instrument of its rule an ascendant minority of the subdued population. This, unfortunately, has been the plan which has been adopted for 800 years in Ireland, and which has not yet been wholly discontinued. ... Ireland is at variance with England because she is not at one with herself. Her internal dissensions must be healed before she can assume her proper place in the imperial system.

Dillon was the most conspicuous of the new Irish members elected in 1865. John O'Hagan had forecast that he would be swept into parliament by the power of popular opinion.[3]

While canvassing during the Tipperary by-election, Dillon 'was met with the question—why I was not the candidate selected by the archbishop [of Cashel]. ... I was asked by many would I consent to stand for Tipperary at the general election, on condition of being returned free of expense, and I evaded a direct answer by saying it would be time enough to make up my mind whenever the offer should made.'[4]

He wrote at a time when priests constituted almost the entire local leadership of the liberal party in rural Catholic Ireland, and the National Association had no electoral machinery except the voice of the clergy. Moreover, candidates frequently spent thousands of pounds on securing a parliamentary seat.

Dillon could not afford this expense, nor attend Westminster without receiving a salary. He made a novel proposal to Bishop Gillooly, who was a member of the board of the Catholic University, by pointing out that the chairs of law and political economy were vacant.

> They cannot be left permanently vacant if the university aspires to be anything more than a high school. It so happens that I obtained the highest prize in political economy when a student in Trinity College, and since then I have kept tolerably *au courant* with the progress of the science ... [if appointed] I should be able to go into parliament and to devote myself mainly to the objects of the association, and would hold myself specially bound to forward the cause of sound education. In both ways I think I would give fair value for whatever salary might be assigned to the united chairs of law and political economy.

In any event, 'the enterprise in which we have engaged will have as much service from me as I can render without serious injury to myself.'

In his last letter to Gillooly (15 December 1865) Dillon wrote sadly: 'I conjecture from Yr. Ldship's silence on the subject that some difficulty has arisen which you do not see how to get over. ... If I could look forward to the probability of such an arrangement as I speak of being made within a short time, I would enter on my new career without any misgiving.'

Episcopal confidence in Dillon may not have extended to the education question, the issue on which their lordships were most paternalistic. He had drafted the education resolution for the aggregate meeting in consultation with Gillooly, adding the comment: 'The right insisted on in the above resolution is the right of *the parent*. When that is conceded by the state there arises the right of *the church* to direct the parent. From such a government as we live under it would seem that we can reasonably expect no more than that it will *let us alone*, leaving the Catholic parent and the Catholic bishop to settle the matter between them.'[5]

Cullen did not welcome unauthorised lay initiatives on the education question. He had, furthermore, warned Newman to preserve the Catholic University from Young Irelandism. The rector found the archbishop so distrustful of everyone that he wondered Cullen did not 'cook his own dinners.'[6]

But whatever about a professorship, Cullen helped to launch Dillon in the prestigious constituency of Tipperary. Archbishop Leahy was already disillusioned with the senior member for the county, Laurence Waldron, when Cullen wrote to him on 30 June: 'Some friends called on me today to state that they are most anxious to get Mr Dillon returned for Tipperary. It appears that Gill will oppose Waldron and Moore, but that if Moore were to coalesce with Mr Dillon and pay his expenses there would be no contest. Mr Moore could afford to expend a few thousands as he is worth nearly a million of ready money.'[7]

Dillon considered he had 'a very fair chance of being his successor' after Waldron retired from the contest.[8] Peter Gill did stand and again attracted local Fenian support. The *Irish People* took an inordinate interest in Dillon's candidacy; being opposed to 'parliamentary humbug', the official organ of the revolutionary organisation declared that 'an ex-rebel leader is the very worst enemy Ireland could have in the foreign parliament'.[9] Accordingly, on arrival in Clonmel Dillon was greeted with shouts of: 'Dillon the '48 renegade' and 'Go back to Paul Cullen.' After trying to speak for twenty minutes he was said to have broken down.[10]

Duffy, pressed by Dillon to remain in Ireland, had accompanied him to the hustings. He thought it 'a significant illustration of the senseless and stupid policy, which the Fenians borrowed from the Chartists, that a Fenian mob in the capital of the county silenced by clamour the most distinguished and best-tested nationalist then in the country'.[11]

Dillon had complained to John O'Leary, whom he met as a Fenian representative in the early 1860s, 'of the danger of the popular ostracising of worthy, trusted public men'. Nevertheless, when one of the Tipperary hecklers was arrested during the Fenian crackdown, he wrote to the attorney general appealing for his release.[12]

'In parliament my efforts would be directed towards securing for my country substantial self-government', Dillon asserted in his election address:

> All the prominent grievances of Ireland, in my opinion, resolve themselves into one—that in the making of our laws and in the administration of our affairs the will of the Irish people counts for little or nothing. The wrongs endured by the Irish tenantry, the misappropriation of our ecclesiastical revenues, our defective system of education, the drain of our wealth to England, the flight of our people to America—what are they all but symptoms of our organic disease—the subjection of our national will to the dominant will or another people? ...
>
> To the state of the laws regulating the tenure of land I have devoted some laborious consideration, and I entertain little doubt that, without encroaching on the legitimate rights of property, a modification of the present system of land tenure may be effected

which would speedily check the outflow of our population. I venture to hope that, if returned to parliament, I could materially contribute towards a successful solution of that vital question, by giving shape and precision to the proposals of its friends and by disarming the prejudices of its opponents. ...

Even a dozen men acting together in good faith, and commanding respect by the exhibition of integrity and good sense, could accomplish much that we require. But my hope for the future mainly rests upon the growth of a political organisation which will deserve and possess the confidence of the country, and which, while keeping a vigilant eye on the conduct of Irish representatives, will, by its power and by its spirit, make manifest to every English statesman that the empire is not safe while Ireland is aggrieved.

The *Irish People* claimed Dillon was blessed from the altars from which he had been cursed in 1848. 'The priest who prayed to see his corpse dangling from the gallows was his staunch supporter at the election, while the priest who was most prominently identified with the national cause in '48 stood upon the hustings to denounce him.'[13] This, as we have seen from Father Kenyon's performance during the attempted rising, was a misreading of history.

On nomination day that cleric delivered an harangue about the green flag on behalf of Gill. Dillon said he had heard eloquent words from the same lips before: 'We might all do better than go talking about raising the green flag, though when it was real talk I was there. My principles are now as they were then, viz. that Ireland should be ruled by Irishmen from the centre to the sea.'[14]

Charles Moore and Dillon were elected members for Tipperary. They received 2,722 and 2,662 votes respectively, to 938 for Gill, in an electorate of 9,000.

Dillon, in expressing his appreciation of tenant farmer support, warned against the Fenian conspiracy (shortly to result in mass arrests).

I perceive, not without bitter regret, and not without lively apprehensions for the future, that the minds of the young men of Ireland, most of them sincere, patriotic, high-spirited and brave, are being misled. I grieve to think that most of our young men are being misled to their own destruction, and that of their country as well. Men have attacked me as a deserter from my colours. I want to know at what period of my life did I range myself among the enemies of my country that I should be accused of deserting my colours? Did I ever preach or countenance doctrines unfavourable to this country? When did I preach against parliamentary agitation, and yet come to advocate its principles on the hustings? What I claim credit for is this—I am a man of action. It is now many years since I first came to this county and looked down upon the lovely valley of the Suir. I was then a young enthusiast in the cause of my country. I then heard men talk of raising the green flag, and I said to them if the green flag is to be raised, in God's name let us go and raise it. I am one of those who would rather raise a hundred flags and fight a hundred battles against any odds, and even with the certainty of defeat, than for ever to be talking of battles and never to fight them, or of green flags and never to raise them.[15]

Having disposed of his own rebel past, and completed Kenyon's discomfiture, Dillon outlined his parliamentary strategy.

First make Ireland successful, then I say to assert the rights of the Irish people to make their own laws and to be the arbiters of their own destiny. I have heard, in the course of my travels in this county of Tipperary, a sentiment that all attempts at improving our present condition will be thrown away. I have met many men who are firmly prejudiced that such is the case. I respect that sentiment, I admit there is some ground for it; promises have been broken more than once, still I do not despair. I believe that some good may yet be effected for Ireland. If we have 20 Irish members to stand together in the house, they can make the government feel by their aid and by their votes, that their support entirely depends upon the measures which the government will give to this country. I do believe that great things could be thus effected for the people of Ireland, and my highest ambition in now entering upon my parliamentary career is to be one of such a party—a party who will hold their place in parliament independent of all governments; at the same time making every party there feel that their support will be given on condition of that party doing good things for this country.

G.H. Moore, who amazed Duffy 'by a rooted prejudice against Dillon', wrote from Mayo: 'Well, it's all one to me and am glad I was not made a fool of. Dillon has got his seat in parliament, and so has [Sir John] Gray. Dr Cullen has a right to chuckle, and I have the right of a cynic and a prophet to snarl and smile.'[16] Moore may have been an embittered cynic but he was no prophet.

During the autumn of 1865 Dillon concentrated on organising a conference of Irish liberal MPs to 'agree on a plan of action' before parliament
met the following spring. Although only about a dozen members (in an
Irish representation of 105) were committed fully to the objects of the
National Association, he told a committee on 18 October: '... from
communications made to myself by a good many of the representatives, I
have no doubt we shall have a very influential meeting of members of
parliament in Dublin within a month.' He favoured going with an agreed
programme to the liberal government 'and saying that upon the condition
alone of giving us these measures would they have our support'.[17]

The ministry needed Irish votes to carry the franchise reform bill. Dillon
assured the bishops in November: 'English opinion inclines more to a
redress of Irish grievances at the present juncture than at any former period
in our history. ... All these signs on the political horizon encourage the
belief that providence has afforded us an opportunity for achieving, by a
comparatively short and easy effort, reforms which (under less favourable
circumstances) might cost the labour of many years.'

The conference of MPs was held eventually on 5-6 December, largely
through the efforts of Dillon,[18] who persuaded the twenty two members
present to adopt a comprehensive programme of reform.

The aims of the National Association—which remained a clerical-
dominated Dublin-based pressure group—were grafted skilfully on to the
parliamentary body. A committee chaired by Dillon was appointed to draft
a land bill 'providing adequate compensation for all tenants' improvements and to induce the granting of leases'; the state church was declared
to be an intolerable grievance; and the conference requested a denominational system of education. Resolution 13 noted 'that, inasmuch as the
"advanced" section of the English liberal party largely share our political
views and sympathise with our efforts, we are anxious to co-operate with
them in anything calculated to advance our common interests, and hope
for their assistance in the promotion of measures beneficial to Ireland'.

In January 1866, on the eve of going to parliament, Dillon achieved
notoriety with a speech in response to the Fenian arrests. He asserted that,
at the end of the American civil war,

> a great military and naval power, destined in all probability to
> become at no distant day the greatest power on earth, has sprung
> suddenly into existence ten days' sail of the Irish shores; that those
> in whose hands mainly rest the guidance and control of that power
> are animated by the deepest resentment against England; that this

resentment is inflamed and stimulated to activity by the presence and influence of ten millions of citizens of Irish blood; and, finally, that deep and widespread disaffection pervades the population of at least three of the provinces of Ireland.[19]

The association sought to disarm disaffection by justice, Dillon continued. 'We want change but we want neither Jacobinism, nor anarchy, nor spoliation. We want rather to advance with safe and steady steps towards the goal we have in view, under the guidance of religion and intelligence.' He referred to impending evictions in Tipperary and concluded:

> Here is the key to all this Irish disaffection by which the people affect to be so bewildered. The law robs and exterminates the people; the people naturally hate and defy the law. For my part, I shall content myself with saying that such laws do not deserve to be respected, and that the perpetrators of such outrages as I have described are greater enemies of law, of peace and prosperity in Ireland than those heroic through mistaken men who have been sent to penal servitude during the last six weeks.

The Dublin tory press wondered if Dillon's clerical associates agreed with his views, which would be used to justify disloyalty. The *Daily News* said he had marred his fledgling parliamentary career, while the *Daily Telegraph* remarked that Pentonville prison would be a more appropriate destination for him than the House of Commons.[20]

On the other hand, as Dillon informed Adelaide, Archbishop Henry Edward Manning of Westminster saw nothing in the speech but a bold enunciation of the truth. Manning said also 'that the Fenians in Pentonville have sent a request to the government that they may be allowed to have Mass. And the government, although they have always bitterly refused, have granted their request'.[21]

John Mitchel observed from Paris, where he was installed briefly as a Fenian agent, that Dillon's speech 'shows that the fire of '48 is not yet quite extinguished under the snows that now whiten his head'.[22] (Mitchel had been jailed after the American civil war together with Jefferson Davis, president of the vanquished, slave-owning south.) Dillon thought 'our friends the yankees have to answer for a good deal of coarse brutality' towards the prisoners.

O'Hagan had shown extraordinary foresight in a letter to Adelaide. He was 'becoming a southerner on the American question through fear of the north. The truth is our northern instincts in Ireland all had their root in the danger to England which was sure to follow the success of the north. But is it England alone that will be endangered [?] I have not got I confess to love her more than in my youth, but I am a European to the core and I tremble to think of our poor Europe with its splendid civilisation being overrun in another century by victorious yankeedom.'[23]

Dillon attended parliament regularly to familiarise himself with proceedings. He found the company of English radicals most congenial. He established a rapport with the *bête noire* of the tories, John Bright, who 'came and sat by me yesterday in the dining room. After inter-change of compliments, I said what bitter enemies you have. I never saw so much malignity displayed towards any human being. "Yes", he said, "they are miserable fellows and they hate me because they know I am not looking for anything for myself while they think of nothing else".'[24]

Bright went on to say that he thought Sir John Gray should not have attacked the Fenians in his speech. Dillon agreed, 'although they don't deserve any sympathy. There is no intellect in their movement, and I fear but a small share of honesty.' Bright's main objection to the Fenian movement was 'its entire hopelessness. There are certainly causes enough in Ireland to justify insurrection if this could only succeed.' He added: 'You like myself have got a reputation for entertaining very violent opinions.'

On the previous evening in the commons tea room Dillon had introduced himself to John Stuart Mill as a friend of Gavan Duffy. Mill 'shook hands very warmly and said I was just the man whose acquaintance he desired to make—that he had been reading my evidence about the land question'. Dillon got on 'famously' with the author of *Principles of political economy*.

At the beginning of the parliamentary session William Ewart Gladstone, then chancellor of the exchequer, stated it was the intention of the government to legislate for Ireland according to Irish exigencies and no longer according to English routine. Dillon found Gladstone's speech particularly encouraging: 'I was sitting nearly opposite him and he spoke fairly *at* me—looking straight at me and I at him. I suppose he saw that I was drinking in every word he said. He is certainly a *great man*. ... He is *fearfully* persuasive and much of his power is certainly due to his elevated moral character. Mill said to me that his speech portends good things for Ireland.'[25]

Dillon delivered his maiden speech on 17 February when the Habeas Corpus Act was being suspended in Ireland again. He spoke directly after John Bright, describing his speech 'as one of the most generous, most true and most noble utterances which it has ever been my fortune to listen to'.[26]

In opposing the habeas corpus suspension bill Dillon stated: 'I have no sympathy with Fenianism, and those who have had an occasion to investigate the transactions and the peculiar literature of that movement must know very well that I am one of the most prominent objects of the hostility of its leaders. I believe I was the only candidate at the last general election in Ireland that had to encounter the organised opposition of the Fenians. ... The facility with which I overcame it in one of its reputed strongholds has always made me sceptical of the force which has been popularly attributed to this movement.'

Whatever capacity Fenianism might have for mischief was based on the disaffection arising from misgovernment: 'The Irish people feel bitterly that the laws which are made by the imperial parliament have been generally made in the interests of a class and against the people.' Dillon wanted

> to know in what state Ireland must be before she is fit to receive her full measure of justice at the hands of the imperial parliament. If she is silent and there is an absence of complaint, then the inference is that she has no grievance to complain of. On the other hand, if she is turbulent and seditious, then it it said that it would not be compatible with the dignity of the imperial government to make any concession under such circumstances. It seems to me that the only appropriate time for doing justice is always the present hour; and until the government of this country give some specific assurance that they mean to do justice to Ireland I, for one, cannot aid them in any effort to quell the discontent and disaffection which have been caused by the denial of justice.

Almost as soon as he arrived in London Dillon began to prepare a land bill. Enclosing a copy of his bill to Dr Cullen, he wrote: 'Although Mr Gladstone has pronounced it "fair and moderate" I have little hope that the landlords will be satisfied with it. However, if the government should take it up there is a fair prospect of its being carried though the House of Commons. What I fear most is that a clamour may be got up in Ireland by those who will think it too moderate. These people little understand the difficulties we have to encounter.'[27]

He informed Adelaide on 19 February: 'I am very busy drafting a land bill for the Irish members—ie, about 25 of them. We meet tomorrow at 2 o'c. when "my bill" will be considered in detail. It is now in the hands of the printer.' Six days later he reported: 'I was engaged a good deal yesterday and will be again today in trying to get the Irish members to agree to a decent land bill. I fear I shall have hard work to succeed. They always pretend that their only objection is the impossibility of carrying it in the house. But it is plain enough that they have no desire to carry anything that is worth having.' Mill, who was present at Dillon's invitation, whispered: 'I see what a difficult business you have in hand. ...'

The *Nation* underlined this point by criticising 'Mr Dillon's bill' as inadequate.[28] At a meeting of the National Association he defended it as the best measure that could be obtained in the prevailing circumstances; moreover, 'if this bill had been in operation for the last fifty years the occupiers of the land would have as much interest in the land at least as the proprietors have in it.'[29] He refuted his critics: 'If we want measures that can be carried only by revolution, and if we will accept no measure short of that, our only plan is to become revolutionists.'

A motion endorsing Dillon's bill 'as the minimum of the tenants' just demands' was passed unanimously. In a letter to the press he explained further that a moderate bill had been drafted in the hope that the government would accept it.[30] Gladstone requested a second copy of the bill.[31] After meeting him with a Louth MP, Tristram Kennedy, Dillon announced: 'It is nearly certain that the government will adopt our land bill.'[32] In fact it was accepted as 'simple, clear and definite in character'.[33]

During the struggle for reform Dillon supported the franchise extension bill unconditionally. He outlined his position in a letter to the association:

> This is not merely a question of confidence in a whig government, but a question on the decision of which depends the future political status of the true liberal party in England. Should this bill become law that party will rule the state. ... It becomes necessary that Ireland should make choice of friends and allies, and upon the wisdom of that choice the destiny of our country will depend for many a year to come. ... [Gladstone] has more than once admitted that the discontent of the Irish people is the natural result of the misgovernment to which they have been subjected. He has said that the future government of that country ought to be different from the past or the *present*, and that Irish questions ought to be

dealt with in accordance with the views and sentiments of the Irish people. ...

If any man will tell me that, as a member of the National Association, I am bound to take the earliest opportunity to put that government out of office, and for that end to inflict a grievous injury on the working classes of England, and to alienate and outrage the only party in the House of Commons from which we can expect any aid or sympathy, I can only say that his arguments will be very cogent and persuasive if they convince me that his conclusion is not unwise, unpractical and absurd.[34]

He told Cullen: 'If this reform bill could only pass we would have equality in religion and education within five years.'[35] Many MPs had expressed approval of his letter. 'Since I came into personal contact with them, I have learned fully to appreciate the mischief done by systematic *denunciation* in Irish politics, and I have often congratulated myself that I earned the reproach, cast upon me by the *Nation*, of being "too amiable".'

The force of Dillon's argument was evident on 27 April when all but three of the independent opposition members supported the government on the second reading of the reform bill and the ministry surivived with a majority of five votes. Their decision has been interpreted as marking 'the effective inauguration in parliament of that phase of alliance with the liberals which eventually produced disestablishment'.[36] At a meeting of the association on 26 May Dillon said it would be 'fatal to let pass an opportunity for forming an honourable alliance, not with a government but with a great and powerful party, whose interests and sympathies are in the main identical with our own'.

When the government published its Irish tenant bill he asserted that if it was passed 'leases or compensation would become the law'. He confided to Adelaide (14 May): 'My heart is literally broken writing letters chiefly defending the tenant bill. ... I am so fagged.' He promised to make the speech which she had suggested. The *Dublin Evening Mail* caricatured Dillon as 'Mr Gladstone's Irish tail'; while the *Nation* accused him of sliding, like O'Connell, into a whig alliance (at a time when the difference between 'liberal' and 'whig' was blurred).[37]

Dillon spoke during the second reading of the Tenure and Improvement of Land (Ireland) Bill on 17 May,[38] supporting his case for land reform by quoting from Edmund Burke and John Stuart Mill. He tried to persuade Irish landlords that they had nothing to fear from the bill; claims for compensation would arise only in the event of eviction. But he could not refrain from pointing out that special legislation was necessary for Ireland because Britain had placed 'a proprietory of one race and one religion over a peasantry of another race and another religion'.

In his own speech Mill recognised the significance of a British administration introducing an Irish land bill into parliament; nothing which any government had yet done—not even Catholic emancipation—'has shown so true a comprehension of Ireland's real needs, or has aimed so straight at the very heart of Ireland's discontent and of Ireland's misery'.[39] The house had a golden opportunity for reconciliation, he said. 'When I think how small a thing it is which is now asked of us ... I confess I am amazed that those who have suffered so long and so bitterly are able to be conciliated or calmed by so small a gift.' There was nothing in the proposed measure 'so alarming that we need be afraid to try, as an experiment, what is so ardently wished for by a country to which we owe so much reparation that she ought to be the spoilt child of this country for a generation to come—to be treated not only with justice but with generous indulgence.'

At a meeting of the association Dillon recommended that, in the event of the bill being rendered worthless by the House of Lords, tenant farmers should form an agricultural union:

> Such a union, extending into every parish in Ireland, ruled by a committee sitting in Dublin, acting strictly within the law, aiming at nothing but justice, enforcing its rules by no deeds of violence, but by the same species of moral sanction which secures obedience of the rules of trades' unions—such a union would, in my opinion, as in the opinion of the London *Times*, set the question of tenant right in Ireland at rest speedily and for ever.[40]

Before the debate on the second reading of the land measure could be resumed, however, the liberals were defeated on 18 June when the opposition carried an amendment to the reform bill. Faced with a resumption of tory rule, Dillon wrote characteristically: 'Irish prospects here look now so gloomy that I feel half-tempted to give the thing up.' Although the land bill for which he had striven so hard was withdrawn, Dillon need not have been so despondent because 'from then on the expectations of the Irish rose'.[41]

He returned to London with a number of other Irish MPs to oppose the continued suspension of habeas corpus sought by Lord Derby's ministry on 2 August. In his speech he noted that the Habeas Corpus Act had been suspended five times in Ireland since the Union. 'So inveterate was the habit of passing these coercive laws for Ireland, that he feared the simple request of the government for unconstitutional powers would be considered a sufficient reason for granting them. During the sixty five years that had elapsed since the legislative union, not one had passed in which some law had not been enacted for the curtailment of the liberties of the Irish people.'[42]

Dillon observed that the tories wanted to have it both ways. They had opposed the land bill mainly on the ground that it was special legislation for Ireland. The Irish people would not be dragooned into loyalty; discontent could be removed by implementing the wise, generous policy recommended by his colleague, John Francis Maguire. The Fenian conspiracy had been exaggerated by the apprehensions of the gentry and the 'officious loyalty' of the police. He paid tribute to those landlords 'with whose honest and zealous efforts on behalf of the Irish tenantry it was my privilege in the course of the present session to co-operate'; nevertheless, the average Irish country gentleman was a man who would 'ride twenty miles to a meeting of guardians for the purpose of preventing a Catholic schoolmaster from being appointed to teach Catholic paupers'.

In a passage omitted from the *Hansard* record, Dillon concluded his last speech in the House of Commons:

> I trust—not whig or tory—but the English people. I believe their instincts are sound and generous; I believe their cause is our cause; I believe they would do us justice if they could. The speeches delivered by their trusted leaders in this house during the present session have sunk into the heart of Ireland, and awakened there a hope to which it had long been a stranger—the hope that Irish freedom is not incompatible with British connexion. If I understand those declarations they hold out a promise that Ireland shall be ruled with a regard to the requirements of its social condition, and in accordance with the opinion and convictions of its people. These are not the principles avowed by the present government. They promise no concession. The millions who till the soil are to be retained in servile dependence and insecurity. The church of the minority shall remain the church of the state. The church of the people shall be officially insulted and defamed. In all things, not our will but their will shall be law, and that law shall be enforced through the old machinery of jailors, policemen and spies. And this being so, I appeal to the liberal members who hear me, not to arm them with special powers against—not a conspiracy, which is extinct, but against that discontent which is the natural and just result of the misgovernment in which they are resolved to persist.[43]

During a two-day debate in Dublin corporation later in August 1866 Dillon maintained that, while the crisis was exaggerated, in so far as Fenianism contemplated the overthrow of the government it 'had extensive sympathy from the people'. The *Nation* proclaimed that 'home rule' was once more at the head of Irish demands.[44]

Glasnevin

The key to liberty is love. It leads us
out of earthly into heavenly life.
BETTINA VON ARNIM TO GOETHE

Dillon was at the height of his powers when, having embarked on an auspicious parliamentary career, he died suddenly.

On the Sunday before his death he told a church meeting in Glasthule, County Dublin, that the condition of Catholics had improved 'thanks to the patriotic efforts of their forefathers—thanks to the great O'Connell, and the people who sustained him through his long and arduous struggle. Thanks also to the liberality and justice of a large section of the English people. But much remained to be done still.'

Dillon contracted cholera which was rampant in Dublin; his fatal illness started with a cold on Wednesday; by Friday his doctor held out no hope of recovery. 'He raved of Ireland on his death-bed', according to the *Nation*, and expired at 8.20 p.m. on Saturday, 15 September.[1] Adelaide would inform Duffy: 'John's death was as beautiful as his life—calm, perfectly resigned—sustained by firm and lively faith. It is all my consolation to think he is with God.'[2]

Dr R.R. Madden, who heard Dillon speak at the wooden chapel in Glasthule, was present at his end in Druid Lodge:

> He was a man indeed most worthy of being loved and honoured. He had the happiest combination of intellectual gifts, of social qualities, of manly, earnest, straightforward views, of tolerant opinions, of kindly feelings, all the gentleness of a woman's nature in alliance with the firmness of a character constituted for the accomplishment of heroic purpose. He loved his country well, but he loved his religion better. He was a lawyer and a sound one, he was a liberal in the true sense of the word, but he did not think it ungenteel or unprofessional, or unworthy of acceptance in what is called good society, either Catholic or Protestant, to make any

apologies for being, as the French say, *foncièrement Catholique.*
John Dillon thought it one of the greatest blessings of his life to
possess a firm faith in all the doctrines of his church. ...[3]

His funeral was an exercise in Victorian necrophilia. At noon on
Monday a hearse and four horses bearing black plumes received the body,
which was enclosed in an oak coffin lined with cedar and lead. The 'sad
cortege—monster procession' extended over one and a half miles, and
from Baggot street 100 carriages followed it to Glasnevin cemetery.
However, according to one correspondent the long line of carriages could
not compare 'with the spontaneous gathering of the sons of toil, upon
whose brawny shoulders he was lovingly borne into the mortuary chapel
and from thence to the grave' near the O'Connell tower.[4]

Prominent mourners included: John Martin, James Cantwell, James
Haughton, Sir Colman O'Loghlen, MP; Sir John Gray, MP; Major
Laurence Knox, founder of the *Irish Times*; and Sir William Wilde. On
Wednesday seventy priests assisted at requiem high Mass attended by a
'vast congregation' in the pro-cathedral. Cullen performed his first office
for the dead since becoming the first Irish cardinal in June.[5]

At a special meeting of Dublin corporation, A.M. Sullivan said Dillon's
public career had been characterised by an 'intense desire to cause men to
sink their differences for the sake of the country'. The lord mayor-elect,
William Lane Joynt, wrote from the Burren in north Clare, where he was
land agent to Lord Annaly, proposing a memorial fund: 'I only knew
Dillon since his return from America; but I have never known a more
gentle, well-informed or refined person—one more thoroughly moderate
in his political views, and tolerant of those of others. His devotion to the
interests of his country rendered his attention to professional pursuits
impossible.'[6] (It is possible that Lane Joynt heard about Dillon's '48
exploits from Father Ryder, who had sheltered him at his house in
Glenfort, outside Ballyvaughan.)

From London the Reform League expressed 'its deep sympathy with
the family of the deceased and with Ireland in the loss they have sustained'.[7] The last letter Dillon received was a note from John Bright
accepting an invitation to a banquet in Dublin in October.[8] The dinner
went ahead despite his death. Bright (who believed ultimately that Irish
nationalism must be contained in the interests of Britain and its empire)
said: 'I had not the pleasure of a long acquaintance with Mr Dillon, but ...
during the last session of parliament I formed a very high opinion of his
character. There was that in his eye and in the tone of his voice—in his

manner altogether—which marked him for an honourable and a just man. I venture to say that his sad and sudden removal is a great loss to Ireland.'[9] He told Adelaide during a visit of sympathy: 'I never saw a man make the same way in the same time; he did not speak much but everyone felt he was an able man.'

The London *Times* noted admiringly that Dillon had been returned to parliament without expense, and said he was trusted by the Roman Catholic bishops more than any other politician since O'Connell.[10]

The *Irish Times* said: 'By those who differed with him in political views he was sincerely respected for the candour and independence which distinguished his public character and for the gentlemanly tone of his address.' As a member of Dublin corporation Dillon was 'an earnest advocate of sanitary reform and works of public utility. In private life the deceased gentleman was greatly beloved for the amiability and benevolence of his disposition.'[11]

'The great advance made by the land question during the last session' was due principally to Dillon, Gray acknowledged in his *Freeman's Journal*.[12] Its leading article stated:

> No man will hesitate to say that there is not left either in the association or in the Irish representation a man who combined all the qualities possessed by John Dillon—the gentleness of manner—the practised skill as a speaker—the readiness as a writer—the persuasive firmness, and the unbounded confidence of all the members of his party in his honour, in his zeal and in his singleness of purpose. These qualities enabled him to keep men together, and to bring them to sink minor differences for the sake of a great public purpose. Patient and conciliatory in council, Mr Dillon won men round to his views, or banished hostile dissent without exciting the envy and jealousy of any person, and every man who took part in Irish parliamentary politics looked forward to the time when, by the gradual exercise of the qualities which won the confidence of friends and the respect of foes, he would be able to cement the Irish representatives into a compact united mass, able to enforce good measures for the country and to resist bad ones. ...
>
> The gifted and gentle member for Tipperary, whose ambition it was to live to carry out a good tenant-right bill—who laboured assiduously to frame that bill—who did so much to induce the late

government to accept that bill—and in this success but indicated the future triumphs which the exercise of the same patient, laborious work could achieve—now rests from his labours. ...

The *Nation* appeared with black borders (as it had done when Davis, O'Connell and O'Brien died). Dillon, it recalled, was 'the most undemonstrative of men. His qualities were not for show; and with all his splendid attainments and his intellectual superiority, he was to the last as simple, as guileless, as unostentatious as a child'.

> None of his contemporaries resembled Davis in manner and character more than Dillon did; and as in life the friends were so much alike, so it has happened that in death their fate has been much the same. Like Davis, Dillon has fallen suddenly and unexpectedly on the threshold of what promised to be a great, an active and a useful career; and, as in the case of Davis, all creeds and parties amongst Irishmen have been fused in grief for his loss. ...
>
> In 1848 he was amongst the last to yield to the resistless current of wild enthusiasm that, much against his protests, swept the Irish Confederation from his original foundations. But they who judged his protests to be the utterances of pusillanimity little knew the man and ... it was remarked of him that his whole nature seemed transformed as the peril grew the greater. He who in council had been calmest, was the boldest and most daring in the field. ... He proceeded to Tipperary ... utterly against his judgment, but resolved not to flinch as the issue had been forced upon the country. His worst anticipations, his own frequent warnings, were soon verified. In a few weeks the chief he loved and followed was a prisoner, and he himself, with many a gallant comrade, was a fugitive with a price on his head. But not all the gold that England offered could prevail upon the noble peasantry of Munster to betray the proscribed chiefs. ... In New York Mr Dillon was joined by his wife; that devoted, brave-hearted young heroine wife, the history of whose adventures during the period of his outlawry in August, September and October 1848 leaves romance far behind.[13]

On returning to Ireland, the *Nation* continued, Dillon resisted entreaties to re-enter public life after the disillusionment of his early career: 'but every day it was felt more keenly that Ireland had too much need for such a man'. In parliament he was an able but not a brilliant speaker; 'he had a horror of clap-trap ...'

He was a man of deep and earnest religious feeling; not osten-
tatiously indeed but, withal, scrupulously and edifying attentive to
the practices of faith. He had the most generous toleration for the
conscientious convictions of his fellow-men, whether in harmony
or at variance with his own; but he viewed with utter distrust and
aversion the man who disregarded or condemned religion. With
him liberality did not mean indifference, nor did earnestness mean
bigotry; and there could be no more fitting tribute to his character
in this respect than that afforded by the sight of the Protestant
minister and the Catholic priest of the parish in which he had
resided following his coffin.

The *Dublin Evening Post* asserted: 'Unlike so many, however, who, in
parting with the illusions of their patriotism, part also with the substance
of it, the experiences of John Dillon's early miscalculations served only
to enable him to comprehend the case of Ireland without any illusions, and
to understand it in all its difficulties and all its realities.' It added: 'He had
learned to restrict his efforts to the attainment of the possible. ... He has
taught us all by example how possible it is to conduct political argument
and to carry on political contests without the personal antagonisms which
have been so marked and so repelling a feature of public life in Ireland.'[14]

The *Ulster Observer* said in hope: 'Goodness like his survives great-
ness, and remains not only in history and tradition, but in the affections of
the people.'

The *Clare Journal* commented that as a public speaker Dillon
'hesitated—not from a lack of words, but because of thoughts, strong and
gushing. The power of the scholar, the orator and the writer was felt when
he warmed with his subject, and few ever heard him speak that were not
charmed with the natural simplicity of his manner.'[15]

John O'Hagan wrote in the *Kilkenny Journal* that his death was a
calamity to Ireland. Dillon was 'cut off in the prime of manhood when his
hopes were highest, and when the sorrows and trials of a chequered life
seemed to have passed away, and a career of honour and usefulness was
opening to him in the service of the country he loved so well'.[16] During a
short parliamentary career 'his hand, his head, his heart were in everything
that could promote the prospects and happiness of his country; yet there
was no ostentation, no display, but that humility which shows the true
worker as well as the true patriot.'

O'Hagan revealed that in the summer of 1865 'at least a dozen
invitations from counties and boroughs, seeking the honour of his name
and services, summoned him from the retirement of his happy home to

undertake the duties of public life and struggle once more for his native land.'

Duffy would write: 'The same courage which placed him in the front of the barricade at Killenaule, without a spark of fanaticism to blind him to the peril, enabled him to do his duty' in parliament. At the time he confided to Adelaide that her husband's death had altered his long-term plan of retiring to Ireland.[17]

> Never since the death of Thomas Davis did I hear news as disastrous and appalling as that which awaited me on landing ... [in Melbourne]. There remained but one man in whom I trusted for any sustained and unwavering attempt to obtain concessions for Ireland—and that man was a friend whom for more than 20 years I loved, because I never saw the taint of selfishness or deceit in any act or thought of his; with whom I never had a moment's difference, because his sweet and generous nature and transparent sincerity made it impossible to misunderstand him. ... May heaven console you, my dear Mrs Dillon, or at least sustain you under a burden so hard to bear.

John Pigot wrote from Bombay, where he was practising at the bar: 'It is as I knew it would be. God gives you full *power*, as it is promised. There is *nothing* in this world that all *can* not bear, and in full cheerfulness, by his grace. And God be thanked you are evidently granted it in full.'[18]

John Mitchel told her: 'I have known in my time many good men, but one nobler, more generous-hearted, more pure and gallant than John Dillon I never knew—never hope to know.' Mitchel wrote to his brother, William: 'The death of John Dillon is a real and bitter sorrow to me. There were few men of his type in the world. He was all wrong, about almost everything. Nevertheless, he was better than most folk who are all right.'[19]

Adelaide observed to Duffy: 'Is it not a strange fate, the three men still alive who, having known John well, could best have told others what he was are in three different quarters of the globe—India, Australia, America: John Pigot, you and John Mitchel. Characteristic too of John that you three, who in many things have differed, have all united in the same deep sorrow over his grave.'[20]

In his recent study Professor Emmet Larkin concluded that Dillon had leadership qualities in abundance: courage, integrity, energy, determination and intelligence. ...[21] Dillon's friend, John Martin, wrote: 'His personal influence was already great and was fast growing greater'; he would probably have become a considerable power in Irish politics.

Dillon had foreseen that Martin's attempt to revive the repeal agitation through the National League would fail abjectly. Martin added that since his death The O'Donoghue had 'gone over formally to the English side. No wonder the poor Fenians so pant for revolution to clear our political atmosphere.'[22]

The diarist O'Neill Daunt summed up Dillon as

> a good Catholic and an excellent Irishman. A few days' illness hurried him off—so frail is our hold on life. He will be much missed, not only on private but on public grounds. Earnest in his religious belief, he was full of tolerance for all sectarians. He saw as clearly as possible the mischief to Ireland resulting from sectarian divisions, and would have neutralised that mischief in the only effectual way—by abolishing every scrap and vestige of the ascendancy of any one body of religionists over any other, thus establishing the perfect political equality of all. His place will not be speedily filled.

Archbishop Leahy told Daunt that 'Dillon has not left his like behind'.[23]

Denis Florence MacCarthy wrote a poem in his memory, the twelfth (and final) verse of which reads:

> Enough, that in thy death, as in thy life,
> To them and us thou'rt still a guiding star;
> Thou leav'st thy country widowed as thy wife—
> Thy friends made orphans as thy children are.

Three years later Adelaide lost her next dearest companion, her daughter Rose, who died of consumption, aged twenty. She recorded the keening of two women who comforted her in Ballaghaderreen.[24] She resolved to be sister and mother to her sons after the death of 'so sweet, so sensible, so clever and good an elder sister'.

Mitchel wrote from Brooklyn on 30 November 1870:[25]

> You do not think I have been indifferent all this time to your great trials and troubles, any more than you have been to those of me and mine. I am so bad a correspondent that there is really no hope of me—although I greatly admire such people as John Martin (for example) who keep friendship alive by constant and conscientious correspondence. He gives a great deal of pleasure by this to a wide circle of friends in many parts of the world.

Many thanks, dear Mrs Dillon, for your cordial letter and the photograph enclosed. Of course I cannot recognise in the portrait of your son 'Jack' any likeness to the little boy I knew of old: but can well recognise in it the impress of both father and mother. Ano[ther] very fine photograph I have to thank you for—that of John Dillon himself, brought to me three years ago by a clergyman. It is indeed precious to me and all my household, and is itself a most admirable likeness recalling vividly the noblest head I ever saw. And he was my friend, if I ever had a friend.

Thank you also for the copy of your son Willie's inaugural address before the Catholic University. This I have read with surprise but a highly agreeable kind of surprise—not surprise at the talent and elegance and the evidence of a deep and thoughtful nature, but at the bold stand which he makes against the 'spirit of the age', a most pestilent spirit indeed. If I thought he had ever read my own address delivered at the University of Virginia, I might flatter myself that he had got some ideas from *me*. ...[26]

You name two old friends of mine as still feeling an interest in us—John O'Hagan and John Pigot. I am glad to hear that they remember us kindly, though in the case of J. O'H. I scarcely expected that. We have been severed so widely, though gradually—it is like the slow kind of severance described in Jean Ingelow's poem, 'Divided'. I suppose we shall never meet again, but whatsoever may be our public and political differences, it is grateful to me to receive a word from him, through you, recalling old friendship. Pray ask him, when you see him, if he remembers our walk in Donegal. But I am sure he does. ...[27]

As to that continuation of MacGeoghegan, it is a book that requires to be rewritten—but I never have time even to *write*, let alone rewrite.[28] It is very defective, and nobody is so well aware of its defects as I am. Yet as a kind of summary of the history for a century and a half it is more satisfactory than any *single* book on the subject. I wish I could take just one year to make it right. The villain of a publisher here ruined it with a bad index.

My wife wrote to you on hearing of the death of your dear daughter, Zoë—but never expected any answer under such circumstances. She desires to send you her most affectionate love. ...

Adelaide died aged forty four and was buried with her husband in Glasnevin. The inscription on their tombstone contains much truth: 'This Irish cross is dedicated to the memory of John B. Dillon, member of parliament for the county of Tipperary, whose life was one of single-minded and unfailing devotion to the cause of Ireland. Born 5 May 1814, died 15 September 1866. With his honored name is united that of his dear wife, Adelaide Dillon, who in love of country and deep religious faith was one heart and one soul with him. She died 29 May 1872.'

Subsequently, Anne Deane, remembering her uncle's kindness, 'looked on his children as her own'.[29] John Dillon would commission Patrick Pearse's father to erect a monument to her in Strade, County Mayo.[30] William O'Hara had provided for the boys' education.

William Dillon went to Colorado to avoid succumbing to tuberculosis. He wrote the authorised biography of Mitchel, whose militant nationalism captured the imagination of young John Dillon.[31] The third son, Henry, was called to the bar. He practised for a short time and then became a Franciscan—Father Nicholas—renowned for his commitment to the vow of poverty.[32]

In common with most of his associates at the time, John Blake Dillon did not realise the enormity of the Great Famine. Nineteenth century intellectuals tended to be preoccupied with theories rather than people. Nevertheless, Dillon's unsigned articles in the *Nation* 'made a deep impression on the more thoughtful of his readers'.[33] Two decades later he was moved to act with the bishops by conditions which had produced 'forced, unprepared and excessive emigration'.[34] But the National Association failed to capture the popular imagination, Dillon being the only eminent layman to identify fully with it. Nonetheless, the land bill of 1866 reversed the presumption in law that improvements were the landlord's property.

Dillon made a remarkable impression during one year in parliament. His performance influenced Gladstone's reshaping of Irish policy and left its mark on that statesman's reforming ministry of 1868-74. His strategy of supporting the new liberal leadership proved dramatically successful.[35] Although not a systematic thinker, he outlined ideas which would be implemented under Parnell, ably assisted by John Dillon, *fils*.

The permanent legacy of John Blake Dillon lies more in his personality and principles than in his achievements. He was in the highest sense of the term a gentleman. He had a rare gift for making and keeping friends. He was a man of large mind: serious but not solemn. Sometimes 'melancholy mark'd him for her own'.

The rights Dillon sought for Catholics he claimed for all the Irish people. He worked to establish friendship between the peoples of Ireland and Britain. He had a mind that could lift him above national limitations and provide a vision of the oneness of humankind.

Politics ended in mysticism for Dillon. After his death a correspondent suggested that Adelaide might commune with him in the spirit of God.[36] His 'extraordinary conformity and abandonment to God's holy will, without regrets for the work he had so successfully begun ... show the perfection of a soul that merits ... immediate union with God after death'.

Shortly before he died Dillon wrote a meditation, 'Words of a believer',[37] in which he affirmed that all people were created equal and that, through unity, the oppressed would inaugurate an era of universal brotherhood. 'The man who says in his heart: I am not like other men but other men have been given to me that I may rule them and that I may dispose of them and all that is theirs at my pleasure: that man is a son of Satan. And Satan is the king of this world for he is the king of all those who think and act in this way; and those who think and act in this way have made themselves by his counsels the masters of the world.'

God 'commanded men to love one another that they might be united and that the weak might not fall beneath the oppression of the strong'. Towards the end of his *pensées* Dillon confronted the problem of evil:

> My soul was sad and hope went forth from it. ... And God sent a deep sleep upon me. And in my sleep I saw as if a luminous form standing before me, a spirit whose look sweet and searching penetrated to the bottom of my most secret thoughts. ... And the spirit said to me, 'why are thou sad'. And I replied weeping: 'Oh behold the evils which prevail throughout the earth.'
>
> And the divine form smiled with ineffable sweetness and this word came to my ears. 'Thine eye seeth all things through a deceitful medium which men call time. Time exists only for you. With God there is no time.'
>
> And I was silent for I did not understand. Suddenly the spirit said, 'behold' ... I saw at once that which men in their weak and faltering language call the present, the future and the past. ... And the entire human race appeared to me as one man. And this man had done much that was evil, little that was good; had experienced a great deal of grief and but little of joy.
>
> And there he lay in his distress on a soil at one time frozen, at another time burning. ... And behold a ray of light came forth from the east and a ray of love from the south and a ray of strength from the north. And these three rays united upon the heart of that man. And when the ray of light came forth a voice cried: 'Son of God, brother of Christ, know that which you ought to know.'
>
> And when the ray of love came forth a voice cried: 'Son of

God, brother of Christ, love those whom you ought to love.' And when the ray of strength came forth a voice cried: 'Son of God, brother of Christ, do that which ought to be done.' And when the three rays had united the three voices also united and there was formed of them a single voice which cried: 'Son of God, brother of Christ, serve God and serve but him alone.'

And then what had seemed to me up to that time as one man appeared to me as a multitude of peoples and of nations. ... And those peoples and those nations awakening on their bed of anguish began to say: 'Whence come our sufferings and our weakness and the hunger and the thirst which afflicts us and the chains which bind us to the ground and enter into our flesh.' And their understanding was opened and they felt that the sons of God, the brethren of Christ, had not been condemned by their father to slavery and that this slavery was the source of all their ills.

Each of them tried to break his chains but none succeeded. And they regarded each other with great pity, and love acting within them they cried: 'We have all the same thought; why should we not have all the same heart? Are we not all the sons of the same God and brothers of the same Christ? Let us love ourselves or die together.'

And having said this they felt within them a divine strength and I heard their chains crack, and they fought for six days against those who had bound them and on the sixth day they were victorious and the seventh was a day of repose. And the earth which was withered resumed its verdure and all might eat of its fruits and go and come without anyone saying to them: 'Whither are you going? You pass not here.'

And the little children gathered flowers and carried them to their mother who smiled sweetly on them. And there were neither poor nor rich, but all possessed in abundance what supplied their wants because all loved one another and assisted one another like brothers.

Dillon's reflections are encapsulated in the neo-Platonic triad of faith, love and knowledge. They are redolent of Christian socialism and of the poet, Adam Mickiewicz, who saw Poland fulfilling a messianic role among the nations of Europe by her self-sacrifice and eventual redemption.

Notes

INTRODUCTION

1   R.V. Comerford, 'Representation at Westminster, 1801-1918; in William Nolan (ed.), *Tipperary: history and society* (Dublin, 1986), p. 331.
2   Charles Gavan Duffy, *Four Years in Irish history, 1845-1849* (London, 1883), p. 95n.
3   H.G. Schenk, *The mind of the European romantics* (London, 1966), pp 152-3.
4   Duffy to Adelaide Dillon, December 1867 (this recently-discovered letter is now with the rest of the Dillon papers in Trinity College, Dublin).
5   Duffy, *Young Ireland* (2 vols., London, 1896 ed.), i, pp 38-9.
6   Adelaide Dillon memoir (TCD, Dillon Papers, MS 6457e).
7   Thomas N. Brown, *Irish-American nationalism, 1870-1890* (New York, 1966), p. 18.
8   Cecil Woodham-Smith, *The great hunger* (New American Library ed., 1964), p. 262.
9   Kerby A. Miller, *Emigrants and Exiles: Ireland and the Irish exodus to North America* (Oxford, 1985), p. 295.
10 Cullen to Monsignor Tobias Kirby, 30 September 1866 (Dublin Diocesan Archives).
11 Gearóid Ó Tuathaigh, *Ireland before the Famine, 1798-1848* (Dublin, 1972), pp 204, 206.
12 See pages 182-3.

CHAPTER ONE

1   Adelaide Dillon memoir.
2   F.S.L. Lyons, *John Dillon: a biography* (London, 1968), p. 1.
3   Interview with James Dillon, 18 April 1984. James Dillon believed that Luke Dillon was descended from a younger son of a Viscount Dillon who married a local Catholic (interview with Mrs Maura Dillon, 10 January 1987).
4   Registry of Deeds Office: 325-433-224630, 418-158-27288, 419-325-274168, 682-506-469679.
5   Ibid.: 564-188-388-377273, 125-104-8364.
6   NLI MS P5312 lists two Luke Dillons in the Loughglynn Cavalry; Burke's *Irish Family Records* (1976).
7   Adelaide Dillon memoir.
8   Leon Ó Broin, *An Maidíneach* (Baile Átha Cliath, 1971), p. 124.
9   Dublin University Calendar, 1842.
10 Lyons, *Dublin*, p. 2; *Ireland since the Famine* (London, 1971), p. 94.
11 Charles Gavan Duffy, *Thomas Davis: the memoirs of an Irish patriot 1840–1846* (London, 1890), p. 64; Denis Gwynn, *Young Ireland and 1848* (Cork, 1949), p. 4.
12 John Dillon, *An address read before the Historical Society, Dublin Institute, at the close of the session 1840–41* (Dublin, 1842).
13 T.W. Moody, *Thomas Davis, 1814–45* (Dublin, 1945), p. 9.
14 Duffy, *Four years*, p. 100.
15 Brian Inglis, *The freedom of the press in Ireland, 1741–1841* (London, 1954), p. 227.

16   Moody, *Davis*, p. 25.
17   Duffy, *Davis*, p. 52.
18   Duffy, *Young Ireland*, i. p. 30.
19   Dillon to Davis, n.d. (RIA, Duffy papers, MS 12P151(3)); Leon Ó Broin, *Charles Gavan Duffy—Patriot and Statesmen—the story of Charles Gavan Duffy 1816–1903* (Dublin, 1967), p. 7.
20   Quoted by R. Dudley Edwards, 'The Contribution of Young Ireland to the development of the Irish national idea' in *Feilscríbhinn Torna* (Cork, 1947), pp 124-5; *Irish Citizen*, 7 Mar. 1868.
21   Duffy, *Young Ireland*, p. 30.
22   Duffy, *Davis*, p. 72.
23   Adelaide Dillon memoir.
24   Duffy, *Young Ireland*, p. 32.
25   *Nation* prospectus in Thomas Davis: *Essays and poems, with a centenary memoir* (Dublin, 1945), p. 13.
26   Ó Tuathaigh, *Ireland before the Famine*, p. 186.
27   R.B. McDowell, *Public opinion and government policy in Ireland, 1801–1846* (London, 1952), p. 231; Liam de Paor, *The peoples of Ireland* (London, 1986), p. 241.
28   Duffy, *Young Ireland*, pp 132-3; *Irish Citizen*, 7 Mar. 1868.
29   Moody, *Davis*, p. 36.
30   Donal A. Kerr, *Peel, priests and politics: Sir Robert Peel's administration and the Roman Catholic Church in Ireland, 1841–1846* (Oxford, 1982), pp 233-5.
31   Ibid., pp 4, 87, 330-31.
32   Moody, *Davis*, pp 36-7.
33   R. Dudley Edwards (ed.), *Ireland and the Italian Risorgimento* (Dublin, 1960), pp 31, 53; Kevin B. Nowlan, *The politics of Repeal: a study in the relations between Great Britain and Ireland, 1841–50* (London, 1965), p. 9.
34   Oliver MacDonagh, *States of mind: a study of the Anglo-Irish conflict, 1780–1980* (London, 1983), p. 76; Kevin B. Nowlan, 'The meaning of repeal in Irish history' in *Historical Studies*, iv (London, 1963), p. 8.
35   Moody, *Davis*, p. 46.
36   Lyons, *Dillon*, p. 4.

CHAPTER TWO

1   Kevin McGrath, 'Writers in the "Nation", 1842-5' in *Irish Historical Studies*, vi (1949), pp 205-6, lists 50 articles; Dillon also wrote a leading article on the Dungarvan election (11 July 1846); the National Library collection, MS 3656, is incomplete.
2   T.F. O'Sullivan, *The Young Irelanders* (Tralee, 1944), p. 41.
3   *Nation*, 22 Oct. 1848.
4   Ibid., 10 Dec 1842.
5   'Ubi solitudinem faciunt, pacem appellant.'
6   The Quaker, Richard Webb, observed that Mayo people 'made no battle for their lives' but displayed 'an extraordinary amount of patient endurance' (Miller, *Emigrants and exiles*, p. 310).
7   *Nation*, 3 Dec. 1842.
8   Ibid., 31 Dec. 1842.
9   Ibid., 24 Dec. 1842.
10   Ibid., 28 Jan. 1843.
11   Quoted in Miller, *Emigrants and exiles*, p. 241.
12   *Nation*, 19 Nov. 1842.
13   Moody, *Davis*, p. 50.

14 De Paor, *The peoples of Ireland*, p. 236.
15 Duffy, *Young Ireland*, i, p. 63; *Nation*, 31 Dec. 1842.
16 *Nation*, 26 Nov. 1842.
17 Ibid., 7 Jan. 1843.
18 Ibid., 17 Dec. 1842.
19 Ibid., 5 Nov. 1842.
20 Ibid., 19 Nov. 1842.
21 *Nation*, 4 Feb. 1843; Dillon to Davis, 21 Mar. [1844] (NLI, Davis papers, MS 2644/47).
22 Kevin B. Nowlan and Maurice R. O'Connell (eds.), *Daniel O'Connell: portrait of a radical* (Belfast, 1984), p. 14.
23 McDowell, *Public opinion and government policy*, p. 240.
24 *Nation*, 11 Feb. 1843.
25 Ibid., 19 Nov. 1842, 14 Jan. 1843.
26 Kerr, *Peel, priests and politics*, p. 92.
27 Nowlan, *The politics of repeal*, p. 49.
28 *Nation*, 7 Jan. 1843.
29 Ibid., 26 Aug. 1843.
30 Ibid., 5 Aug. 1843.

CHAPTER THREE

1 MacDonagh, *States of mind*, p. 58, 'The contribution of O'Connell' in Brian Farrell (ed.), *The Irish parliamentary tradition* (Dublin 1973), p. 166; Maurice R. O'Connell, 'O'Connell, Young Ireland and violence' in *Daniel O'Connell: the man and his politics* (Irish Academic Press, 1990), p. 68.
2 Daniel Murray to John Hamilton, 13 Oct. 1843, quoted in Kerr, *Peel, priests and politics*, p. 91. Murray was harping back to 1014.
3 *Nation*, 14 Oct. 1843; Nowlan, *Politics of repeal*, p. 52.
4 Dillon's club membership card was among the papers found recently by the family. Now in the National Museum, Dublin, it has inscriptions such as 'Volunteers of 1782 revived' and 'Repeal Year 1843', and engravings ranging from Brian Boru to O'Connell.
5 *Nation*, 18, 25 Mar. 1848.
6 Moody, *Davis*, p. 35.
7 NLI, Duffy papers, MS 5756/ pp 31-6.
8 Davis to John Pigot, 24 Mar. 1844 (*Irish Monthly*, May 1888).
9 Duffy, *Davis*, p. 197; *Four years*, pp 20-21.
10 Pigot to Davis, 13, 18 Sept. [1844] (NLI, Davis papers MS 2644/425).
11 See Griffith's biographical notes for his 1913 edition of John Mitchel's *Jail Journal*.
12 Davis to Pigot, 24 Mar. 1844, *op. cit.*
13 De Paor, *Peoples of Ireland*, pp 241-3, 251.
14 Pigot to Davis, 18 Sept., *op. cit.*
15 Kerr, *Peel, priests and politics*, p. 120.
16 Paradoxically, as the college began to supply more priests the population started to decline. In 1834 the ratio of diocesan clergy to the Catholic population was 1:2,985; by 1861 it had shrunk to 1:1,783. (Ibid., p. 353).
17 Ibid., pp 309-11.
18 Denis Gwynn, *O'Connell, Davis and the Colleges Bill* (Cork, 1948), p. 64; Duffy, *Young Ireland*, ii, p. 174.
19 *Nation*, 17 May, 14 June 1845.
20 K. Theodore Hoppen, *Elections, politics and society in Ireland, 1832-1885* (Oxford, 1984), p. 333.
21 Moody, *Davis*, p. 42.

22 Duffy, *Young Ireland*, ii, p. 162; O Broin, *Duffy*, p. 24.
23 Dillon to O'Brien [n.d.] (NLI, W.S. O'Brien papers, MS 434/1302).
24 MS 2644.
25 In December Duffy edited a collection of Davis's essays dedicating it to 'John B. Dillon, his dear and trusted friend and mine' (Davis, *Literary and historical essays*, Dublin, 1845); in *Young Ireland*, ii, pp 211-12, Duffy did not transcribe accurately: see MS 5756/129.
26 Adelaide Dillon memoir; Lyons, *Dillon*, p. 5; William Dillon, *Life of John Mitchel* (2 vols, London, 1888), i, p. 87; P.J. Hooper's note for a biography of J.B. Dillon (Dillon papers, MS 6908).
27 Duffy, *My life in two hemispheres* (2 vols, London, 1898), i, p. 126; *Young Ireland*, ii, p. 212.
28 Dillon papers, MS 6457/512.
29 See my article, 'Mitchel letter throws new light on capture of Tone', *Irish Times*, 30 May 1986. This letter, dated 17 Dec. 1845, is the only part of the Mitchel-Dillon correspondence known to have survived.
30 *Nation*, 6 June 1846. Davis had assigned biographical projects to members of the *Nation* group.
31 William Wilde (Oscar's father) considered the climate would do more to ward off consumption, or arrest it in the incipient stages, than any he knew of (Terence de Vere White, *The parents of Oscar Wilde* (London, 1967), p. 42).
32 Extract from Dillon's journal preserved by his wife (MS 6457e).
33 Dillon to Jane McDonagh, 18 May 1846.
34 Duffy, *Four years*, p. 198.
35 Nowlan, 'The meaning of repeal in Irish history', pp 9, 13; MacDonagh, *States of mind* p. 78; Maurice O'Connell, 'O'Connell, Young Ireland and violence', *op. cit.*, pp 82-88.
36 Quoted in my brief monograph, *John Mitchel* (Dublin, 1978), p. 18.

CHAPTER FOUR

1   Lyons, *Ireland since the Famine*, pp 195-6; Nowlan, *Politics of Repeal*, p. 110.
2   Nowlan, 'The meaning of repeal in Irish history' in *Historical Studies*, IV, p. 14; 'The Catholic clergy and Irish politics', ibid., IX, p. 130.
3   John Saville, *1848: The British state and the Chartist movement* (Cambridge, 1987), p. 69.
4   De Paor, *Peoples of Ireland*, p. 243; Woodham-Smith, *Great Hunger*, pp 59, 165.
5   Helen Burke, *The people and the poor law* (Women's Education Bureau, 1987), p. 30.
6   Woodham-Smith, *Great Hunger*, p. 145.
7   Nowlan, *Politics of repeal*, p. 119.
8   Ibid., pp 130, 136.
9   Woodham-Smith, *Great Hunger*, p. 314.
10 Nowlan, *Politics of repeal*, p. 219.
11 W.E. Vaughan, *Landlords and tenants in Ireland, 1848-1904* (Economic and Social History of Ireland, 1984), p. 16.
12 Mary E. Daly, *The Famine in Ireland* (Dublin Historical Association, 1986), p. 110; *Returns by provinces and counties of cases of evictions which have come to the knowledge of the constabulary, 1849-80*, HC, 1881 (185), LXXVII.
13 MacDonagh, *States of mind*, p. 36.
14 Woodham-Smith, *Great Hunger*, pp 150-51; Nowlan, *Politics of repeal*, p. 165.
15 Saville, *The British state and the Chartist movement*, p. 6.
16 MacDonagh, 'Irish emigration …' in R.D. Edwards and T.D. Williams (eds.), *The Great Famine* (Dublin, 1956), p. 336.
17 Saville, *op. cit.* pp 4, 95.
18 Edwards and Williams (eds.), *Great Famine*, p. 179.
19 Woodham-Smith, *Great Hunger*, p. 160.

20 Ó Tuathaigh, *Ireland before the Famine*, pp 220-21.
21 *Times*, 12 Dec. 1876.
22 Woodham-Smith, *Great Hunger*, pp 99, 146.
23 John Pigot to William O'Hara, 31 Mar. 1847 (Dillon Papers, MS 6455/30).
24 Dillon to Duffy [n.d.] (Duffy papers, MS 5756/265).
25 Haughton's epitaph in Mount Jerome cemetery, Dublin, reads: 'A follower of Christ he did his best. He was a well-known advocate of universal freedom, peace and temperance.'
26 McDowell, *Public opinion and government policy*, p. 256.
27 *Nation*, 5 Dec. 1846; *Proceedings of the Young Ireland party at their great meeting in Dublin, 2 December 1846, with a correct report of the speeches and resolutions* (Belfast, 1847).
28 Duffy, *Four years*, p. 334.
29 S.H. Bindon to Smith O'Brien, quoted in Gwynn, *Young Ireland and 1848*, p. 94.
30 G.A. Hayes McCoy, *History of the Irish flags from earliest times* (Dublin, 1979), p. 145.
31 *Nation*, 12 Dec. 1846.
32 Ibid., 19 Dec. 1846; W.J. Fitzpatrick (ed.), *Correspondence of Daniel O'Connell* (2 vols., London, 1888), ii, pp 391, 395.
33 Gwynn, *Young Ireland and 1848*, p. 94.
34 Dillon to O'Brien, 10 Dec. [1846] (O'Brien papers, MS 434/1, 298).
35 Dillon to O'Brien, 11 Dec., MS 434/1, 299.
36 *Nation*, 28 Nov. 1846.
37 Ibid., 12 Dec. 1846.
38 Dillon to O'Brien, [n.d.], MS 434/1, 300.
39 Richard Davis, *The Young Ireland movement* (Dublin, 1987), p. 114.
40 Dillon to O'Brien, 19 Dec. 1846, MS 434/1, 301.
41 *Nation*, 26 Dec. 1846.
42 Gwynn, *Young Ireland*, p. 93; *Nation*, 2 Jan. 1847.
43 L. Fogarty, *James Fintan Lalor, patriot and political essayist* (Dublin, 1919), p. 5.
44 *Nation*, 16 Jan. 1847. George Henry Moore was elected MP for Mayo in 1847. Henceforth, his interests alternated between politics and racing. George Moore remarked: 'Nobody but Archbishop MacHale was allowed punch in my father's house.' (*Hail and Farewell*, 1985 ed., p. 69.)
45 Nowlan, *Politics of repeal*, pp 127, 139.
46 See my 'John Mitchel: the great contradiction', *Irish Times* 1 February 1983.
47 Maurice R. O'Connell, 'John O'Connell and the Great Famine' in *Irish Historical Studies*, xxv (1986), p. 140.
48 *Nation*, 6 Mar. 1847.
49 Gwynn, *Young Ireland*, p. 138; Duffy, *Four years*, p. 506.
50 Dillon to O'Brien, 11 Dec. 1846; [n.d.], MSS 434/1, 299, 440/2,168.
51 Dillon to O'Brien, 3 Jan. 1848, MS 441/2,347.
52 Davis, *Young Ireland movement*, p. 121; *Irish Citizen*, 7 Mar. 1868.
53 Duffy, *Four years*, p. 364.
54 Dillon to Duffy, 7 Aug. 1847 (Duffy papers, MS 5757/47).
55 *Nation*, 28 Aug. 1847.
56 Gwynn, *Young Ireland*, p. 115.
57 Nowlan, *Politics of repeal*, p. 42.
58 William O'Hara to James O'Hara, 20 May 1853 (Dillon papers, MS 6456/239). Appropriately, this affair was in Cahir House, Feakle, in the countryside associated with the Rabelaisian poet, Brian Merriman.
59 Adelaide Hart to Dillon, 2 Aug. 1847 (Dillon papers, MS 6455/43).
60 Ibid., 14 Aug. 1847, MS 6455/52. As the Dillon correspondence in Trinity College, Dublin, is excellently catalogued, henceforth letters between John and Adelaide in MSS 6455-7 will generally be identified by the date in parenthesis.
61 MS 6457e. The important letter, MS 6455/34, was not transcribed correctly.

62 Ibid. This valuable section is missing from the letters. It was probably lost in transmission to Duffy, who used it in *Four years*, pp 424-5.
63 Nowlan, *Politics of repeal*, 181; Davis, *Young Ireland movement*, p. 147.
64 Dillon to O'Brien, [n.d.], MS 440/2,101.
65 John to Adelaide Dillon (Duffy papers, MS 5758/pp 9, 86).

CHAPTER FIVE

1   Lyons, *Ireland since the Famine*, p. 98.
2   *Nation*, 8 Jan. 1848.
3   Lyons, *Ireland since the Famine*, p. 98; Duffy, *Four years*, p. 549; W.J. Lowe, 'The Chartists and the Irish Confederates: Lancashire, 1848' in *Irish Historical Studies*, xxiv (1984), p. 174.
4   Duffy, *Four years*, p. 542.
5   *Nation*, 4 Mar. 1848.
6   *United Irishman*, 4 Mar. 1848.
7   *Freeman's Journal*, 1 Mar. 1848.
8   Dillon to William O'Hara, [n.d.], MS 6455/61b.
9   Meagher to Dillon, MS 6455/83; *Nation*, 11 Mar. 1848.
10 Ibid., 4 Mar. 1848.
11 Nowlan., *Politics of Ireland*, p. 182.
12 D.N. Petler, 'Ireland and France in 1848' in *Irish Historical Studies*, xxiv (1985), pp 495-6.
13 NLI, Larcom papers, MS 7698.
14 Saville, *The British state and the Chartist movement*, p. 94.
15 MS 6455/61b; *Nation*, 11 Mar. 1848.
16 Ibid., 11 Mar. 1848.
17 Ibid., 18 Mar. 1848.
18 *Nation*, 25 Mar. 1848; Davis, *Young Ireland movement*, p. 150; Nowlan, *Politics of repeal*, p. 184; Saville, *British state and Chartist movement*, p. 92.
19 MS 6457b; *Nation*, 25 Mar. 1848.
20 *Nation*, 25 Mar. 1848.
21 Saville, *op. cit.*, p. 102.
22 Petler, 'Ireland and France in 1848', p. 493.
23 Nowlan, *Politics of repeal*, pp 187-91; Saville, *op. cit.*, p. 80.
24 Saville, *op. cit.*, p. 87; Petler, 'Ireland and France in 1848', p. 499.
25 Petler, 'Ireland and France in 1848', p. 499.
26 Ibid., p. 497.
27 Ibid., p. 503; Nowlan, *Politics of repeal*, pp 189- 91, 'The meaning of repeal in Irish history', p. 11.
28 Petler, *op. cit.*, pp 501-2.
29 D. Thomson and M. McGusty (eds.), *The Irish journals of Elizabeth Smith* (Oxford, 1980), pp 175-6.
30 McCoy, *History of Irish flags*, pp 144-5.
31 In 9 D'Olier Street, Dublin, which today forms part of the *Irish Times* complex.
32 *Tipperary Vindicator*, 5 April 1848.
33 *Nation*, 8 April 1848.
34 Ibid.
35 *Limerick Reporter* quoted in *Nation*, 15 April 1848.
36 *Journals of Elizabeth Smith*, p. 182.
37 Quoted in Saville, *British state and Chartist movement*, p. 104.
38 Cecil Woodham-Smith, *Queen Victoria: her life and times* (2 vols, London, 1972), i, pp 288-9; Saville, *British state and Chartist movement*, pp 120, 126.
39 Ibid., p 74, 120, 125; Lowe, 'Chartists and Irish confederates', p. 177.

40 Cf. A.L. Le Quesne, *Carlyle* (Oxford, 1982), p. 81; G.D.H. Cole, *Chartist portraits* (London, 1941), pp 331-3.
41 Saville, *op. cit.*, pp 162, 202, 223; Lowe, *op. cit.*, pp 182, 186.
42 Saville, *op. cit.*, pp 111, 126.
43 *Hansard* (3rd series), xcviii, cols. 73-102.
44 *Nation*, 6 May 1848.
45 Davis, *Young Ireland Movement*, p. 154.
46 Gwynn, *Young Ireland*, p. 180.
47 *Journals of Elizabeth Smith*, p. 185.
48 Woodham-Smith, *Great Hunger*, p. 341.
49 Michael Cavanagh, *Memoirs of Gen. Thomas Francis Meagher* (Massachusetts, 1892), p. 191; *Nation*, 13 May 1848.
50 *Nation*, 11 Jan. 1868.
51 Duffy, *Four years*, p. 595; Woodham-Smith, *Great hunger*, p. 342.
52 Duffy, *Four years*, p. 608; Woodham-Smith, *Great hunger*. p. 343.
53 *Nation*, 3 June 1848.
54 Nowlan, *Politics of repeal*, p. 203; *Nation*, 3 June 1848; Lowe, 'Chartists and Irish confederates', p. 177; Saville, *British state and Chartist movement*, pp 131-8.
55 *Journals of Elizabeth Smith*, pp 185, 187.

CHAPTER SIX

1 Edwards, 'The contribution of Young Ireland to the development of the Irish national idea', p. 133.
2 Philip Fitzgerald, PP, *Personal recollections of the insurrection at Ballingarry in July 1848* (Dublin, 1861), p. 6.
3 Saville, *British state and Chartist movement*, p. 161.
4 Duffy, *Four years*, pp 644-5.
5 Meagher's narrative (slightly abridged), appendix 1, Gwynn, *Young Ireland*, pp 275-98.
6 Michael O'Farrell, O'Brien's junior counsel after his arrest, recorded this statement (TCD MS 9786/27). O'Brien would write in 1857: 'The fact was that I had long been fully convinced that resistance to the British parliament was the duty of every Irishman, but I had been extremely anxious to avert, as long as possible, a collision on account of the terrible and uncertain hazards of such a strife, and it was not until the Irish nation had been deprived of the right of trial by jury, by the suspension of the Habeas Corpus Act (of which proceeding I first became apprised when I was in the county of Wexford), that I resolved finally to call upon the people to take up arms in open resistance to misgovernment' (Dillon papers, MS 6456/328).
7 Gwynn, *Young Ireland*, p. 297; Philip Fitzgerald, *A narrative of the proceedings of the Confederates in '48, from the suspension of the Habeas Corpus Act to the final dispersion at Ballingarry* (Dublin, 1868), p. 26.
8 Duffy, *Four years*, p. 608.
9 Ibid., p. 609; Nowlan, *Politics of repeal*, p. 209.
10 Duffy, *Four years*, p. 560; *My life*, i, p. 278. 'Mr O'Flaherty was sent to America to purchase arms and ammunition and to bring them with officers and volunteers and land them on the western Irish coast' (Patrick O'Donoghue's account of 1848, NLI MS 770, p. 21).
11 O'Hagan to Dillon, Christmas 1848 (NLI MS 5758/104); Duffy, *Four years*, pp 639, 693.
12 Ibid., p. 612; Nowlan, *Politics of repeal*, p. 206; Davis, *Young Ireland movement*, p. 156.
13 *Nation*, 24 June 1848.
14 Davis, *Young Ireland movement*, p. 157.
15 *Nation*, 24 June 1848.
16 Duffy, *Four years*, p. 618.

17 Ibid., p. 619.
18 Woodham-Smith, *Great hunger*, p. 343; Saville, *British state and Chartist movement*, p. 96.
19 Duffy, *Four years*, p. 632.
20 *Nation*, 8 July 1848.
21 J.G. Hodges, *Report of the trial of William Smith O'Brien for high treason at the special commission for the County Tipperary, held at Clonmel, September and October 1848* (Dublin, 1849), p. 817.
22 Davis, *Young Ireland movement*, p. 160; Cavanagh, *Memoirs of Meagher*, p. 238; Nowlan, *Politics of Repeal*, p. 211.
23 *Times*, 24 July 1848.
24 Nowlan, 'The political background' in *Great Famine*, p. 203.
25 Quoted in Saville, *British state and Chartist movement*, p. 157.
26 Herbert Maxwell, *The life and letters of George William Frederick, 4th earl of Clarendon* (London, 1913, 2 vols), i, p. 289.
27 'To suppress the rebellion of 1798 the castle entered into an informal alliance with the Orangemen.' (Donal McCartney, *The dawning of democracy: Ireland 1800-1870*—Dublin, 1987—p. 35.)
28 Saville, *British state and Chartist movement*, pp 152, 154, 156.
29 Duffy, *Four years*, pp 641-2; Robert Kee, *The green flag: a history of Irish nationalism* (London, 1972), pp 276-7.
30 Gwynn, *Young Ireland*, pp 318-21.
31 Ibid., p. 281; Michael Doheny, *The felon's track* (Dublin, 1951 ed.), p. 290.
32 Letters from Dillon and his wife, 20, 26 July 1849.
33 *Irish Felon*, 22 July 1848.
34 Gwynn, *Young Ireland*, p. 284.
35 Hodges, *Report of the trial of O'Brien*, p. 133.
36 Duffy, *Four years*, p. 646.
37 Woodham-Smith, *Great hunger*, p. 347.
38 Gwynn, *Young Ireland*, pp 242, 298; Desmond Ryan, *The Fenian chief: a biography of James Stephens* (Dublin, 1967), pp 8-13.
39 Meagher's narrative, *op. cit.*
40 Ryan, *Fenian chief*, pp 14-15.
41 *Freeman's Journal*, 1 Aug. 1848; Gwynn, *Young Ireland*, pp 247, 252; Duffy, *Four years*, p. 651.
42 K. Theodore Hoppen, 'National politics and local realities in mid-19th century Ireland' in *Studies in Irish history presented to R. Dudley Edwards*, A. Cosgrove and D. McCartney (eds., Dublin, 1979), p. 195; *Tipperary Vindicator*, 5 Aug. 1848.
43 Mayor John Luther to the under-secretary, Thomas Redington: 'I have committed the boys to gaol for further examination at next court day' (SPO, Outrage reports, Tipperary, 1848, 27/1327, 2352).
44 Outrage reports, 27/1435, 1437; *Tipperary Vindicator*, 5 Aug. 1848.
45 Duffy, *Four years*, p. 658.
46 Outrage reports, 27/1410, 1534, 1599.
47 *Times*, 31 July 1848.
48 Duffy, *Four years*, p. 661.
49 Fitzgerald, *Personal recollections*, p. 14.
50 Duffy, *Four years*, p. 662.
51 Thomas G. McAllister, *Terence Bellew MacManus* (Maynooth, 1972), p. 12.
52 Duffy, *Four years*, p. 664.
53 James Stephens, *Irishman*, 11 Mar. 1882.
54 *Annual Register*, 1848, p. 409; Hodges, *Report of the trial of O'Brien*, p. 354.
55 *Irishman*, 1 April 1882.
56 Duffy, *Four years*, p. 666; John Devoy, *Recollections of an Irish rebel* (Shannon, 1969 ed.),

p. 267.
57   Thomas Dwyer to Smith O'Brien, 10 Sept. 1858 (NLI MS 446/3064).
58   Duffy, *Four years*, p. 667.
59   Ibid.
60   O'Donoghue narrative [28 Aug. 1848], MS 770, p. 25; *Irishman*, 18 Mar. 1882.
61   Duffy, *Four years*, pp 667, 678.
62   Woodham-Smith, *Great Hunger*, p. 354; Fitzgerald, *Narrative of proceedings of the Confederates*, pp 28-31.
63   Duffy, *Four years*, pp 526, 628.
64   Denis Gwynn, 'Father Kenyon and Young Ireland' in *Irish Ecclesiastical Record* (1949), p. 226ff; Duffy, *Four years*, pp 669-70.
65   T.C. Luby, *Irish Nation*, New York, 25 Feb. 1882.
66   Duffy, *Four years*, p. 671n.
67   Doheny, *Felon's track*, p. 152.
68   Fitzgerald, *Narrative of proceedings of the confederates*, pp 23-4.
69   Father Fitzgerald quoted in Gwynn, *Young Ireland*, p. 253.
70   Hodges, *Report of the trial of O'Brien*, p. 475.
71   *Times*, 1 Aug. 1848; *Freeman's Journal*, 31 July 1848.
72   *Tipperary Vindicator*, 12 Aug. 1848.
73   Kee, *The green flag*, p. 284.
74   Duffy, *Four years*, pp 682-88. According to Trant, who claimed to have averted a general rising, six insurgents were killed and thirteen wounded (NLI MS 4325).
75   Fitzgerald, *Narrative of proceedings of the Confederates*, pp 24-9.
76   Larcom papers, MS 7698.
77   Hodges, *Report of the trial of O'Brien*, pp 455-62.
78   *Tipperary Vindicator*, 12 Aug. 1848.
79   McAllister, *MacManus*, p. 23.
80   Duffy, *Four years*, p. 666.
81   Gwynn, *Young Ireland*, p. 270.
82   McGee's 'narrative' in Doheny, *Felon's track*, pp 289-97.
83   *Times*, 31 July 1848.
84   *Freeman's journal*, 5 Aug. 1848. Nowlan, *Politics of repeal*, p. 216.
85   Fitzgerald, *Narrative of proceedings of the confederates*, p. 26.
86   Woodham-Smith, *Great Hunger*, pp 363, 378.
87   O'Brien prepared but did not deliver a speech from the dock (Gwynn, *Young Ireland*, pp 227-38); *Annual Register*, 1848, p. 410.
88   Patrick O'Donoghue's account of 1848 (NLI MS 770, pp 19-20); John O'Mahony's narrative of the attempted rising (MS 868, pp 10, 12).
89   Duffy, *Four years*, p. 687.
90   Tom Garvin, *The evolution of Irish nationalist politics* (Dublin, 1981), p. 52.
91   *Tipperary Vindicator*, 2 August 1848.
92   NLI MS 464, p. 133.
93   John to Adelaide Dillon, 12, 19 Dec. 1848 (TCD MSS 6455/75, 76).
94   MSS 6457d, e.
95   I am indebted to Professor Dillon and Elgy Gillespie for this information.
96   *Kilkenny Journal*, 9 Aug. 1848.
97   E.G. Ryan, RM, to Redington, 1 Aug. 1848 (Outrage reports, Galway, 11/679).
98   Philip Orrusly, Aran dispensary, to Redington, 27 Sept. 1848 (Outrage reports, 11/768); P.A. Ó Síocháin, *Aran: islands of legend* (Dublin, 1962), p. 173.
99   MS 6455/68; Irish Catholic Directory, 1849.
100 John to Adelaide Dillon, 6 Aug. 1849 (MS 6455/128).

CHAPTER SEVEN

1 Séamus Ó Duilearga a bhailigh agus a chuir in eagar, Dáithí Ó hÓgáin a chóirigh (Comhairle Bhéaloideas Éireann, 1981). 'An old man who was born and reared in Glínn Mheáin told me a long time ago that the father of John Dillon was taken out from a rock in Glínn Mheáin in a currach—that is the father of the man we call Honest John Dillon—and that he went from there on board a vessel. He went everywhere in priest's clothes. And there was a priest in Ballyvaughan named Father [Patrick] Ryder and it was his suit he wore until going ashore at New York quay, if that was where he landed.'
  I am indebted to Dr Ó hÓgáin for this reference from folklore. I am also grateful to Father William Rooney, PP, for helping to locate Glínn Mheáin in Craggagh: Derreen, south of Fanore. Mr James Dillon told me shortly before his death that while in Chicago in 1923 he was approached by an old Clare man, named Pat Behan, who told him: 'My father pulled an oar for your grandfather.'
2 O'Sullivan, *Young Irelanders*, p. 256. Dillon's choice of pseudonym was ironic. James Hughes, PP, Claremorris, was among the clergy who denounced the rebels 'as the enemies of order, religion and country' (Duffy, *Four years*, p. 693).
3 A.M. Sullivan, *New Ireland* (London, 1877), p. 99; *Irish Citizen*, 7 Mar. 1868.
4 William O'Hara, Ghent, 25 Aug. 1848, to C.T. Hart (MS 6455/67).
5 MS 6464 (typescript 6906).
6 Meagher presented an autographed copy of his speech to 'Mrs John Dillon' (MS 6455/109).
7 Nowlan, *Politics of repeal*, p. 216.
8 Blanche M. Touhill, *William Smith O'Brien and his Irish revolutionary companions in penal exile* (University of Missouri Press, 1981), p. 10.
9 Ó Broin, *Duffy*, p. 67.
10 Moira Lysaght, *Father Theobold Mathew: the apostle of temperance* (Dublin, 1983), p. 41.
11 Richard Ellmann, *Oscar Wilde* (London, 1987), p. 8.
12 O'Cathaoir, 'Smith O'Brien's retribution' in *North Munster Antiquarian Journal*, xxvii (1985).
13 Hart journal, p. 33.
14 Ibid., p. 82.
15 John O'Leary, *Recollections of Fenians and Fenianism* (2 vols, Shannon 1969 ed.), i, p. 72.
16 Clarendon to Sir George Grey, 4 Feb. 1849, quoted in Nowlan, *Politics of repeal*, pp 215-6n.
17 Letters from Dillon to his wife, MSS 6455/76, 90.
18 Dillon to his wife, n.d., MS 6455/88.
19 Ibid., 3 Mar. 1849, MS 6455/94.
20 O'Sullivan, *Young Irelanders*, p. 40; *Irish Citizen*, 7 Mar. 1868.
21 O'Hagan to Dillon, Christmas 1848 (Duffy papers, MS 5758, p. 105).

CHAPTER EIGHT

1 John to Adelaide Dillon 25 Nov. 1851, MS 6456/168.
2 Ibid., 10 April 1849, MS 6455/99.
3 Hart journal, p. 58.
4 Dillon to McGee, 22 May 1849, MS 6455/107 a, b.
5 John to Adelaide Dillon, Brooklyn, 7 May 1849, MS 6455/104.
6 Duffy, *My life*, ii, p. 6.
7 Lucas, an English Catholic convert, was the founder of the *Tablet* journal.
8 Ó Broin, *Duffy*, p. 90.
9 John to Adelaide Dillon, 7 July 1849, 2 July 1851, MSS 6455/123, 6456/148a.
10 MS 6462a. In all probability Meagher left the tricolour sash, later preserved by the Dillon family, with his admirers in Druid Lodge.

11 John to Adelaide Dillon, 25 July 1851, MS 6456/152.
12 See page 28.
13 John to Adelaide Dillon, c. July 1849, MS 6455/127; Woodham-Smith, *Great hunger*, p. 390.

CHAPTER NINE

1 Friedrich Schlegel, a German Catholic philosopher, maintained women had a greater propensity for religion and poetry then men, and that lovers should be intellectually congenial.
2 Walter S. Sanderlin, 'Galway as a transatlantic port' in *Éire-Ireland*, v (1970), p. 20.
3 John to Adelaide Dillon, 5 Aug. 1851 (MS 6456/154a).
4 See the author's 'Terence Bellew MacManus: Fenian precursor' in *Irish Sword*, xvi (1985).
5 Terence Bellew MacManus to R.J. Tyler, Philadelphia, 14 July 1851 (Dillon papers, MS 6456/150).
6 *Nation*, 21 Feb. 1852.
7 I am indebted to Dr Blanche Touhill for this reference.
8 John Cussen, 'William Smith O'Brien in Van Diemen's Land, 1849-54' in *Old Limerick Journal*, 23 (1988), p. 81.
9 O'Brien, New Norfolk, VDL, to Dillon, 23 Nov. 1852 (MS 6456/220).
10 Dillon to O'Brien, 12 Dec. 1852 (NLI MS 445/2841).
11 John to Adelaide Dillon, 22 July 1851 (MS 6456/207).
12 *Nation*, 17 Jan. 1852.
13 John to Adelaide Dillon, 20 Dec. 1851 (MS 6456/172).
14 Ibid., 5 Jan. 1852.
15 Ibid., 23 Jan. 1852.
16 A.M. Sullivan watched them go and asked: 'What were they fitted for? Many of them had never seen a town of 10,000 inhabitants; and in a large city, even in their own country, they would be helpless and bewildered as a flock of sheep on a busy highway. ... Landing in such masses, everything around them so strange, so new, and sometimes so hostile, they inevitably herded together, making a distinct colony or "quarter" in the city where they settled. Destitute as they were, their necessities drove them to the lowest and most squalid lanes and alleys of the big towns. At home in their native valleys poverty was free from horrors that mingled with it here' (*New Ireland*, pp 125-6).
17 O'Hagan to Dillon, n.d. (MS 6456/175).
18 *Irish-American*, 27 Mar. 1852.
19 John to Adelaide Dillon, 30 Nov. 1852 (MS 6456/221).
20 Gordon N. Ray (ed.), *The letters and private papers of William Makepeace Thackeray* (London, 1946), iii, p. 228.
21 *Citizen*, 1 July 1854.
22 Dictionary of American Biography.
23 *Citizen*, 22 July 1854.
24 *Irish-American*, 15, 29 Jan. 1853.
25 Dillon to Martin O'Flaherty, 18 Jan. 1853 (Dillon papers, recent acquisition).
26 In 1851 the Irish bishops appealed for funds to launch the Catholic University and raised £18,000. (Emmet Larkin, *The consolidation of the Roman Catholic Church in Ireland, 1860-1870* (University of North Carolina Press, 1987), p. 13.)
27 MS 6456/318a.
28 John to Adelaide Dillon, n.d. (MS 6456/234).
29 Doheny, New York, to O'Brien, 20 Aug. 1858 (NLI MS 446/3058).
30 John Boyle O'Reilly quoted in the author's 'John O'Mahony, 1815-1877' in *Capuchin Annual* (1977).
31 John Mitchel, *Jail Journal* (Sphere ed., 1983), pp 278, 280, 349.
32 *Citizen*, 6 May 1854.

33 Smyth to Kevin O'Doherty, 28 Feb. 1856 (Dillon papers, MS 6457h/10).
34 Dillon to O'Brien, 9 Oct. 1858 (O'Brien papers, MS 447/3141).
35 MSS 447/3139, 3140.
36 W. Dillon, *Mitchel*, ii, p. 58.
37 Adelaide Dillon to Charles Hart, 4 Dec. 1854 (MS 6456/269).
38 Duffy, *Four Years*, p. 764n; *Irish Monthly*, xiv (1886), p. 624.
39 Duffy, *My life*, ii, p. 61.
40 John to Adelaide Dillon, 6 Nov. 1855 (MS 6456/308).

CHAPTER TEN

1   Sullivan, *New Ireland*, p. 303.
2   *Nation*, 12 July 1856; *Old Limerick Journal*, no. 23 (1988), p. 81.
3   Newman's address to medical students, November 1858.
4   See author's 'Smith O'Brien retribution', *op. cit.*, pp 70-4.
5   Michael Davitt, *The fall of feudalism in Ireland* (New York, 1904), pp 73-4.
6   Joseph Denieffe, *A personal narrative of the Irish Revolutionary Brotherhood* (Irish University Press ed., 1969), p. 15; Devoy, *Recollections*, p. 19.
7   Dillon to Stephens, 11 Jan. 1858 (Dillon papers, MS 6456/331).
8   O'Leary, *Recollections*, i, p. 13, ii, p. 22n; Duffy, *My life*, ii, p. 266; Ryan, *Fenian chief*, p. 102; R.V. Comerford, *The Fenians in context* (Dublin, 1985), p. 50; Justin McCarthy, *Ireland since the union* (London, 1887), p. 155.
9   Dillon to O'Brien, 27 Aug. 1858 (not 1856 as incorrectly identified, NLI MS 445/2928).
10 Duffy, *Four years*, p. 771n.
11 Dillon to Moore, 11 Mar. 1861 (NLI, Moore papers, MS 894/679).
12 Dillon to Moore, 13 June 1861, Martin to Moore, 13 Dec. 1861 (MSS 894/689, 696).
13 O'Brien to Moore, 4 Jan. 1862 (MS 894/698). See Martin's copy of Mitchel's address (MS 894/697).
14 Smyth to Moore, 27 Mar. 1863 (MS 894/726).
15 *Nation*, 14 Feb. 1863.
16 Ibid., 21 Mar. 1863.
17 *Limerick Chronicle*, 4 July 1863.
18 *Nation*, 25 April 1963.
19 John Blake Dillon, *Report on the state of the public accounts between Ireland and Great Britain* (Dublin, 1882).
20 Dillon to O'Brien, 23 Jan. 1864 (O'Brien papers, MS 8657).
21 O'Brien to Dillon, 16 Jan. 1863 (Dillon papers, MS 6457/339).
22 *Nation*, 25 June 1864.
23 SPO, Fenian police reports 2, 1864, 28/1-4, 31/1; Touhill, *William Smith O'Brien*, p. 229.
24 P.A. Sillard, *The life and letters of John Martin* (Dublin, 1901), p. 174.
25 Larkin, *Consolidation of Catholic Church in Ireland*, p. 54.
26 Cullen to Archbishop Spalding of Baltimore, 2 Nov. 1864 (Dublin Diocesan Archives—DDA).
27 J.H. Whyte, *The Tenant League and Irish politics in the 1850s* (Dublin Historical Association, 1963), p. 17.
28 Dillon to Bishop Laurence Gillooly, 19 Dec. 1864 (Gillooly papers, NLI microfilm). He had supported mixed education in 1845, cf. p. 28.
29 Sillard, *John Martin*, pp 165, 172.
30 *Nation*, 13 Aug. 1864; *Irish Times*, 26 Feb. 1970.
31 *Freeman's Journal*, 16 Sept. 1873. I am indebted to Dr C.J. Woods for drawing this to my attention.
32 Larkin, *Consolidation of Catholic Church*, p. 290; Comerford, *Fenians in context*, p. 105.

33 O'Neill Daunt journal, 5 Nov. 1864 (NLI MS 3041).
34 Guest-house register, 18-21 Nov. 1864. Father Patrick Ryan, OCSO, helped with this discovery.
35 Larkin, *Consolidation of Catholic church*, p. 291; E.R. Norman, *The Catholic Church and Ireland in the age of rebellion, 1859-1873* (London, 1965), pp 139-40.
36 *Nation*, 26 Nov. 1864.
37 Gillooly to Dillon, 30 Nov. 1864 (Gillooly papers). At Cullen's suggestion an organising committee had been formed comprising Cullen, Dillon, McSwiney and Alderman Richard Devitt.
38 *Dublin Evening Post*, 21 Feb. 1865.
39 Larkin, *Consolidation of Catholic Church*, pp 305, 312.
40 Ibid., p. 314.
41 Moore to Dillon, 13 Feb. 1865; Dillon to Moore, 15 Feb. 1865 (Moore papers, MSS 894/728, 729); Dillon to Cullen, 16 Feb. 1865 (DDA).
42 Larkin, *Consolidation of Catholic Church*, p. 316; David Thornley, *Isaac Butt and home rule* (London, 1964), pp 42, 44, 55, 89-91; J.H. Whyte, *The independent Irish party, 1850-9* (Oxford, 1958), p. 154ff.
43 E.D. Steele, *Irish land and British politics: tenant-right and nationality, 1865-1870* (Cambridge, 1974), p. 19.
44 *Report and proceedings from the select committee on tenure and improvement of land (Ireland) act.* HC, 1865 (402), xi, clauses 1,598, 1,805, 2,092-2,102.
45 Ibid., clauses 1,833, 1,896-7, 2,155.
46 Larkin, *Consolidation of Catholic Church*, pp 337-8; Patrick J. Corish, 'Cardinal Cullen and the national association of Ireland' in *Reportorium Novum*, iii (1962), pp 35-6.
47 *Nation*, 1 July 1865.

CHAPTER ELEVEN

1 *Freeman's Journal*, 19 April 1866.
2 *Daily News*, 31 Jan. 1866.
3 O'Hagan to Adelaide Dillon, 19 Feb. 1865 (Dillon papers, MS 6457/347).
4 Dillon to Gillooly, 3 Mar. 1866 (Bishop Gillooly papers, NLI microfilm P7622).
5 Ibid., 19 Dec. 1864.
6 Ian Ker, *John Henry Newman: a biography* (Oxford, 1988), pp 417, 461; Larkin, *Consolidation of Catholic Church*, pp 364, 367. The 'pecuniary position' of the university was the reason given for postponing the development of the law faculty (minutes of board meetings on 23 June 1865 and 24 Oct. 1866, Catholic University records, vol. 3, Archives Department, University College, Dublin).
7 Quoted in Larkin, *Consolidation of Catholic Church*, p. 358.
8 Dillon to Gillooly, 12 July 1865.
9 *Irish People*, 15 July 1865.
10 Ibid., 22 July 1865.
11 Duffy, *My life*, ii, pp 268-9.
12 Thomas Clarke Luby to John O'Leary, 20 April 1892 (NLI, Luby papers, MS 331-3); Michael J. Lennon, 'In the footsteps of the Fenians', *Irish Independent*, 22 Nov. 1956.
13 *Irish People*, 22 July 1865.
14 *Nation*, 22 July 1865.
15 Ibid., 29 July 1865.
16 Duffy, *My life*, ii, p. 269; NLI MS 894/731.
17 Larkin, *Consolidation of Catholic Church*, p. 363.
18 Daunt journal, 5 Dec. 1865.
19 *Freeman's Journal*, 24 Jan. 1866.

20   *Dublin Evening Mail, Saunders' News-letter*, 24 Jan. 1866.
21   John to Adelaide Dillon, n.d. [21 Feb. 1866] (MS 6457/364).
22   W. Dillon, *Mitchel*, ii, p. 236.
23   John O'Hagan to Adelaide Dillon, 19 Feb. 1865 (MS 6457/347).
24   John to Adelaide Dillon, 20 Feb. 1866 (MS 6457/351)
25   John to Adelaide Dillon, n.d. [9 February 1866] (MS 6457/366).
26   *Hansard*, 181:701-4.
27   Dillon to Cullen, 5 Feb. 1866 (DDA).
28   *Nation*, 24 Mar. 1866.
29   Larkin, *Consolidation of Catholic Church*, p. 377.
30   *Dublin Evening Post*, 24 Mar. 1866. Dillon thought 'it would be a great gain to get the law
     on the side of the improving tenant, and to place the landlord in the position of being obliged
     to evade or defeat the law whenever he desired to commit an act of injustice or oppression'.
31   J.B. Dillon and Tristram Kennedy wrote to Gladstone twice on 22 Feb. 1866 (BL Add. MSS
     44,409 ff 213, 216. I am indebted to Eugene J. Doyle, MA, for this reference.)
32   John to Adelaide Dillon, 7 Mar. 1866 (MS 6457/352).
33   R.D. Collison Black, *Economic thought and the Irish question, 1817-1870* (Cambridge,
     1960), p. 50.
34   *Freeman's Journal*, 19 April 1866.
35   Dillon to Cullen, 21 April 1866 (DDA).
36   Comerford, *Fenians in context*, p. 142.
37   John to Adelaide Dillon, n.d. MSS 6457/359, 365; *Dublin Evening Mail*, 26 May 1866;
     Nation, 2 June 1866; Larkin, *Consolidation of Catholic Church*, pp 384, 386.
38   *Hansard*, 183:1097-1102. Dillon's bill was entitled: 'A Bill further to amend the law relating
     to the Tenure and Improvement of Land in Ireland.'
39   *Hansard*, 183:1087.
40   *Freeman's Journal*, 26 May 1866.
41   John to Adelaide Dillon, n.d. [19 June 1866] (MS 6457/363); E.D. Steele, *Irish land and
     British politics*, p. 70.
42   *Hansard* 184:1969-71.
43   *Dublin Evening Post*, 4 Aug. 1866.
44   *Nation*, 18 Aug. 1966.

CHAPTER TWELVE

 1   *Nation*, 22 Sept. 1866.
 2   Quoted in Ó Broin, *An Maidíneach*, p. 318-9.
 3   Adelaide Dillon to Duffy, 16 Feb. 1867 (MS 6457/378).
 4   A meeting of tradesmen in County Clare passed a motion identifying with the large number
     of Dublin workers who attended Dillon's funeral (*Irishman*, 22 Sept., 6 Oct. 1866).
 5   *Kilkenny Journal*, 19 Sept. 1866.
 6   *Irish Times*, 22 Sept. 1866.
 7   *Freeman's Journal*, 24 Sept. 1866; George Howell, secretary, to Adelaide Dillon, 4 Oct. 1866
     (MS 6457/376).
 8   John Bright, Rochdale, to Dillon, 1 Sept. 1866 (MS 6457/372).
 9   Quoted in McCarthy, *Ireland since union*, p. 165.
10   *Times*, 18, 20 Sept. 1866.
11   *Irish Times*, 17 Sept. 1866.
12   *Freeman's Journal*, 17 September 1866.
13   *Nation*, 22 Sept. 1866.
14   *Dublin Evening Post*, 17, 20 Sept. 1866.
15   *Clare Journal*, 20 Sept. 1866.

16 *Kilkenny Journal*, 19 Sept. 1866.

17 *Four years*, p. 771; Gavan Duffy to Adelaide Dillon, 23 Nov. 1866 (MS 6457/377).

18 John Pigot to Adelaide Dillon, 27 Sept. 1867 (MS 6457/383).

19 Dillon, *Mitchel*, ii, pp 249, 262.

20 Adelaide Dillon to Duffy, 16 Feb. 1867, *op. cit.*

21 Larkin, *Consolidation of Catholic Church*, p. 356.

22 John Martin, Rostrevor, to Eva O'Doherty, 24 Feb. 1867 (MS 6457h).

23 Daunt journal, 17 Sept., 2 Oct. 1866.

24 'An chuslah ma chrie och och hone [a chuisle mo chroí ... och ochón]. Sure she's in heaven—sure it's happy for you—she's with God and the B. Virgin and her own father alanna—ocoo musha musha [a leanbh ... och ú ... muise, muise]. Sure we'll be *all together in heaven soon*, with the blessing of God and the help of the Blessed Virgin.' (MS 6457/399).

25 This letter from John Mitchel to Adelaide Dillon is in the author's possession. The Mitchels had lost an eldest daughter also and two of their three sons were killed in the American war.

26 Cf. Mitchel's *Jail Journal*, pp 391-4. Adelaide wrote the 'great part' of her sons's inaugural address to the Literary and Historical Society (MS 6457/410).

27 Cf. 'Ulster in the summer of 1845' by 'Slieve Gullion', *Irish Monthly*, 1913, for O'Hagan's diary of his walk with Mitchel, Duffy and Martin. Judge O'Hagan died in 1890, aged 68. His grave is close to Dillon's and that of John Edward Pigot (1822-71). O'Hagan's epitaph reads: 'Faithful till death to God and Ireland.'

28 John Mitchel, *The history of Ireland from the treaty of Limerick to the present time: being a continuation of the history of the Abbé MacGeoghegan* (Cameron & Ferguson, Glasgow and London, n.d.).

29 Mrs William [Sophia] O'Brien, 'Mrs Deane of Ballaghaderreen' in *Irish Monthly*, July 1937, p. 477.

30 Its inscription reads: 'In this grave is buried Anne Deane, wife of Edward Deane. Born Anne Duff, of Ballaghaderreen, she was a great friend of the poor and the oppressed, a lover of Ireland and of liberty. This monument is erected to her memory by her cousin, John Dillon, member of parliament for east Mayo, who owes his life and all that he possesses to her loving kindness and generosity.'

31 Lyons, *Dillon*, p. 15.

32 Interview with Father Cathaldus Giblin, OFM, 16 May 1989.

33 Cavanagh, *Memoirs of Meagher*, p. 34.

34 Cf. Archbishop John Lynch's 1864 pamphlet on emigration in *Eire-Ireland*, xviii (1983).

35 Steele, *Irish Land and British politics*, pp 46, 49; Norman, *Catholic church and Ireland*, p. 387; R.V. Comerford in *A new history of Ireland*, v (Oxford, 1989), p. 434.

36 Sister M.M. Lavin to Adelaide Dillon [Oct. 1866] (MS 6457/373).

37 MS 6457a.

Bibliography

Primary sources

UNPUBLISHED DOCUMENTS

Trinity College, Dublin
John Blake Dillon papers
Charles Hart journal
Michael O'Farrell, statement from William Smith O'Brien on 1848

National Library of Ireland
Smith O'Brien papers
Charles Gavan Duffy papers
Thomas Davis papers
Collection of Dillon articles from the *Nation*
John O'Mahony and Patrick O'Donoghue, accounts of '48; Sub-inspector Thomas Trant's
annotations on Michael Doheny's *Felon's track*.
W.J. O'Neill Daunt journals
Laurence Gillooly papers (on microfilm)
G.H. Moore papers
Thomas Larcom papers

Royal Irish Academy
Gavan Duffy papers
Records of Irish Confederation

State Paper Office
Outrage reports from Counties Clare, Galway and Tipperary in 1848
Fenian police reports, 1864

Dublin Diocesan Archives
Paul Cullen papers

Registry of Deeds Office

University College, Dublin, Archives
Catholic University records

NEWSPAPERS

Citizen (New York)
Dublin Evening Mail
Dublin Evening Post
Freeman's Journal
Irish-American
Irish Citizen (New York)
Irishman
Irish People

Irish Times
Kilkenny Journal
Nation
Saunders' News-letter
Times (London)
Tipperary Vindicator
United Irishman

CONTEMPORARY PAMPHLETS, OFFICIAL REPORTS, WORKS OF REFERENCE

Dillon, John [Blake], *An address read before the Historical Society, Dublin Institute, at the close of the session, 1840-41*, Dublin, 1842.

___, *Report on the state of the public accounts between Ireland and Great Britain*, Dublin, 1882.

Proceedings of the Young Ireland party at their great meeting in Dublin on 2 December 1846, with a correct report of the speeches and resolutions, Belfast, 1847.

Report and proceedings from the select committee on tenure and improvement of land (Ireland) Act, HC, 1865 (402), xi.

Returns by provinces and counties of cases of evictions which have come to the knowledge of the constabulary, 1849-80, HC, 1881 (185), lxxvii.

Hansard's parliamentary debates, third series

Annual Register

Irish Catholic Directory

Crone, J.S., *Concise dictionary of Irish biography*

Webb, A.J., *A compendium of Irish biography*

Dictionary of national biography

Dictionary of American biography

Secondary sources

BOOKS, ARTICLES, ETC.

Black, R.D. Collison, *Economic thought and the Irish question, 1817-1870*, Cambridge, 1960.

Bowen, Desmond, *Paul Cullen and the shaping of modern Irish Catholicism*, Dublin, 1983.

Brown, Thomas N., *Irish-American nationalism, 1870-1890*, New York, 1966.

Burke, Helen, *The Irish people and the poor law*, Dublin, 1987.

Cavanagh, Michael, *Memoirs of Gen. Thomas Francis Meagher*, Massachusetts, 1892.

Cole, G.D.H., *Chartist portraits*, London, 1941.

Comerford, R.V., 'Representation at Westminster, 1801-1918' in W. Nolan (ed.), *Tipperary: history and society*, Dublin, 1986.

___, *The Fenians in context*, Dublin, 1985.

___, 'Gladstone's first Irish enterprise, 1864-70' in W.E. Vaughan (ed.), *A new history of Ireland*, Vol. 5, Oxford, 1989.

Corish, Patrick J., 'Cardinal Cullen and the National Association of Ireland' in *Reportorium Novum*, iii (1962).

Cronin, Seán, *Irish nationalism: A history of its roots and ideology*, Dublin, 1980.

Cussen, John, 'William Smith O'Brien in Van Diemen's Land, 1849- 54' in *Old Limerick Journal*, no. 23 (1988).

Daly, Mary, E., *The Famine in Ireland*, Dublin, 1986.

Davis, Richard, *The Young Ireland movement*, Dublin, 1987.
___, *William Smith O'Brien: Ireland—1848—Tasmania*, Dublin, 1989.
Davis, Thomas, *Literary and historical essays*, Dublin, 1845.
Davitt, Michael, *The fall of feudalism in Ireland, or the story of the Land League revolution*, New York, 1904.
Denieffe, Joseph, *A personal narrative of the Irish Revolutionary Brotherhood*, Irish University Press ed., 1969.
Devoy, John, *Recollections of an Irish rebel*, IUP ed., 1969.
De Paor, Liam, *The peoples of Ireland*, London, 1986.
Dillon, William, *Life of John Mitchel*, 2 vols, London, 1888.
Doheny, Michael, *The felon's track*, Dublin, 1951 ed.
Doyle, Eugene, J., 'Victoria through Irish eyes: Sir Charles Gavan Duffy in Victoria, 1856-1869' (MA thesis/UCD, 1983).
Duffy, Charles Gavan, *Young Ireland: a fragment of Irish history*, 2 vols, London, 1896 ed.
___, *Four years of Irish history, 1845-1849*, London, 1883.
___, *Thomas Davis: the memoirs of an Irish patriot, 1840-1846*, London, 1890.
___, *My life in two hemispheres*, 2 vols, London, 1898.
Edwards, R. Dudley, 'The contribution of Young Ireland to the development of the Irish national idea' in Seamus Pender (ed.), *Féilscríbhinn Torna*, Cork, 1947.
___ (ed.), *Ireland and the Italian risorgimento*, Dublin, 1960.
___ and T. Desmond Williams (eds.), *The Great Famine: studies in Irish history, 1845-52*, Dublin, 1956.
Edwards, Owen Dudley (with G. Evans, J. Rys and H. MacDiarmid), *Celtic nationalism*, London, 1968.
Ellmann, Richard, *Oscar Wilde*, London, 1987.
Farrell, Brian (ed.), *The Irish parliamentary tradition*, Dublin, 1973.
Fitzgerald, Philip, PP, *Personal recollections of the insurrection at Ballingarry in July 1848*, Dublin 1861.
___, *A narrative of the proceedings of the confederates in '48, from the suspension of the Habeas Corpus Act to their final dispersion at Ballingarry*, Dublin, 1868.
Fitzpatrick, W.J. (ed.), *Correspondence of Daniel O'Connell*, 2 vols, London, 1888.
Fogarty, L[ilian], *James Fintan Lalor, patriot and political essayist (1807-1849)*, Dublin, 1919.
Foster, R.F., *Modern Ireland, 1600-1972*, London, 1988.
Garvin, Tom, *The evolution of Irish nationalist politics*, Dublin, 1981.
Gibson, Florence E., *The attitudes of the New York Irish towards state and national affairs, 1848-1892*, New York, 1951.
Griffith, Arthur (ed.), *Meagher of the sword: speeches of Thomas Francis Meagher in Ireland, 1846-1848*, Dublin, 1916.
Gwynn, Denis, *Young Ireland and 1848*, Cork, 1949.
___, *O'Connell, Davis and the colleges bill*, Cork, 1948.
___ 'Father Kenyon and Young Ireland' in *Irish Ecclesiastical Record* (1949).
___, *Thomas Francis Meagher*, Cork, 1961.
Hill, Jacqueline R., 'Nationalism and the Catholic Church in the 1840s' in *Irish Historical Studies*, xix (1975).
Hodges, J.G., *Report of the trial of William Smith O'Brien for high treason at the special commission for the County Tipperary, held at Clonmel, September and October 1848*, Dublin, 1849.
Hoppen, K. Theodore, *Elections, politics and society in Ireland, 1832-1885*, Oxford, 1984.
Hynes, Liam, 5 'letters' in *Western People*, Aug.-Dec. 1968.
Inglis, Brian, *The freedom of the press in Ireland, 1741-1841*, London, 1954.
Kee, Robert, *The green flag: a history of Irish nationalism*, London, 1972.
Ker, Ian, *John Henry Newman: a biography*, Oxford, 1988.
Kerr, Donal A., *Peel, priests and politics: Sir Robert Peel's administration and the Roman*

Catholic Church in Ireland, 1841-1846, Oxford, 1982.

Larkin, Emmet, *The consolidation of the Roman Catholic Church in Ireland, 1860-1870*, University of North Carolina Press, 1987.

Lee, Joseph, *The modernisation of Irish society, 1848-1918*, Dublin, 1973.

Le Quesne, A.L., *Carlyle*, Oxford, 1982.

Lowe, W.J., 'The Chartists and the Irish Confederates: Lancashire, 1848' in *Irish Historical Studies*, xxiv (1984).

Lyons, F.S.L., *John Dillon: a biography*, London, 1968.

___, *Ireland since the Famine*, London, 1971.

___, and R.A.J. Hawkins (eds.), *Ireland under the Union: varieties of tension: essays in honour of T.W. Moody*, Oxford, 1980.

MacManus, M.J. (ed.), *Thomas Davis and Young Ireland*, Dublin, 1945.

McDowell, R.B., *Public opinion and government policy in Ireland, 1801-1846*, London, 1952.

McAllister, Thomas G., *Terence Bellew McManus*, Maynooth, 1972.

McCoy, G.A. Hayes, *History of Irish flags from earliest times*, Dublin, 1979.

McCartney, Donal, *The dawning of democracy: Ireland, 1800-1870*, Dublin, 1987.

___ and Art Cosgrove (eds.), *Studies in Irish history presented to R. Dudley Edwards*, Dublin, 1979.

McDonagh, Oliver, *States of mind: a study of the Anglo-Irish conflict, 1780-1980*, London, 1983.

___, *Daniel O'Connell*, 2 vols (*The hereditary bondsman* and *The emancipist*), London, 1988-9.

MacGrath, Kevin, 'Writers in the *Nation*, 1842-5' in *Irish Historical Studies*, vi (1949).

Macintyre, Angus, *The Liberator: Daniel O'Connell and the Irish party, 1830-1847*, London, 1965.

McCarthy, Justin Huntly, MP, *Ireland since the Union*, London, 1887.

MacSuibhne, Peadar, *Paul Cullen and his contemporaries with their letters from 1820-1902*, 5 vols, Naas, 1961-77.

Maguire, John Francis, MP, *The Irish in America*, London, 1868.

___, *Father Mathew: a biography*, London, 1863.

Maxwell, Herbert, *The life and letters of George William Frederick, 4th earl of Clarendon*, 2 vols, London, 1913.

Moody, T.W., *Thomas Davis, 1814-45: a centenary address*, Dublin, 1945.

Moran, Gerard P., *The Mayo evictions of 1860*, Westport, 1986.

Miller, Kerby A., *Emigrants and exiles: Ireland and the Irish exodus to North America*, Oxford, 1985.

Mitchel, John, *Jail Journal*, Sphere ed., 1983.

___, *The last conquest of Ireland (perhaps)*, Dublin, 1861.

Newsinger, John, 'John Mitchel and Irish nationalism' in *Literature and History*, vi (1980).

Norman, E.R., *The Catholic Church and Ireland in the age of rebellion, 1859-1873*, London, 1965.

Nowlan, Kevin B., *Charles Gavan Duffy and the repeal movement*, Dublin, 1963.

___, *The politics of repeal: a study in the relations between Great Britain and Ireland, 1841-50*, London, 1965.

___, 'The meaning of repeal in Irish history' in *Historical Studies*, iv (1963).

___, 'The Catholic clergy and Irish politics in the 1830s and '40s' in *Hist. Studies*, ix (1974).

___ and Maurice R. O'Connell (eds.), *Daniel O'Connell: portrait of a radical*, Belfast, 1974.

Ó Broin, Leon, *An Maidíneach*, Dublin, 1971.

___, *Charles Gavan Duffy—patriot and stateman—the story of Charles Gavan Duffy, 1816-1903*, Dublin, 1967.

O'Connell, Maurice R., 'John O'Connell and the Great Famine' in *Irish Hist. Studies* xxv (1986).

___, 'Young Ireland and the Catholic clergy in 1844: contemporary deceit and historical falsehood' in *The Catholic historical review* (Washington DC), lxxiv (1988).

___, *Daniel O'Connell: the man and his politics*, Irish Academic Press, 1990.

___ (ed.), *The correspondence of Daniel O'Connell*, 8 vols, Dublin, 1972-80.

O'Cathaoir, Brendan, 'The pattern of Ulster riots', *Irish Times*, 26 February 1970.

___, 'John Mitchel: the great contradiction', *Irish Times*, 1 February 1983.

___, 'John O'Mahony, 1815-1877' in *Capuchin Annual* (1977).

___, *John Mitchel*, Dublin, 1978.

___, 'Terence Bellew MacManus: Fenian precursor' in *Irish Sword*, xvi (1985).

___, 'Smith O'Brien's retribution' in *North Munster Antiquarian Journal*, xxvii (1985).

[Cahir], 'Isaac Butt and the Limerick by-election of 1871' in *North Munster Antiq. Journal*, x (1966).

O'Conner, Rebecca, *Jenny Mitchel: Young Irelander: a biography*, Dublin, 1988.

O'Hegarty, P.S., *A history of Ireland under the Union*, London, 1952.

O'Leary, John, *Recollections of Fenians and Fenianism*, 2 vols, IUP ed., 1969.

O'Reilly, Bernard, *John MacHale, archbishop of Tuam, his life, times and correspondence*, 2 vols, New York, 1890.

Ó Síocháin, P.A., *Aran: islands of legend*, Dublin, 1962.

O'Sullivan, T.F., *The Young Irelanders*, Tralee, 1944.

Ó Néill, Tomás P., *Fiontán Ó Leathlobhair*, Dublin, 1962.

Ó Tuathaigh, Gearóid, *Ireland before the Famine, 1798-1848*, Dublin, 1972.

Pearl, Cyril, *The three lives of Gavan Duffy*, New South Wales, 1979.

Petler, D.N., 'Ireland and France in 1848', in *Irish Hist. Studies*, xxiv (1985).

Phelan, Josephine, *The ardent exile: life and times of Thomas D'Arcy McGee*, Toronto, 1951.

Ryan, Desmond, *The Fenian chief: a biography of James Stephens*, Dublin, 1967.

Sanderlin, Walter S., 'Galway as a transatlantic port' in *Éire-Ireland*, v (1970).

Saville, John, *1848: The British state and the Chartist movement*, Cambridge, 1987.

Schenk, H.G., *The mind of the European romantics*, London, 1966.

Sillard, P.A., *The life and letters of John Martin*, Dublin, 1901.

Smyth, Patrick James, *The life and times of Thomas Francis Meagher*, Dublin, 1867.

Sullivan, A.M., *New Ireland*, London, 1877.

Steele, E.D., 'Cardinal Cullen and Irish nationality' in *Irish Hist. Studies*, xix (1975).

___, *Irish land and British politics: tenant-right and nationality, 1865-1870*, Cambridge, 1974.

The Irish journals of Elizabeth Smith, 1840-1850, eds. D. Thomson and M. McGusty, Oxford, 1980.

Thornley, David, *Isaac Butt and home rule*, London, 1964.

Touhill, Blanche M., *William Smith O'Brien and his Irish revolutionary companions in penal exile*, University of Missouri Press, 1981.

Trant, Thomas, *Reply to Father Fitzgerald's pamphlet entitled his 'Personal recollections of the insurrection at Ballingarry in July 1848'*, Dublin, 1862.

Vaughan, W.E., *Landlords and tenants in Ireland, 1848-1904*, Dublin, 1984.

White, Terence de Vere, *The parents of Oscar Wilde: Sir William and Lady Wilde*, London, 1967.

___, *The road of excess*, Dublin, 1945.

Whyte, J.H., *The independent Irish party, 1850-9*, Oxford, 1958.

___, *The Tenant League and Irish politics in the 1850s*, Dublin, 1963.

Woodham-Smith, Cecil, *The great hunger*, New American Library ed., 1964.

___, *Queen Victoria: her life and times*, 2 vols, London, 1972.

Index